## ADVANCE PRAISE FOR *NOT F..R FROM ME*

"Every Ohioan should read *Not Far from Me*. Statistics might help us cope objectively with the opioid crisis, but numbers make it too easy to forget that people are suffering. To heal and be healthy, we need the empathy and insight that literature can provide. Written by addicts, families, first responders, and civic leaders, *Not Far from Me* captures the human story of addiction and the ways in which communities are struggling to find hope and preserve lives."
    —Pat Williamsen, Executive Director, Ohio Humanities

"As I've traveled throughout Ohio, I've heard many personal stories of opioid addiction similar to those in *Not Far from Me: Stories of Opioids and Ohio*. These powerful stories will increase awareness, reduce stigma, and help us better understand the complex issue of addiction so we can turn the tide of this epidemic and save lives."
    —Senator Rob Portman

"So much has been written, so much news reported, so many hands have been wrung in response to Ohio's—and the nation's—collective dope sickness. Too often, though, the voices of those affected have been lost in the din. *Not Far from Me* helps redress this loss by allowing Buckeyes to tell their own stories in their own ways. I loved hearing those voices in all their tear-inducing, maddening, uplifting, defiant bravery."
    —Brian Alexander, author of *Glass House: The 1% Economy and the Shattering of the All-American Town*

"There's not a community in our state that hasn't been affected by opioid addiction, and it's so important to hear the voices of the families who are being torn apart. Their stories are a powerful call to action for us to work together to fight this public health crisis."
    —Senator Sherrod Brown

NOT FAR FROM ME

# NOT FAR FROM ME
## STORIES OF OPIOIDS AND OHIO

EDITED BY DANIEL SKINNER
AND BERKELEY FRANZ

FOREWORD BY TED STRICKLAND

TRILLIUM, AN IMPRINT OF
THE OHIO STATE UNIVERSITY PRESS
COLUMBUS

Trillium, an imprint of The Ohio State University Press.

Library of Congress Cataloging-in-Publication Data
Names: Skinner, Daniel, author. | Franz, Berkeley A., author.
Title: Not far from me : stories of opioids and Ohio / Daniel Skinner, Berkeley Franz ; foreword
      by Ted Strickland.
Description: Columbus. : Trillium , 2019. | Series: Trillium books
Identifiers: LCCN 2019002910 | ISBN 9780814255384 (paperback)
Subjects: LCSH: Opioid abuse—Ohio. | Drug abuse—Social aspects—Ohio. | BISAC: BIOG-
      RAPHY & AUTOBIOGRAPHY / Personal Memoirs. | PSYCHOLOGY / Psychopa-
      thology / Addiction.
Classification: LCC RC568.O45 S55 2019 | DDC 362.29/309771—dc23
LC record available at https://lccn.loc.gov/2019002910

Cover design by Angela Moody
Text design by Juliet Williams
Type set in Adobe Caslon

# CONTENTS

## PART TWO: PROCESSING LOSS

# PART THREE: MAKING SENSE

# PART FOUR: DEVISING SOLUTIONS

## PART FIVE: CHALLENGING ASSUMPTIONS

# GEOGRAPHIC TABLE OF CONTENTS

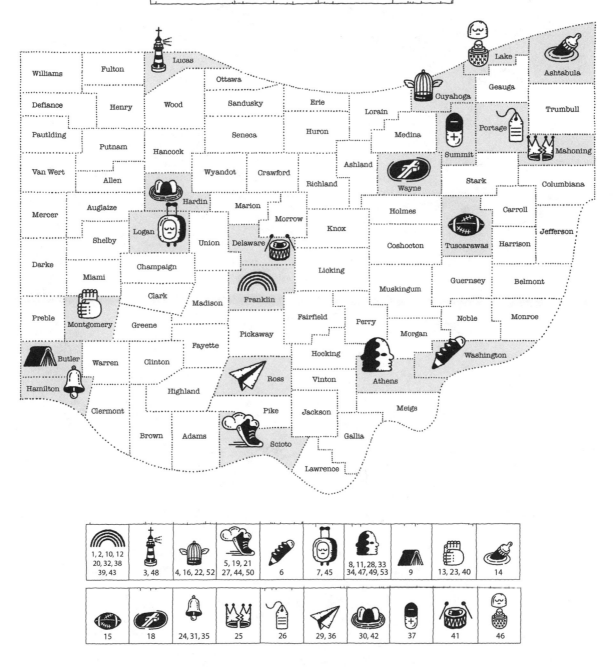

Numbers correspond to the submissions listed in the table of contents. Use the symbols to locate the county of each contributor. Designed by Maryam Khaleghiyazdi, an MFA candidate in Graphic Design at Ohio University.

# FOREWORD

I'll never forget that day. April 1, 2016. I was standing at the graveside of my forty-two-year-old nephew who, three days earlier, had lost his life by accidentally overdosing on Oxycodone. The family had asked me to share some final thoughts about Bruce. But as I tried to speak I was overcome by my own grief and was only able to mumble a few garbled words in an effort to comfort those who loved him and were heartbroken by his death.

As a former congressman and governor, I'd been called upon to speak words of comfort following many tragedies that occurred in my district and state while I was serving in office. But this tragedy was so painfully personal because my family was experiencing the grief and sense of loss that so many thousands of other Ohio families have endured in recent years as the opioid epidemic has spread across the state and throughout our nation.

It's a tragic fact that we are losing more Americans to drug overdoses in a single year—over 62,000 deaths in 2017—more than the number of American soldiers killed during the entire twenty years of the Vietnam War.

That's why I so strongly support the publication of this book. We need to hear the truth about what is happening to us. We cannot, nor should we even try to, escape the painful reality that lives are being lost in such great numbers to drug abuse. Our families are being torn apart.

Children are growing up without their parents. Babies are coming into this world already addicted to opioids.

I've always thought of Ohio as a large, diverse collection of mostly decent, hardworking, wonderful people. And it is tragic beyond words to know that so many of our fellow Ohioans are losing their lives or are living greatly diminished lives because of drug addiction.

But there is hope. The editors of this book, Daniel Skinner and Berkeley Franz, are providing us with information and needed inspiration that can help stem the ravages of Ohio's opioid epidemic. You should know that this book is not an academic or theoretical discussion of addiction. Rather, it's a collection of real-life, first-person stories by people from different parts of Ohio whose lives have been touched and, in some cases, forever changed as a result of drug addiction.

This book is filled with stories of people who have opened their hearts, shared their experiences, and demonstrated the magnificent ability of the human spirit to overcome the worst that life could throw at them. It's written by people of many different backgrounds: students, teachers, recovering addicts, parents who have lost children, medical professionals, law enforcement officers, elected officials, addiction counselors, leaders in the African American community, and LGBTQ advocates. They represent different genders, ethnicities, races, professions, ages, and socioeconomic backgrounds. The one thing they have in common is the experience of dealing with opioid addiction, either by becoming addicted themselves or by trying to help others who are addicted. They are all people who care deeply about Ohio.

Although the problem of drug addiction has been part of American life since the beginnings of our nation, the current opioid crisis is more deadly and widespread than ever in the past. How did it happen? Many factors have brought us to where we find ourselves now. New and more powerfully addictive drugs were created for the worthy purpose of relieving human pain and suffering. However, many well-meaning physicians were given false and misleading information regarding the addictive nature of these new medications by pharmaceutical companies hell-bent on promoting the widespread use of their drugs in order to maximize their profits. The situation was made much worse by some unscrupulous doctors opening financially lucrative "pill mills" to take advantage of those who were addicted. And, as these things were happening, cheap "black tar" heroin began flooding into our country from Mexico and became easily available throughout Ohio's large cities, small towns, and rural areas. The result was a convergence of events, occurring somewhat simultaneously, providing easy access to both legal and illegal narcotics and creating the explosion of a deadly epidemic of drug abuse.

The book includes many stories that will inspire you and make you proud to be an Ohioan. You will meet young people who share their struggles with poverty and addiction through original poetry that is both raw and primitive yet profoundly insightful and inspiring. A mother writes about her talented teenage son who sustained a sports injury and was prescribed narcotic pain medication resulting in a six-year night-mare of opioid dependency before breaking free of his addiction. You will read about the gut-wrenching experience of a child welfare case-worker who was called to a home where a young mother was found on the floor, having died of a drug overdose, while her six-month-old child lay smiling and cooing in a nearby crib.

You will meet little Abby, a kindergarten-aged child living with addicted parents in a house with dirt floors, missing windows, and no running water. Her elementary school principal writes, "They were liv-ing in an unforgiving cycle of poverty, disability, and drug use." But your heart will nearly burst with pride and gratitude as you learn how her teachers came to her rescue. If you want to be inspired and made to feel proud of Ohio, Abby's story alone is more than sufficient reason to read this book.

While most citizens now have at least a general awareness of this ever-expanding public health crisis, we are still not doing what needs to be done to deal with it. There's a lot of talk from state and national leaders, but there is also a lack of effective action. We need to convince the public that addiction is a disease and that everyone—certainly every family—is at risk. We need to make medically assisted treatments avail-able to those who are addicted. We need to reform our laws to reflect the fact that addiction is a disease and not a moral failure. We need to provide sufficient state and federal funding consistent with the enormity of the crisis. And we need to encourage all segments of our communities to come together to provide the full range of supportive services needed to help those fighting addiction.

It is my hope that this book—that these stories—will provide us with the insight, the determination, and the hope we need to fight for poli-cies and programs that will bring an end to this crisis.

Ted Strickland
Former Governor of Ohio

# INTRODUCTION

DANIEL SKINNER AND BERKELEY FRANZ

In 2017 when we began working on this collection, opioids were a subject of intense debate in Ohio and across the nation. Politicians were holding an endless stream of listening sessions, accompanied by carefully staged photo opportunities and followed up with manicured press releases. A few bills were passed. In some cases funds were being allocated for prevention, for treatment to help those in recovery, or for providing Narcan to save those in the grips of an overdose. Many health care professionals were promoting their efforts to turn off the steady stream of prescription opioids flowing from their offices; some remained adamant they were not to blame. Pharmaceutical manufacturers and distributors as well were investing time and resources to downplay their role in covering up the addictive potential of prescription opioids.

We also began to learn that across Ohio, a wave of new activism was arising to promote a better understanding of opioid abuse and identify possible solutions. Educators were stretching resources as far as they could to help struggling students. Law enforcement officers were rethinking their approach and retraining to acquire necessary skills. Most important, countless family members and community leaders were working to stem the growing problem at home. Too many were not successful.

What unites these people is that they all care deeply about the growing crisis and aim to build a more robust dialogue around causes and potential cures. But much of this work continues to occur behind the scenes or in isolation. We hope that collecting first-person perspectives into one volume might bring some overlooked stories and new perspectives out into the open where they can be heard—an admittedly modest goal in a seemingly intractable crisis.

Clearly there has been no shortage of public narratives about opioid abuse in Ohio. In fact, they are everywhere. Ohio is the "overdose capital of America," an "epicenter," "ground zero." We know that Ohio is in the midst of a growing calamity, but we don't know why. Widely read authors have floated explanations for growing opioid abuse and asked, What could be behind the staggering numbers and seemingly endless list of worsts and firsts? The journalist Sam Quinones has emphasized the role that national economic and social trends played in laying a foundation for opioid abuse to flourish; he included among his list of causes Americans' long-standing attraction to individualism and a tendency to stigmatize addiction, poverty, and mental illness. While the drugs originated outside of Ohio, Quinones insists that the social conditions in our state made us especially vulnerable. Other writers, such as J. D. Vance, emphasize cultural values and, in the process, give credence to stereotypes that have long beset Appalachian communities. For Vance, personal responsibility—yet more individualism—seems to be the answer.

The public historian Elizabeth Catte helps us understand how in Appalachia specifically, dominant narratives have largely come from the outside, tending to universalize the region as a passive victim to economic crisis and addiction. What we need instead, according to Catte, is to let individuals speak for themselves. Only then will we understand how dominant narratives are contested and how counternarratives have been obscured in public dialogue. Most glaring in the opioid epidemic has been the omission of narratives recounting the experiences of family members, public officials, health care providers, community leaders, and others who are intimately familiar with opioid abuse and the attempts to find new options for prevention and long-term recovery. In short: the voices of everyday Ohioans are missing.

Although these stories are not new, stigma and other barriers have prevented their public telling. As we learned after putting out a call for stories in the fall of 2017, many people are ready to share their perspective and are tired of the culture of silence that exists around opioid abuse. In a speech at Ohio University, Quinones argued that only recently had stories begun to emerge, largely as a result of the efforts of community members and leaders. When he was working on *Dreamland,* this openness just did not exist. "Every place I went," he explained, "I could not find families who wanted to talk about this topic. It was just hidden. There were just a few people, and I put them all in my book; everybody else was afraid or ashamed or mortified." The very existence of *Not Far from Me: Stories of Opioids and Ohio*—and the fact that so many Ohioans have freely shared how opioids have affected their lives, their families, their work, and their communities—is evidence that something is beginning to change.

While the public narratives about opioids in Ohio have helped us learn something about ourselves, our state, and our connection to larger trends related to opioids, the stories and experiences are only now reaching the public conversation. These stories may be a crucial part of reducing stigma and underscoring the efficacy of communities working together to solve challenging social problems. Shifting the dialogue to the personal helps us move away from abstractions such as "crisis" and "epidemic" to understand the day-to-day and lived experiences. In doing so, we'll hear from a wide range of contributors who are economically, geographically, politically, and socially diverse. Across these perspectives, we do not attempt or claim to piece together a once-and-for-all account of opioids in Ohio, but we hope that by engaging these stories we will offer a more humane window into opioid addiction and use stories as a starting point for new and often difficult conversations.

## THE SETTING

Ohio is known for many things. In politics, Ohio is a pivotal swing state that presidential candidates must win to claim the White House. But beyond the mandatory photo ops eating local fare at the Ohio State Fair, politicians must quickly learn how to balance a complex set of identities and interests if they are to connect with Ohioans. They must be equally at home talking about tractor parts, steel tariffs, biotech, and God. For more than a century Ohio has had a strong identification as a blue collar state at the forefront of many of the nation's largest industries, from automobiles to manufacturing to aerospace. Ohio is also the birthplace of the American Federation of Labor, reminding us that many of the jobs that once sustained Ohio paid well and were reliable. Though some of these companies still have a foothold in the state, and others have moved in, the pensions are largely gone. Ohio's cities are dotted with looming but vacant buildings. One of Ohio's strongest, more recent identities is that of a postindustrial "rust belt" state.

Like many other Midwestern states, Ohio is known for its polite residents, sprawling suburbs, and city centers that are but a stone's throw from farmland. Ohio also is known for its fierce sports culture, where high school football is a Friday night ritual, college football is a religion, and professional sports—until recently—has been a source of perennial disappointment. Win or lose, people go in droves and often start early. Ohioans of all stripes seem to cope with economic struggle by finding hope elsewhere.

In the area of health, Ohio is a state of paradoxes. In 1967, on the heels of the Hough uprising in Cleveland's East Side, Martin Luther King Jr. chose another East Side institution—Glenville High School— to declare that "the goal of America is freedom." Today, however, it is hard to see freedom as an accurate descriptor when Ohio continues to have some of the worst health indicators and race-based disparities in the nation. These disparities exist in spite of world-renowned medical centers such as Cincinnati Children's Hospital in Southwest Ohio, the Cleveland Clinic in the Northeast, and a vast network of community health centers across the state. Ohio pairs enormous potential with persistent challenges.

To those who love the state and have great hope for it, it is depressing to realize that Ohio is now nationally known for being an epicenter of opioid addiction and overdose. We have learned not only of ethical lapses within the state's medical, pharmaceutical, and health care industry but also of class- and race-based disparities in the criminalization of drug users. While many of the state's leaders have come to acknowledge the problem, with most taking an empathetic approach, there are still strongholds of resistance. As the Sheriff of Butler County, who refuses to let his deputies carry life-saving Narcan, has declared, "I'm not the one that decides if people live or die. They decide that when they stick that needle in their arm." Clearly, we have a long way to go before we can say that we are addressing the multifaceted causes of addiction— instead of reducing it to a moral failing.

But given our history and the tremendous potential of Ohio institutions and communities, there is reason to believe that being the worst also positions us to be innovative in responding to widespread opioid addiction. As one contributor notes, Alcoholics Anonymous was first established in Akron in 1935. Although Ohio's license plates declare Ohio the "Birthplace of Aviation," another contributor notes that Ohio might be also considered the "birthplace of recovery." Yet the story becomes a good deal more complicated when one realizes that those steel license plates are fashioned by inmates in a Warren County correctional institution. This facility houses, among other convicted criminals, those caught up in Ohio's historically punishing code for drug-related crimes, most of whom were—and remain, as some of our contributors note—Ohioans of color.

Many of the stories in this book make clear that Ohioans have responded in force to the challenges opioid abuse has created in their communities. They have done this in a myriad of ways: by developing new social service programs, medical options for recovery, better ways to support youth, and new opportunities for community dialogue, all of which may prove to be key in preventing or responding to drug addiction. When you're facing the most deadly drug epidemic in recent history, it makes sense that the state with some of the worst outcomes might also lead the way out.

## STORYTELLING IN A CRISIS

Many Ohioans have suffered from the stifling stigma of addiction and the absence of fruitful dialogue. At the same time, we have been inundated by headlines and studies communicating the severity of drug use. At some point, the crisis became a brand, at least politically—a thing to talk about and reference instead of an issue to be engaged seriously and with focus. As editors, we've struggled with how to raise important issues related to opioid abuse without furthering stereotypes, isolating struggling communities, and adding to existing sensationalism. And as two white academic researchers not originally from Ohio, we have also wrestled with how to insert ourselves into the work, acknowledging that our own biases and social position matter when publicly sharing stories that are not our own.

We ask that you read this book within the context in which it was conceived, created, and published. As we contemplated launching this project in early 2017, we discussed, in frank terms, whether such a volume was needed, whether we were the right people to undertake it, and—most importantly—whether such a project would be construed as jumping on a bandwagon or exploiting a popular topic. In the early stages of the project, we spoke with one law enforcement professional to see if he might want to contribute to the book. "Let me tell you," he explained, "we were talking about opioids before it was cool to talk about opioids." He did not want to contribute. Opioids had worn him down and he was tired of the pandering.

Yet as we further discussed our aims, it became clear that the dominant narratives surrounding the opioid situation had already become stale and unhelpful. Too many—though certainly not all—politicians around the state seemed more interested in publicity than bold solutions. Institutions around the state promoted all of the good things they were doing to combat the opioid crisis, but many of these efforts seemed more concerned with assuring others that they were poised to do something instead of really doing something. The motivating impulse of this book, in other words, was our belief that if the narrative about opioids in Ohio were to impact policy in a meaningful way, then it would have to be revised. We thought that this revision was best carried out by actually listening to Ohioans who had experienced opioid abuse firsthand and providing them a platform on which to tell their stories.

Changing the narrative about opioid abuse, however, is not an easy task. Many contributors in this book struggled with the right words. Ohio's experience with opioids has eroded trust to such an extent that we are not always sure which words are appropriate, which are to be trusted, and which are part of an attempt to either evade responsibility or score political points. Throughout the book, for example, many contributors use scare quotes to call into question words such as "crisis," "epidemic," and even "overdose." This wasn't something we anticipated at the outset, but as we read submission after submission it dawned on us: one of the things that Ohioans' experiences with opioids have done is to make them sensitive to the use and abuse of language in trying to make sense of those experiences.

Take "crisis" as one interesting example of how language can be both problematic and telling. A crisis, according to the Greek origins of the word, is an event that ideally gives rise to a "critique," which is the product of "critical" thinking. In the case of growing opioid abuse, the language of crisis or epidemic often served to preclude critical thinking and sensationalize the complex social and economic factors that supported the rise in abuse. The alarmist and lofty language of crisis and epidemic is often evoked to try to make sense of the state's experience as a whole.

How do we refer to something that is so big, but also so personal? Our writers also struggle from time to time with what to call things: Is it opioid use? Abuse? Or misuse, as most clinical experts now agree? Are the people themselves addicts? Patients? Individuals? Or just—more humanely—people? Then there are the words that individuals use to describe their feelings and their struggles, as well as those of others. Pieces vacillate between anger, sadness, hope, resignation, blame, and back again.

Each of the stories in this book provides a vantage point. Our contributors change the narrative surrounding opioid use in Ohio in several ways. In large part because of influential texts like Quinones's and Vance's, certain parts of the state have received the lion's share of attention, especially with Quinones's focus on Portsmouth and Columbus and Vance's focus on Appalachia and southwestern Ohio. And while these areas were certainly hit hard, and our book contains a number of pieces from and about them, the more interesting story about Ohio and opioids also casts a light on other regions. Accordingly, readers will learn about changes in law enforcement in Toledo, historical memory and racial reckoning in Cleveland, addiction counseling in Ashtabula, pain acceptance and perspective shifting in Cincinnati, and football coaching in New Philadelphia.

Our contributors also challenge our understanding of whom opioids have affected and why certain populations have been overlooked. We hear accounts from Ohio's lesbian, gay, bisexual, transgender, and queer communities; a Mennonite nurse working in Amish country; and faith communities who are addressing opioid abuse as part of their religious commitments. The collection also includes reflections on how opioid addiction relates to the scourge of human trafficking, sports fanaticism, and both poverty and affluence.

Some contributors provide important historical perspective on the changes in cultural perceptions of pain and within medical institutions. Clinicians who worked on the front lines during the height of HIV-AIDS make connections between different public health challenges. And given the recent attention on opioid addiction in white communities, particularly rural and Appalachian, some of our contributors ask what role race is playing in the growing public response that has established special drug courts, legal dispensations, and forgiveness for criminals willing to seek treatment. Several of our contributors do raise the question of race explicitly, especially in light of the nation's and state's responses to the crack-cocaine epidemic of the 1980s, which was met not with the kindness and "all-hands-on-deck" response that have become more common with opioid addiction, but with mass incarceration and mandatory minimum sentences that primarily targeted communities of color. Instead of the empathy we see today for babies born with neonatal abstinence syndrome, we had the stigmatizing language of "crack babies." These and other stories have profound potential to dislodge our deep-seated biases about drugs of abuse, and of Ohio communities more generally.

## CONSTRUCTING THE BOOK

In 2017 we put out a public call for contributors and also reached out personally to individuals across the state whose work we thought might intersect with opioid abuse in some way. Throughout this process, we were surprised when so many of our colleagues, students, friends, and families shared anecdotally how they had been affected personally by opioid abuse and overdose. These are just not the kind of conversations we are used to having in our communities. As researchers we knew how stigmatizing opioid abuse was; we just didn't know it was lingering just below the surface in the lives of so many of our personal and professional contacts. When you're editing a book on opioids in Ohio, people start to open up. From our very limited vantage point, it seems that very few Ohioans have escaped the last decade without scars. The first part of the book's title, *Not Far from Me* comes from a line in a poem by one of our contributors, Gerald E. Greene, and is entirely fitting given the seeming impossibility of escaping the pain of opioid abuse in Ohio.

Of course, there are many other stories that did not end up in this collection and are left still needing to be told. In some cases, we received enthusiastic inquiries from Ohioans who thought that contributing would be a healing or cathartic process, only to realize that they were not yet ready to speak. Other people who wished to contribute were overruled by the objections of their loved ones, who were not willing to participate, even anonymously, in such a public project and face the very real social and legal consequences. In some cases, enthusiastic contributors who were excited to tell their story of pain management ended up simply being in too much physical pain to write. We were able to see in our daily interactions with contributors just how complicated and how difficult many Ohioans' lives are. It will take time to unpack the effects of opioids on the lives of people across the state.

The fact that opioids have impacted so many individuals also meant that we at times had to exclude stories due to lack of space or thematic overlap. It was a challenge to figure out which stories fit together and which complement or challenge others. The process included hours on the phone with prospective contributors, working through hard issues, listening, crying, and processing frustration and uncertainty. We received so many inquiries, especially from family members who had lost loved ones. It was hard to tell some of these people, especially parents who had lost children, that we simply didn't have the space for their story. Each is important and valuable, but books have finite space. There are just too many dead children in Ohio.

We've tried to include a broad set of stories, reflections, and perspectives. Yet even in their diversity, they are linked by recurrent themes. Following these connections, we have organized the book not only to take readers through a series of thematic clusters but also to create categories that readers may find useful for generating conversations of their own. While we offer these themes as lenses for processing the complexities and raw edges of contributors' perspectives, we also acknowledge that many of these pieces are multifaceted and could well have been placed in a different part. The fact that they cannot be easily contained or categorized speaks to their depth.

Part One, "Establishing Place," illuminates the various spaces and landscapes that opioids have affected across the state, as well as our contributors' attempts to rebuild and reclaim places for recovery. Part Two, "Processing Loss," provides readers with examples of coping with the extraordinary loss our state has undergone—both as a historical moment and, for many, as a matter of permanent loss. Part Three, "Making Sense," offers a range of perspectives on how our state arrived where we are. In attempting to understand the situation we find ourselves in, we explore social currents and forces, emerging data trends, and psychosocial states such as alienation and loneliness. The pieces engage questions of responsibility and how to move forward with a more informed view of how we got here. Part Four, "Devising Solutions," features Ohioans who are involved in transformative work motivated by personal experiences with addiction. They describe solutions arising out of professional aims or frustrations or an overwhelming sense of responsibility to one's family or community.

The final section, Part Five, "Challenging Assumptions," focuses on the difficult conversations that still need to be undertaken. In this section, our contributors discuss the persistence of stigma, race- and class-based bias, the need to rethink core community institutions, and the problematic characterization of rural America. We end with a consideration of assumptions because it seems to us to be the most intractable piece of the larger puzzle. The stigma surrounding drug use, and opioid use in particular, will remain a challenge moving forward. The problem is that many of the experiences chronicled here are still considered incredible or unlikely. It is a curious feature of humanity the extent to which families and friends can deny what is taking place right in front of them. There is certainly power in the retrospective and reflective aspect of storytelling, and we hope that this collection will serve as another way to keep this discussion going.

————

The sociologist Arthur Frank reminds us to "let stories breathe." For Frank, stories are an essential part of our humanity and we should listen closely to what they tell us, how they challenge us, and how they shape us, for better or worse. In the context of opioid abuse, focusing on individual stories may help to mitigate or even remove stigma. These stories can remind us of the lives behind the larger phenomenon and give us the tools to approach with empathy and understanding the problem facing us. The contributors sharing their stories in this volume are incredibly brave, but mostly they are determined to be a part of a movement that speaks openly and takes opioid abuse out of the shadows. These stories remind us that drug use and addiction are entirely human, created out of our flaws and hopes but also out of the often-inhospitable social environments that we have constructed. Adding more-personal stories to the existing narratives surrounding opioids in Ohio problematizes stereotypes and biases, revealing a set of shared values and diverse individuals fighting for the future of our state.

NOT FAR FROM ME

Men preaching in street. Credit: Toledo Restoration Church.

# PART ONE
# ESTABLISHING PLACE

I N FOCUSING ON OHIO explicitly, we found that the diversity of places across the state arose as an obvious way to read the book spatially and geographically. Some cities—Portsmouth and Dayton especially, but also others—have received an inordinate amount of attention as hotbeds for opioid use. And while available data on overdose rates show variation across the state, the attention on certain areas has overshadowed the ways in which opioid addiction has affected nearly every community, often in quite different ways. As our contributors come from across the state, there is an opportunity to have a conversation regarding how communities, cities, counties, and regions have weathered growing opioid abuse. Contributors in this section describe what different places mean to them and how they're wrestling with places they have lost, currently inhabit, or are trying to rebuild. They describe both rural and urban decay, but also the potential of reclaiming places, histories, and memories.

One of the most important places, of course, is one's home. Most contributors regard Ohio as home to some degree—some do so with pride, others with ambivalence. But many contributors also describe the fragmentation of homes, the desire to return home, and—for some—the fact that their homes will never be the same again.

Place also emerges in more subtle ways. Some contributors hope to repurpose existing institutions and think creatively about how to foster places for recovery, prevention, or community. Others are intentionally designing new spaces to provide comfort, safety, or new social connections. For some, new spaces are necessary to combat isolation and stigma, a hallmark of previous recovery-oriented facilities. Many writers express hope that place-making has the potential to breathe new life into battered communities, families, and towns. Others mourn the loss and the memories of places that are not likely to return. Some of these sites are literal, like industrial-laden towns whose populations have collapsed, while others are the metaphorical spaces of childhood, family, or optimism.

# 1

# ODE TO THE CORNER
# OF THE DRUG HOUSE
# DOWN THE GRAVEL ROAD
# OFF THE TWO-LANE HIGHWAY #29

DARREN C. DEMAREE
(COLUMBUS)

Hardened in the air,
my mouth has gone
thin with the season,

which is no longer fall,
no longer winter,
this season is Ohio,

this season is the drug
season. The body
count is the same

as what it would take
to remove the context
of the stars in the sky.

*Darren C. Demaree is the author of eight poetry collections, most recently* Two Towns Over, *which was selected as the winner of the Louise Bogan Award from Trio House Press.*

# 2

## REFLECTIONS OF A RECOVERY WRITER

ANNIE HIGHWATER
(GROVE CITY)

I am a recovery writer. I do not write as someone in recovery from a substance or an addiction. I write as somebody in recovery from an obsession with someone who has struggled with addiction. I write as an affected family member.

I was born and raised in Ohio—"The Heart of It All," as Ohioans like to say. Home of The Ohio State University (Go Bucks!). Ohioans are hearty, thick-skinned, loyal, and adaptable to weather change. Sometimes we experience all four seasons in just one week. Ohio's official state bird is the cardinal. The male cardinal with his bright red coloring reminds us that passion, warmth, and vibrancy are available to us even under the cloak of winter's gray clouds. Coincidentally, Dublin, Ohio, is also the home of Cardinal Health, a large pharmaceutical distributor included in a group of manufacturers who are accused of fueling the opioid epidemic ravaging the state.

Ohio has been especially hard-hit by the national crisis of addiction. It has been called the "Overdose Capital of America." But to me—Ohio is home.

My journey began on Columbus's West Side. I am the youngest of my parents' six children. Four of my older siblings were born into my parents' unhappy and sometimes violent marriage. Our dad was an alcoholic who quit drinking ten years into the marriage, and later became what is known as a "dry drunk," meaning sober, but miserable and highly dysfunctional. He attained sobriety just before the younger two of their children, my brother and I, were born. Additionally, my dad's sobriety was beginning during a time when the "Jesus Movement" was finding its way from California to Ohio. Many Midwest families were deeply involved with church, faith, faith-healing, prosperity doctrines, rowdy revivals, and various other religious practices.

This theology became the cornerstone of my parents' hope for escape from their misery, poverty, and problems. But they never did seem to find their way out. When my mother was eight months pregnant with me, their house caught fire and burned down. We all moved in with my mother's parents and her college-student brother, who at that time was pursuing the '60s music scene and dropping acid to intensify the experience. It was a medley of confusion, heated conflicts, and crisis.

My family rarely discussed our reality; we children were left to figure it out for ourselves. Depression, arguing, and hair-trigger tempers comprised the rhythm of our homelife. A combination of downtrodden, harsh, and emotionally ill-equipped personalities merged with confusing, sometimes delusional, and strict religious dogma. It was an environment of sadness, madness, and misery.

No one talked about bettering life—we simply lived from crisis to crisis. As the years passed, we moved often around Columbus and its surrounding areas, always struggling with rent, utilities, and having enough food for a family of eight. Our life of turmoil seemed never-ending. After those years, I was catapulted to a new level of urgent awareness when I became a mother at the age of eighteen.

Once my son Elliot was born, I became obsessed with making our way out of the oppression, dysfunction, and chaos I had grown up in. I worked hard to put him through private school and attempted to give him a homelife completely different from the one I experienced. Community activities and sports seemed to be a great way to create a healthy life. Ohioans are passionate about sports. We love our hometown teams. We take our sports and the hope we have for our star players very seriously. Sometimes this passion leads to a cut-throat nature that begins with Little League sports and continues through packed high school stadiums for Thursday night baseball games and football Friday nights under the lights.

My son showed extraordinary talent in baseball and football, climbing the ranks and making a name for his number from kindergarten through his teen years. Unfortunately, crisis again swept through our lives when, at seventeen, Elliot suffered a broken jaw in football practice and was given prescription Percocet to treat the pain. That was the beginning of a six-year nightmare through the darkest depths of opioid addiction.

My son's battle with opioid dependency also exposed the hidden struggle my mother was fighting with prescription pain medication. Her addiction had gone unseen, beginning in a seemingly innocent manner, the result of doctors' orders. Under the direction of her physician, my mother was regularly given narcotic pain medication for a broken leg sustained in a car accident. For more than three decades she did not stop taking the doctor-directed and -prescribed opioids.

Though there had been signs for years, most of our relatives were either unaware of or in denial about her substance problem. The revelation of addiction was a shock. Not only was it difficult to understand that taking what a doctor prescribes could qualify as addiction, but my mother did not at all fit the stereotypical "drug addict" profile. She is the perfect picture of a church lady—speaks French, sketches portfolios, sews, faithfully reads and quotes the Bible, and collects Belva Plain novels. She does not swear, drink, or raise her voice. My mother is a lady—as much as my son is a polite, quick-witted, charming, noticeably well-mannered, all-American athlete. Both have always been loved, liked, and respected. Neither looks like a public-service announcement for drug addiction. In fact, they look like . . . great Ohioans! So, naturally, when the issues with opioid addiction came to the surface and hit the fan, everyone close to us seemed to hit the ceiling.

The first response within our family and from extended family members was to deny the truth and turn against the one telling it. I was an outcast—scapegoated and talked about as though I were an enemy. I had to work through that later, as I did not then have the time, energy, or interest to fight any other battles outside of the one raging under my own roof. All of my attention and focus went into the urgency hovering over Elliot's life. I became completely obsessed, consumed by the belief that I was on the clock against my son's death. I thought it was entirely up to me to solve his problems and reroute his life toward health and safety. Isn't that what a loving, concerned parent does? I took on the battle for my son's life as if it were solely my fight. Until it began to devour me.

After living on what felt like a roller coaster for six years, and as things progressively grew worse, I finally handed Elliot the fight. I threw my hands up, lovingly separated myself from the chaos, and retreated for a week to rest my mind. My son ended up sleeping in a baseball dugout that week—in the park where he'd grown up playing Little League. He weighed less than I did. Life was excruciating.

As it turned out, having to come face-to-face with desperation and misery that week, my son finally took the reins of the situation he found himself in. He booked a flight with what money he had left and entered treatment in Southern California. He has now been working a twelve-step recovery plan for more than six years.

It's important to mention that Elliot relapsed early on. That taught us that going away wasn't necessarily his answer (wherever you go, there you are). When he left the state and all people, places, and things related to the problem, the issues went with him. The misery and languishing that the dependency ignited were internal. I then also realized that my son's recovery is truly up to him, not me.

Parallel to his recovery, I began to aggressively pursue my own sanity, peace, and well-being. Which was critical considering the trauma, primal fear, and brutal codependency I had entered into alongside my son's struggle with opioid addiction. Truthfully, it had just about cost me my mind.

Often, family and friends suffering on the sidelines of an addiction don't realize that they're becoming as sick as (if not sicker than) the struggling person they're affected by. I have spent the last six years working on my own recovery—intentionally doing whatever it takes to settle down, heal, maintain peace/well-being, and extend (as well as ask for) forgiveness.

To me, recovery means the continued pursuit of self-awareness, peace, and stability. As a family we are moving forward triumphantly in life, while fully aware that the work to heal and recover is an ongoing process. My son is a success story, but so am I.

For many years before becoming a recovery writer, I worked in the insurance field in Columbus. Part of the process of insuring a home was inspecting it to identify risks. My eyes were trained to see areas of weakness—such as where the roof might leak, if a porch railing is unstable, if the home is vulnerable to break-ins or fires, and if there were cracks in the foundation. As long as all the major bases were covered and secured, the risk that a calamity might threaten to damage, destroy, or collapse the home was lower.

This is similar to the mindset many of us have when it comes to trusting that addiction will never happen in our family. Families doing their best to lead respectable lives (and I believe that's most of us) honestly believe we are doing the hard work to create healthy, thriving families—isn't it our ultimate responsibility? Isn't it our job to cover the risks? If our kids get good grades, mind their manners, and show talent on their teams—how could they possibly end up becoming dependent upon a narcotic?

We too often think that these things happen only in families who must not have loved or guided their kids. Addiction surely occurs only in those whose parents neglected to teach them the right things, give discipline, or take them to church on Sunday. Addiction happens in families who don't cover the risks, right? Shouldn't those who do the work to create a stable, "normal" home environment and raise good kids be safeguarded from the risk?

This is not a realistic mindset. Addiction can happen anywhere, to anyone. There is, however, always hope: just as the opioid epidemic seemed to rise from Ohio like a Category Five hurricane and sweep across the nation, it's worth knowing that Ohio is also the birthplace of recovery. The Alcoholics Anonymous twelve-step movement began in 1935 in Akron, Ohio. Regardless of which method of recovery one subscribes to, this full-circle fact is a powerful reminder that no matter how dark things seem, hope is potent, and recovery is possible.

We are in the fight of our lives against the epidemic of addiction, but one thing remains unshakably true: we don't give up easily. Ohioans are fighters. With honor and respect for those we have lost, and for all those continuing to fight: Be encouraged to never give up. Hope is powerful, and recovery is possible.

*Annie Highwater is an author, writer, speaker, podcast host, and family advocate. Annie's memoir,* Unhooked: A Mother's Story of Unhitching from the Roller Coaster of Her Son's Addiction, *was published in 2016. Her second book,* Unbroken: Navigating the Madness of Family Dysfunction, Addiction, Alcoholism, and Heartache, *was published in 2018.*

# 3

## A PLACE FOR "TOTAL RECOVERY"

MEMBERS OF TOLEDO RESTORATION CHURCH
(TOLEDO)

Toledo Restoration Church is a "total recovery" church dedicated to serving the needs of families and individuals who have been afflicted by addiction. As our name makes clear, we restore lives that have been broken by this disease. We provide free living in Christian Recovery Homes for men and women who have been afflicted by addiction, alcoholism, and prostitution. Step-by-step, we help them with daily prayer, Bible studies, community involvement, and character development with the word of God. We are well-prepared to do so because we've walked the same roads as the people we hope to help. Our stories are what led us to Toledo Restoration Church in the first place. They are why we believe in church-based recovery. To understand the church, let us share a bit about ourselves.

### EDWARD MENDIVEL JR., PASTOR

My father's side of the family was filled with drug addicts. Like most of my family, out of the pain of rejection and hurt I also started using drugs at a young age. I worked to provide for my family, but all of that soon came to an end when my wife, Evelyn, and I started to do things we thought we would never do—just for drugs. We had five small children from the ages of fourteen years to six months when members of Imperial Valley Ministries, an organization in California, started telling us about the Good News of Jesus and the recovery homes the church provided. At this time, we were living from motel to motel, selling a little bit of drugs just to get by. One day after my wife had been in the recovery home for a week, I decided to go to church. I fell on my face at the altar and cried out to God. I've never experienced anything like it before. I left church and a few days later entered Imperial Valley Recovery Men's Home. I was delivered and set free from addiction. Twenty-nine years later, I have adopted the same model that helped me, and I now serve as the pastor of Toledo Restoration Church.

## EVELYN MENDIVEL

My mother did her best to raise all of her fourteen children, but being a single mother was challenging. I started drinking and smoking at a young age. It was almost like second nature to me. I had grown up around my husband and his family, but it wasn't until I had a one-year-old daughter that we began a relationship. He was a heroin addict, but that didn't seem odd to me because he was still a working man. I was a stay-at-home mother, cooking, cleaning, ironing clothes, but one day that just wasn't enough for me because I had seen my husband getting high. I wanted to know what it felt like. I carried two of my children under the influence of heroin and cocaine. When my second youngest was born, two women from Imperial Valley Ministries came to visit the hospital. The doctors wanted to take my baby, but by the grace of God they let me take her home. I still continued to use heroin, but I was drawn to the church by their love and concern for me and my family. One day I called and went to the Women's Recovery Home. After eight years of training and preparation, my husband, my kids, and I were sent to Toledo to plant a Restoration Church! We were excited. We had a vision in our hearts and a desire to help others who were struggling with the same thing we found ourselves struggling with years and years ago.

## KENNETH IVORY JR., ASSISTANT PASTOR

While working in the field of social work for twenty years, I entertained a life of drug addiction. My addiction spiraled out of control, and I landed in Toledo thinking I was coming to get away from the lifestyle. Things only got worse. In Toledo I began to work just to get high: 128-hour weeks just to maintain the madness. One night after getting high and having nowhere to go, I began to feel hopelessly lost—wondering how I was going to get out of this situation. I began to cry out to the Lord that if He would get me out of this situation, I would serve Him for the rest of my life. The very next day, someone from Toledo Restoration Church came to the house and gave me a flyer. It read "Total Restoration is Possible," and this statement has been true for my family and me.

## MARIA MENDIVEL, SECRETARY

I am twenty-nine years old, born and raised in Toledo. As an adolescent, I carried a lot of pain and anger inside, and I became a bit of a rebel— soon leading me to alcohol and drug addiction. I found myself, as many others do, without purpose or value. I knew I needed help. My family was familiar with Toledo Restoration Church, and I knew that this was a place of refuge to run to in times of trouble. After dropping out of a local community college, and on the verge of losing a job, I came to the realization that I needed help. After swallowing my pride, I entered the Women's Recovery Home.

## MARY MORALES-TORRES, MEMBER

I grew up in a home with an addict father and a mother who did the best she could to raise seven children on her own. At the age of eleven, I started smoking weed and drinking. I was sixteen when I first shot up heroin. At twenty-one, I became pregnant. Around this same time, my best friend was murdered. I was shocked. I thought that that would be my destiny if I didn't stop. My kid's dad said he was going to Ohio to start a job, so I came along with intentions of establishing a better life. But I still had the same lifestyle of heroin addiction. Shortly after I moved, my sister died. God showed me I needed to change, but I was hurt and angry about my sister's death. Only two months after her passing, my baby brother died of a heroin overdose. I thought there was no hope and it was the end for me. My kid's dad sold cocaine, so we would do speedballs, a mixture of cocaine and heroin. After being up for three days, with no sleep and doing drugs, I fell to my knees and asked God to change my life. I had no place to live. I was going through a divorce, and I asked Evelyn if I could move into their recovery home with my four children. It was 1996 when Toledo Restoration Church started its ministry in Toledo in a house on Woodruff Avenue. It was there that God started to restore my heart and mind.

————

We are all individuals who have walked the path of addiction and are hoping to help others who are in need. Whether it be in the office or on the streets, we see firsthand the effects that opioids and the drug epidemic has had on our society. We are able to play a part in stopping or preventing this madness—and we are willing to do our part. Our vision has become the vision of Toledo Restoration Church. We know now what we didn't know then: there is a way out and it's through the love and power of Jesus Christ.

Although we are missionaries to drug addicts, our goal is to restore families who have been afflicted by this disease. When a person commits to coming to our church, we immediately begin the healing process by nurturing, caring, and discipling these individuals—assessing the person's needs, not their wants. Almost all of the men and women who enter the recovery homes are from the inner city; they are often poor and come from dysfunctional families. We want to reverse that cycle by taking back what the devil has stolen from them.

Our ministry spends countless hours in the streets. We have "hotdog rallies" where the church gathers in a neighborhood and provides food to the community. We then set up a sound system, canvas the area with flyers about our ministry, and invite drug-afflicted people over for an evening of witnessing, prayer, food, and fellowship. Our members are out in the streets daily, witnessing to drug addicts. We go to blighted and drug-infested neighborhoods to seek out people in need—many of whom are homeless or working as prostitutes. We meet them one-on-one, often while drug activity is in progress. We are quite comfortable with this because our church is made up of former gang members, prostitutes, and drug addicts—we know firsthand where to go, whom to seek out, and how to interact with them. Some of these individuals feel there isn't another life than the one they're in; they have no hope or vision for themselves. The Bible says the people perish for lack of vision. We bring them a target, a goal, and a vision.

Our Missionary Teams also travel to different cities to start new churches. Our goal is to bring awareness and provide help and hope. We send teams out for days, weekends, and even weeks at a time. If you come to our church, you will find "Training Restoration Church Planters" on banners, because that's exactly what we do: we train members to plant restoration churches in other neighborhoods and cities. Our desire is to travel with the Gospel to every city—to reach whoever will hear us and the Good News. Our church goes into the neighborhoods where other churches won't go. Our organization—born in Ohio—now consists of twenty-three churches throughout the US and Mexico.

Each of our churches has a men's home and a women's home that provide a stable place for people to recover. Bible study and prayer are mandatory. The Bible helps target the bad habits—moral, mental, or otherwise—that one acquires while living a life of drug addiction and prostitution. Second Corinthians 5:17–19 says that if anyone is in Christ, he or she "is a new creation."

When someone enters our recovery home, a gestation period begins. We determine what care and attention that individual needs. We then attempt to nurture that person according to his or her affliction. We know that an individual struggling with heroin or opioids will be "kicking." Their joints and body will ache, they won't want to eat, and they will sweat a lot—even while sleeping. They hallucinate. We walk them through this ordeal, providing care and support as they get clean.

Prayer is vital. We believe in the healing power of Jesus Christ unto salvation. Many of the men and women who enter our homes have never had anyone care about them or their situation. Some have been scarred mentally and sexually. Given the structure and demands, the experience can be startling to those seeking to change their lives and rid themselves of drug addiction. They come from situations where there weren't any rules. They have to be weaned from their previous habits to adjust to a life of order.

Our motto is "Pray, Stay, and Obey." We believe that the church is the key to helping Ohio's opioid epidemic. As we refer to the church, we are not speaking of one individual church, but all churches. If all the churches throughout the nation would get out of their four walls and help the lost, hurting, addicted, and oppressed by preaching the Gospel . . . well, we could lessen—and even eliminate—addiction.

# 4

## BUILDING COMMUNITY IN THE
## B. RILEY SOBER HOUSE

RAFAEL "TONY" CORREA
(CLEVELAND)

I opened the B. Riley Sober House, the first LGBTQ+ halfway house for substance abuse in the eastern US, to commemorate my mother. She was the first person I knew who struggled with addiction—and I resented her for it. The only time I would see or hear from her is when she would show up asking for money or call from jail. She tried again and again to get sober, only to fail to follow through. I didn't think anything was going to change.

One day, when she was living with our grandma, she sent us kids outside. I was a nosy kid so I listened through the window when a case manager broke the news to my mother that she had HIV. She sobbed. Eventually, with the help of a twelve-step program, my mother got sober.

Growing up in this environment, I faced a great deal of grief and trauma. Adding to that, I was molested and struggled with my identity as a gay man because I was told that being gay was wrong. I was unable to accept myself. My role models were drug dealers, prostitutes, and individuals rebelling against society, so I began doing what my "role models" did. People had told me to take another look at my attitude and behavior—I paid no attention.

My life began to spiral out of control and my disease progressed rapidly—from marijuana to club drugs and then to heroin. Getting, using, and finding drugs became my reason to live. I moved away from my grandmother's house to be around people who were behaving like me. During my active addiction, I had little to nothing to do with my mom. All I knew was that she ended up getting her own house and getting her kids back, and she was in love with some man again. I couldn't have cared less—I was caught up in the grips of the continuing and progressive illness known as addiction. I was self-entitled and felt like the world owed me something, and I treated everyone I came across as such. I did not care about other people and their feelings. I harmed a lot of people, but, most of all, I harmed myself.

There I was: Puerto Rican, gay, a two-time convicted felon, and a homeless heroin addict with nowhere to turn. I turned to my mom for help. She allowed me to move in with her and then, in a few months, kicked me out for continuing to leave dirty needles lying around. She tried to get me into counseling, but I always had an excuse. I had already been through four detoxes and thirteen treatment programs. What was left to do?

I was living at a friend's place, doing drugs, when my aunt told me to come stay with her while she was at my mom's house. It would be nice to have me there, she said, especially with my other two brothers coming home from prison in the coming months. I moved back in. My aunt lived close by, and she would come over daily while I lived in the basement. During this time, unbeknownst to me, the man my mother was with for fifteen years took all of her savings. My mom fell into depression and stopped taking her HIV medications. Her health quickly deteriorated.

My brothers were now home from prison. My sister was staying over because my mom was so sick that she could not take care of herself. I felt so disgusted with myself for being the older brother but not being able to comfort my family. I was a wreck, but I would not let anyone know it. Eventually my mom died and we all had to move.

I never got to make amends to mom for the way I treated her. Through my own recovery, which consisted of working a twelve-step program and going to treatment one last time, I was afforded the opportunity to found a new recovery house and honor my mom, Bridget Riley, by naming it after her. The B. Riley House is a structured, recovery-oriented, safe, and affirming living space for all members of the LGBTQ+ community. I wanted to tailor it for the LGBTQ+ community because there was nothing like it here in Ohio. As a gay man who had spent a lot of time at heteronormative treatment centers, I knew from personal experience the difficulties that arise with prejudice and discrimination. I know how tough it is to focus on the drug problem at hand when you have people cracking gay jokes, or staff talking about the way you walk and talk.

Our services—which we provide regardless of ability to pay—are intended to help people recover from the seemingly helpless and hopeless state of mind caused by substance abuse. Members from twelve-step self-help groups come to the house each day. We require that all residents attend ninety in-house group sessions in ninety days. We discuss spirituality, sexuality, powerlessness, unmanageability, relapse prevention, and giving back. Each week, residents do house chores, complete a daily gratitude list, and (on Tuesdays and Thursdays) fill out personal inventory sheets. B. Riley is designed to be a self-supporting therapeutic community democratically run by the residents. Most disputes are resolved by the residents, though we have a residential advocate—who is also a Certified Chemical Dependency Counselor Assistant—available in the event residents cannot resolve disputes.

Several mechanisms help us keep our doors open. When residents successfully complete their ninety days in house and begin working, we ask them to give back—these residents are called our "Three Quarters Residents." These residents help us keep our doors open for the new person who does not have the ability to pay. We fundraise by holding local drag shows, dance parties, and cookouts, all with raffles and door prizes. We receive support from private donors, be it in the form of money or toilet paper. If it were not for the help of our community, and my faith in a higher power, B. Riley just would not be. We are truly a nonprofit organization. Our resident advocate and executive director do not get paid. It is the "Carrying of the Message" to the still sick and suffering addict that encourages and motivates our staff.

Recently, we've been seeing more and more residents who started off with club drugs and meth but have progressed to heroin or other opioids, including pills. This has been most typical of the gay male and the trans-female population who have walked through our doors. Although it is always challenging to help individuals in recovery, it has been particularly devastating to watch these young people be beaten up so badly from the opioid epidemic. In February of 2018, data gathered for our semiannual report indicated that most of our residents had used heroin. Several residents had to be given Narcan to be brought back to life. Others spent many years homeless, and still more had been stuck in the cycle of recidivism. One of our past residents had an almost-fatal overdose and was stuck in a coma for six months—only to use again right after reawakening and being released from the hospital. It's painful to hear residents' stories of friends who have died from heroin. It's not just one distant friend, but often four or five in our residents' immediate circles. The grief is astounding.

The crisis is no longer focused on the club drugs that used to be a part of the LGBTQ+ party subculture; more LGBTQ+ people are progressing to heroin. The results are more HIV/AIDS infections, more homelessness, and more trips to hospitals and institutions than we have ever seen. Gay and transgender people abuse substances at more than twice the rate of non-gay or trans-people. Given this, we at B. Riley have changed our outlook on medication-assisted treatments and strongly support the use of Suboxone, methadone, and Vivitrol.

We especially see the value in Vivitrol, which is an opioid antagonist, meaning it attaches to the same receptors as the drugs would, but it doesn't trigger a release of the feel-good brain chemical dopamine. When someone uses Vivitrol and then tries to misuse opioids, the effects are blocked. Vivitrol is administered as a shot and lasts for a month, which can really help a person's recovery.

It is not easy work, but we are proud to be changing the conversation within the LGBTQ+ community through awareness and action. In my experience, a lot of LGBTQ+ individuals don't even think it's affecting our community. We know the drug exists but believe it to be outside of our realm. "Oh, we don't do those things." Rather vain, I would say!

The good news is that more and more individuals are now seeking treatment because we don't turn them away for being who they are. Many of our residents never sought treatment because of their fear of discrimination and prejudice. Other residents sought treatment but were turned away because they are trans-male or trans-female and recovery houses in Ohio accept only those who live within the gender assigned them at birth. There has not been an equal opportunity for life. But at our home, the opportunity for recovery is a right, not a privilege.

*Raphael "Tony" Correa is founder of the B. Riley Sober House.*

# 5

# WALKING PAST ABANDONED HOUSES, I THINK OF ERIC

### BARBARA COSTAS-BIGGS
### (PORTSMOUTH)

This poem wanted to start in a condemned house, so I took
a walk to show the poem this town and asked: which one?

The poem shrugged. Shattered windows rendered black,
no flicker of blue aquarium television light. Fast food wrappers

an altar, piled on the porch. A small pink running shoe
hole worn in the sole stuck in a chain link fence.

Fifteen years ago, while I was drinking flat beer in a dive bar,
my friend Eric died after getting high from a transdermal

oxycodone patch. He wrote poems I will never
forget: he found his mother dead, her fingers

gnawed to bone by rats. His glasses always broken, crooked,
taped, his cheeks and arms scabbed.

This poem can't imagine. It wasn't this house but probably
one like it, peeling clapboard,

busted plumbing. This town smells burned out
and the burning no longer comes from the foundry

or the coke plant or steel mill. We are falling in
on ourselves, shooting heroin into our veins.

These houses—empty of furniture, food, clean clothes,
laughter, shampoo—are helpless, their dirty glass eyes

begging to see something other than broken smokestacks,
shoes strung on powerlines.

The ears that heard hooves on the brick that sleeps
under pavement are long gone.

There was no Narcan for Eric, and no Narcan
for wrecked Greek Revivals.

*Barbara Costas-Biggs* is a poet who lives in Southern Ohio.

# 6

# HOW ARE THE CHILDREN?

JOY EDGELL
(BELPRE)

In the springtime, the small city streets of Belpre are beautiful with blooming trees. The streets are lined with pink and white dogwoods, pear trees, and azaleas. These blooms remind me every year of the hope we see in our students at Belpre Elementary. Many have faced more trauma in their young lives than we as adults have faced in all our years. Yet they persist and, with the help of a school community who loves them, will blossom, just like our trees in the spring.

Belpre is a town of approximately 7,000 people, founded in the 1700s. We were the second settlement in the Northwest Territory, after our neighbor Marietta. Belpre means "Belle Prairie," a name given by the French trappers who admired the valley. Our city also boasts employing the first female schoolteacher in the state of Ohio. Currently, there is a diverse mixture of residents in our small town. There are many adults over the age of sixty-five who worked locally for the large chemical plants. They raised their children in this small river town that values its community. There are also many young families struggling to survive on minimum wage incomes. We are one of the only areas locally to find inexpensive rentals "in town." We are also located right along the major highway that runs from Columbus to Athens to Marietta, which is an ever-growing drug-trafficking route.

As some of our young families struggle in a chaotic world, their children are growing up with many uncertainties. Some are being raised by parents with severe addictions. Opioids have made a strong presence in our community, and some families have been torn apart fighting to keep their loved ones out of its clutches. As a result, some students have to be raised by a variety of relatives such as a grandma or an aunt—and some children are not sure who will be home in the evening to take care of them. As a principal and a mother, I quickly realized this fact five years ago, as I entered this job. Maslow taught us that if an individual's basic needs are not met, that individual will struggle to grow and progress in other areas of their life. Our kids need the basic foundation of love, acceptance, security, and food in order to focus and learn in a classroom. Unfortunately, in many cases, we have to take hours out of a school day to ensure that a student eats breakfast, has shoes that fit, or is simply clean enough to focus.

Two years ago, we welcomed a kindergarten girl—we'll call her Abby—who faced many obstacles, the simplest one being cleanliness. She would come to school with matted hair, clothes that were three sizes too big and covered in stains, and fingernails caked with dirt. You can imagine the smell connected with this little body. Our elementary used to be a middle school, complete with two locker rooms with shower bays. We knew we had to build enough of a relationship with this family in order to gain permission for her to bathe at school so that we could help her create a positive image with friends and be part of a classroom. We were able to gain the trust of the family, and we discovered their house had dirt floors, many windows were missing, and the water had been turned off. They were living in an unforgiving cycle of poverty, disability, and drug use. We also built a closet for Abby in our locker room. Our team brought clothes, shower items, and hair bows to keep the closet stocked. Every Monday, Wednesday, and Friday, Abby received a shower, with help from the school nurse, and her entire demeanor changed when she entered her classroom. Those are not needs that college courses teach you how to provide, but they are essential if we want children to learn and be loved.

Even though those are not skills "taught" in the college educational curriculum, my staff amazes me every day with their capacity to love and provide these basic foundations for students—way before the "book learning" ever begins. No matter what a family is addicted to, the child is not at fault. I have watched teachers hold children on their laps, cry as a student talks about Dad going to prison, and visit homes to take work to students who have no resources to complete it on their own. Children are experiencing large amounts of toxic stress in their young lives, which can cause their brain to change in many ways. The more adverse childhood experiences a student has faced, the more security and structure they need. Research on childhood stress shows us that we need to shift our focus from "What is wrong with that child?" to "What has happened to that child?" and "What do they need from me?"

When students bring this stress to school, the simplest classroom problem can escalate quickly. When a child's "flight or fight" reaction is always on, due to stress at home, that child soon exhibits extreme emotional dysregulation. It is our job to literally reshape that young brain to function and operate in the public arena.

Over the past five or ten years, my teachers have been forced to evolve into childhood counselors, family resource experts, and drug identification professionals in response to growing opioid abuse. They have completed hours of training, learning about trauma in childhood and how it shapes the young and adolescent brain.

We have to first focus on making sure they are secure in the fact that school is a safe place. This means working through what each child needs to feel secure. At times, it may be a counselor assigned to them, other times it may be one bag of nonperishable food a week (we hand out over one hundred bags of food each week), or it may be as simple as a stuffed animal to hug while they work. We had one student who had experienced physical trauma. He really wanted to go to Hawaii someday. When he would have a behavior meltdown, "Hawaii" became his cooldown location. We created a corner of a room to resemble the islands, complete with posters, sand, and inflatable palm trees. The key to our current way of education is to find what makes each individual child feel safe. When they feel safe, they can learn. When they learn, there is hope. When there is hope, their lives may be changed forever.

Education is evolving at a rapid pace. Technology and our current world climate make it impossible to keep up with the newest craze. We at Belpre Elementary want to go back to the foundation of basic needs that I mentioned earlier. Our students receive security, sustenance, and a caring adult in their life each day when they enter our building. They make mistakes and make us mad, just as any typical child in our lives, but every day is a new beginning. Grit and resilience are going to be pivotal in our helping them build a successful future.

An African proverb counsels asking neighboring villages, "How are the children?" The understanding between villages is that the answer will tell you how the village will be in the future. Some of our children struggle on a daily basis, but with security, mental health intervention, and a staff dedicated to breaking the cycle of addiction, we hope to answer, "Our children are survivors."

*Joy Edgell is principal of Belpre Elementary School.*

# 7

# A HAVEN FROM HUMAN TRAFFICKING AND ADDICTION

JEFF BARROWS
(ZANESFIELD)

Over the past decade, Ohio's opioid epidemic has increasingly been featured in the news. Rarely, however, do these reports mention the connection between illicit drugs and another criminal enterprise in Ohio: human trafficking. The exploitation of one human being by another is usually done for financial gain or some other personal benefit. Human trafficking is far more common in Ohio than people think, and it intersects with drug addiction on several levels.

Drug traffickers have learned that while you can sell drugs only once before needing to replenish the product, human beings can be sold over and over again. With this realization, drug traffickers have added human trafficking to their criminal activities—all without lessening or otherwise changing their involvement within the drug trade. Although human trafficking has been occurring in Ohio for many years, the opioid epidemic has been a major contributor to the increasing incidence of this heinous crime.

A 2009 report generated by the Ohio Human Trafficking Commission under the Ohio Attorney General's Office estimated that there were over 3,400 foreign-born persons in Ohio who were at risk of being trafficked, with an estimated 783 currently being trafficked. In addition, the report estimated that over 2,800 Ohio youth under the age of eighteen were at risk of being trafficked into sexual exploitation, including the 1,078 youth who were trafficked into sexual exploitation in the previous year. Due to insufficient data, the report was unable to give an estimate regarding trafficking among Ohio adults, though it recognized that the number was probably even higher.

Opioids are commonly used as a recruiting tool by traffickers to lure a young girl into sexual exploitation. Once a young girl has been identified as a potential victim, the trafficker is able to freely give her drugs to facilitate addiction so that the trafficker can later use that addiction to force her to pay for her drugs through prostitution, stripping, or the production of pornography.

Gracehaven, an organization I founded in 2008, works to fight and prevent sex trafficking among Ohio youth through prevention education, intervention training, case management, and residential treatment of survivors. Our prevention education coordinator vividly describes the use of drugs, especially opioids, as the "leash" drug traffickers use to pull their unsuspecting prey into prostitution.

Illicit drugs are also used within human trafficking to numb the mental and emotional trauma of sexual exploitation, especially within prostitution. Sex-trafficked women and girls average between ten to fifteen sexual encounters per day, only to repeat the same number the following day. We have served girls at Gracehaven who were forced to have sex up to forty times a day. No human being can endure the emotional (and physical) trauma that is associated with repeated intimate sexual relations with complete strangers. Illicit drugs numb that emotional trauma and become a critical tool used by traffickers to maintain their hold on victims by allowing them to escape both the emotional and physical trauma associated with commercial sex.

Illicit drugs are also used to coerce human trafficking victims to becoming drug traders themselves. Drug traffickers who expand their criminal activities into human trafficking often force their victims to be the purchaser, seller, or transporter of the illicit drugs to mitigate their own risk. Of course, these drugs are often the same ones that put women in their situation in the first place.

A final connection between the opioid epidemic and human trafficking is the issue of parental drug addiction and the subsequent risks to children within the home, often including the risk of being trafficked. It is not uncommon for parental addiction to cause neglect and abuse of children so that when funds to purchase drugs become scarce, it seems to be an easy step to sell the children into sexual exploitation to help fund the drug addiction. A neglected and abused child is exactly the kind of victim traffickers seek because they are more easily controlled. We commonly hear stories of parental drug use and addiction that led to circumstances in which the child was left unattended and vulnerable to strangers or other family members.

This complicated relationship between human trafficking and illicit drug use has been substantiated in multiple studies, but it has also been the case with many of the minors we work with at Gracehaven. A quote by an actual survivor best captures this intersection: "I started doing drugs, specifically cocaine, down at the local go-go bar, and eventually I tried heroin. I was a mess, wrecked my life, wasted it on drugs because I'd been raped and I didn't think I mattered to anyone. When I was thirty-one years old I started dating a guy who was a drug dealer. We dealt together, did crack together, and he started prostituting me to close drug deals."

———

I started Gracehaven to address the multifaceted needs of Ohio minors entrapped within child sex trafficking. My goal was to create a specialized residential treatment facility that would serve as the epicenter of our efforts to prevent and address child sex trafficking in central Ohio. Studies have shown that specialized residential treatment is critical to facilitate recovery for victims of human trafficking. Unfortunately, Gracehaven is the only such facility in Ohio. The girls we care for at the home are usually referred to us through the juvenile court system or by county children's services agencies. While they live in the home, our girls attend school and receive specialized and trauma-informed individual, group, art, and even equine therapy.

Gracehaven partners with drug addiction programs across Ohio so that clients admitted to the Gracehaven home have completed an initial treatment phase and are no longer taking illicit drugs. Then throughout their rehabilitation at the Gracehaven home, our programming regularly includes discussions on drug addiction, such as how to avoid relapse and other tools to help the client through their addiction treatment. Since opening, the home has served approximately forty-nine survivors of child sex trafficking. In 2014, Gracehaven merged with Central Ohio Youth for Christ, an entity that had been working with high-risk youth for over fifteen years. This partnership has provided additional resources that will allow us to lead the fight in Ohio and increase our national scope.

In addition to our residential treatment program and our efforts to educate Ohio youth on child sex trafficking, Gracehaven provides case management to both young girls and boys in central Ohio who are either at risk of being trafficked or are survivors of child sex trafficking. Case management is conducted by licensed social workers and includes advocating and coordinating the care of an individual as well as facilitating their access to various community resources such as mental health therapy. Our caseworkers believe, as we all do, that their efforts are worthwhile if they can keep just one Ohio minor from becoming addicted to drugs and subsequently drawn into sex trafficking. Our prevention trainings are conducted throughout central Ohio, reaching over 6,500 junior high and high school students in 2017. Gracehaven also partners with local drug and alcohol treatment agencies to make sure clients undergo necessary drug testing and complete all prescribed treatments. Over the past three years, we have provided case management to over ninety-two young people in central Ohio. Finally, Gracehaven engages in intervention and awareness training of health care professionals around the state, training over 2,800 professionals in 2017.

It's important for us to realize that Ohio's opioid epidemic is not only directly impacting individuals through drug addiction but has consequences particularly for young women who may be at risk of sex trafficking. Because at Gracehaven we regularly encounter these intersections between child sex trafficking and illicit drugs, we understand the need to discuss drug addiction in all our prevention trainings, as well as in our community case management and residential treatment programs. The two simply cannot be separated. We recognize that any effort that successfully reduces the availability of opioid drugs in Ohio will also reduce child sex trafficking.

*Jeff Barrows, DO, is an obstetrician-gynecologist and founder of Gracehaven.*

# 8

## A NEW HOME

MARY LYNN ST. LAWRENCE
(ATHENS)

Every other Saturday I cofacilitate a group discussion with about fifteen women at a local treatment center, and every Thursday night I take phone calls from any of these women who want to talk outside of the group. Sometimes we talk about a problem they have or their children. Other times we talk about nothing in particular at all.

Most of these women are heroin addicts. Some of them have been in as many as nine treatment centers before ours. For some it is the first attempt. Some are pregnant and have taken court-mandated incarceration as an opportunity to get sober for the sake of their unborn child.

The women come from all walks of life. They are health aides, teachers, high school dropouts, waitresses, and college students. What they have in common is an ever-present desire to get high. A lot of the time, the women come to me concerned that their discharge will only hurt their loved ones more. Facing their health issues, they have an overwhelming concern for the well-being of their loved ones. Over the three years I have worked directly with these women, the opioid crisis has reached the level of a national emergency. Today, heroin and methamphetamine are almost always the group's drugs of choice.

I spent most of my career with patients who were confronting death from cancer or AIDS. Hospice patients fight hard to preserve their quality of life. But at the same time they are at some deep place inside resigned to the reality that they are terminally ill. This is not the case with the women I work with now. These women don't think they'll die from an overdose. The fear of death, which could forestall their use of drugs, is missing. The very mindset that could protect them from danger has been whittled away. Drug experimentation, which is relatively common, leads to addiction. People don't understand the sinister nature of the drugs they use. When people are surrounded by this kind of ideology, it makes sobriety seem that much more impossible. When you're surrounded, it's hard to escape.

Most of the women I work with became addicted through someone they know. Others began to use prescription pain medications, became addicted, and turned to heroin or other street drugs when they could no longer obtain prescription medications. Still others used drugs socially initially and quickly become addicted. And addiction ultimately makes people do some crazy things—I have heard of drugs being kept in the cash drawers at restaurants, held in the parking lot at work, and hidden in the outbuildings on people's properties. Once inside the culture, the addict is surrounded.

We are facing a public health challenge that can't be solved by treatment alone. These people, especially the women we work with, just need a community. A young person relies on peers more than family for emotional support, and leaving that group and moving away for recovery is for them a frightening and sad possibility. To an older person with an established family, leaving home holds a different kind of terror. But finding new, clean, and sober friends and family is the only exit that holds the possibility of recovery.

Imagine spending months in treatment, missing your family, losing your job, and then having to enter a new life alone in an empty apartment—with no associates other than those you met in the treatment center. As long as we keep on releasing addicts from incarceration or treatment right back into their previous homes, I see little hope for change. New and sustained interpersonal relationships can make a difference.

In 2016, our local Alcohol, Drug Addiction and Mental Health Services Board had a meeting with service professionals and community leaders to discuss possible local responses to the addiction crisis. As a result, I continued to meet with a small group of professionals to discuss what could be done.

Visiting the jail, we observed that when they are released, people are often met by someone who offers them drugs on the ride home. Most of the women I work with will go to a transitional home after discharge, but eventually they have to return to their own social network, and it is almost always the same place where they started using. It was a disgrace.

A small group of us, all women, established Women for Recovery, a nonprofit organization, in early 2017. We planned to create a small recovery home for about eight women, all in recovery. This home would be a place where women could go and stay for a few months after discharge from jail or a treatment center. Here they would be able to seek work, go to counseling, get to know their children again, and, most important of all, develop a new set of friends who don't use alcohol or drugs.

We began operations with six residents, a day administrator, and a trained counselor who provides daytime supervision at the house and does community work. Our model is a collaborative one. We have chosen a somewhat isolated and yet beautiful setting for our home, called Serenity Grove. Nature helps women seeking wholeness and health. There are raised-bed gardens, and eventually we hope to keep bees. We have seven acres, a small stream, and ample space for walking and thinking.

All of the women at Serenity Grove follow an organized recovery program. We believe that successful recovery is individually motivated and self-directed. It will work only if a woman sees it as an opportunity to find happiness and success while living among others. Developing such a community takes time. We have our first residents now, and we hope to build a reputation that brings in people from all walks of life.

Our approach is not a panacea. It will not bring back Tracy, who spent two three-month sessions in a treatment center and then went home and died from an overdose within a few weeks. Nor can it help Ellen, who was born to Jackie several weeks premature and addicted and spent the first months of her life in the neonatal unit in Columbus, crying to be held, alone in an isolette. If we keep treating addiction as a medical condition only and fail to address the life changes that must take place in order for people to stay free of substance abuse, we will only further entrench ourselves. The women who come to live in our residence must be convinced that they are facing a life of suffering and perhaps death if they do not get sober. They need a community that is ready to help them heal.

*Mary Lynn St. Lawrence was a founding board member of Women in Recovery and is now an active member of the Serenity Grove community.*

# 9

## COLLABORATION
## IN MIDDLETOWN

TRAVIS BAUTZ
(MIDDLETOWN)

Middletown is the historical center of our library system, dating back to the days when the city was a thriving industrial stronghold for the steel and paper industries. Middletown is a proud community of 45,000. However, it has had some economic downturns over the years, marked by the factory closings and job losses that are typical in rust belt states.

Recently, the opioid epidemic has hit close to home, with overdoses reported in homes and in public venues such as restaurants, stores, and parks. News outlets in 2017 reported that the city of Dayton had the highest per capita opioid use in the country. Cincinnati was not far behind at number six, and Toledo at number ten. All of these cities, including Middletown, are near the I-75 corridor.

The city of Middletown reported that in 2017, $2.3 million was spent on opioid-related expenses, with $1.9 million going to the police. There were 966 opioid overdoses among 798 individuals. Among these overdoses were 77 fatalities—up 45 percent from the previous year. In total, 2,970 milligrams of Narcan were administered by EMS—at 2 milligrams per dose. As overdoses became more frequent, locally and nationally, people began to recognize the wide-reaching effects of the epidemic. It was not uncommon for library patrons, friends, or staff to personally know someone touched by overdoses. Our library staff have even witnessed overdoses firsthand on a couple of occasions.

As the city faced increasing opioid-related costs, overdoses, and fatalities, city leaders worried and even agonized. At a city council meeting, one councilman expressed frustration over the dramatic increases to city expenses. The councilman asked if the city was obliged to answer emergency calls for suspected overdoses, especially for those who were repeat overdosers. The councilman proposed other potential solutions, such as court-appointed community service following overdose calls, and stated, "I want to send a message to the world that you don't want to come to Middletown to overdose because someone might not come with Narcan and save your life. We need to put a fear about overdosing in Middletown."

The councilman's statements quickly circulated among news circuits locally, nationally, and even internationally. Newspaper headlines from prominent news outlets proclaimed:

- One politician's answer to opioid overdosers: "Let 'em die" (*Chicago Tribune*)
- "Ohio councilman wants to save money, 'Send a Message' by letting overdose victims die" (*Huffington Post*)
- "One politician's solution to the overdose problem: Let addicts die" (*Washington Post*)
- "Drug overdoses are soaring in one town. A proposed solution? Stop sending ambulances" (*Tri-City Herald*)
- "Ohio councilman: After 2 overdoses, no more EMS" (*USA Today*)

As with many things that go viral in today's digital age, opinions and reactions to these headlines were many. Some supported the sentiments; others denounced them. Legal and ethical debates ensued in the court of public opinion, among our community members, and across the nation.

Middletown became a destination for national reporters seeking to learn more, many painting the city (unfairly, in my opinion) as a wasteland of addicts and overdoses. Residents and city employees were approached and questioned about the opioid epidemic. In an extreme example, a reporter even pretended to be overheated from jogging as an excuse to enter a fire station seeking emergency treatment. While inside, the reporter then began questioning EMTs about opioids in order to obtain information for his stories. The pressure from inside and outside the community was a lot to bear.

The following month, the councilman did withdraw his proposal and apologized for causing an uproar. Regardless, many were left to wonder about the effect of the opioid epidemic on the city's reputation and long-term viability.

The Middletown Library did not escape the overdoses, as library staff faced overdose situations on several occasions in recent years. Thankfully, none were fatal, though we had some close calls. In the first case, an adult passed out facedown in the toilet before being rescued by a staff member. In the second, an adult passed out behind a restroom door, making it difficult for others to enter and provide aid. These instances were not commonplace in our location, but they made an impact on staff, who are dedicated to promoting the well-being of our patrons and community.

As staff were learning to deal with these worrisome situations, we learned of a regional meeting, the Middletown Heroin Summit, being formed by a private/public partnership between the city and the nearby Atrium Medical Center. Library staff attended the summit and found a citywide turnout, including elected officials, judges, bailiffs, probation officers, faith-based leaders, police, fire, paramedics, social workers, doctors, addiction specialists, rehabilitation centers, school leaders, and more. While we view ourselves as well-connected within the community, the opioid epidemic enhanced and strengthened our community-wide partnerships.

Our city manager led the discussions, with subgroups focusing on rehabilitation, education, and enforcement issues. Collaborative efforts were established to address and assist those affected. A Heroin Response Team of social workers, EMTs, and police personally visited all overdose victims, taking them to rehabilitation options immediately as necessary. Through these meetings, new networking opportunities provided attendees a better understanding of what community resources were available. Library staff were able to use these connections to secure critical resources, including referral documentation for both addicts and their families. Libraries have always been a place for information, a safe and nonjudgmental venue for research and assistance. But now this safe and open environment provides a comfortable location for those in our community seeking assistance with opioid addiction specifically.

Most important, the city's health commissioner provided staff with a no-nonsense, fact-based presentation to offset myths or mistaken ideas held by staff. Our initial discussions on the use of Narcan focused on liability and safety issues for staff. For example, a common misconception is that administering Narcan will produce a violent and reactive overdose victim. The health commissioner's practical advice proved invaluable, as it explained how Narcan works and how even a slow-working, low-dose version (nasal spray) can buy time for the victim until professional medical staff arrive. In response to this new information, library staff expressed an interest in receiving training on how to administer the nasal version of Narcan. I am proud to say that our follow-up discussions focused primarily on how important it is that we do everything we can to assist those in need, especially when it is possible to save a life.

As our collaboration with the Heroin Summit strengthened, we were able to schedule Heroin Response social workers to be on-site during library hours. The social workers met with patrons and their families and provided services as needed.

In 2018, a full year later, Middletown has seen a marked decline in opioid-related overdoses. I believe this decline is in large part due to the collaborative efforts of the regional Heroin Summit members. Unfortunately, challenges remain as many still struggle with other addictions. However, I am convinced that the strong city leadership and collaborations from so many groups, individuals, agencies, and institutions were responsible for such marked improvements in addressing our local opioid crisis. Middletown's collaborative spirit is to be commended as a sign of an engaged citizenry who continuously work together to better our community. It is my privilege to work and serve such a wonderful community.

*Travis Bautz is executive director of the MidPointe Library System, which serves approximately 200,000 patrons in West Chester, Monroe, Trenton, and Middletown.*

# 10

# DEFIANCE, OHIO
# IS THE NAME OF A BAND

HANIF ABDURRAQIB

(COLUMBUS)

& THEY ARE FROM COLUMBUS, OHIO, WHICH IS confusing
to folks on the East Coast when I tell them about the time they played
for four hours at the Newport & it was raining outside but me & everyone I knew still locked arms after the show & walked down High Street
singing "Oh, Susquehanna!" at the top of our lungs till some dive bar
security threatened to kick our asses & he had 20 pounds on all of us
combined & Defiance, Ohio plays folk punk which pretty much means
that sometimes they let a banjo or a cello crawl into bed with the screaming & all of their shows feel like they were made just for you & Geoff
Hing plays guitar for them & makes singing look effortless & I guess it
is kind of because all of their fans know all of the words to their songs
& they sing them so loud it's like the band doesn't even have to & their
fans are often cloaked in tattoos & trucker hats & ironic hand me down
shirts from old car garages or little league baseball teams & they jump
on each other's backs at shows & scream in each other's faces & it's, like,
familial I guess, or I guess it is most times & one time at a show I saw a
dude with some straight edge tattoos knock out some dude who had an
entire school of fish inked on his arm & so okay, it's certainly not always
familial & when the guy hit the floor, Ryan Woods put down his bass &
said, "Hey, listen, don't come to a Defiance, Ohio show and fight. Cut
that shit out. Hold hands with each other or some shit" which is funny

37

to say coming from a band that put the song "I Don't Want Solidarity If It Means Holding Hands With You" on their first album, which was a fine album but it had a little too much acoustic noise for my taste & Defiance, Ohio is a real town in Ohio & the band is not from there & anyone who is from there either leaves or dies & in the summer of 1794, General Mad Anthony Wayne ordered a fort be built at the confluence of the Maumee and Auglaize rivers in Ohio & when it was done, a soldier from Kentucky named Charles Scott stood in front of the fort & said "I defy the English, Indians, and all the devils of hell to take this" & that's how the fort was called Fort Defiance & how a whole city spilled around it by 1904 & that city was also named Defiance & the site of the Fort is a library now, or at least that's what I've been told & me and my pals would drive up to Defiance every now & then when we were old enough for adventure but too young to properly wallow in the depths of Columbus's scene & we would go to Bud's diner & flirt with the waitresses & sometimes we would drive down the backroads screaming the words to some punk dirge out of the open windows of a car we had to have back in someone's parent's driveway by morning & sometimes we would take out mailboxes with a baseball bat & once a man ran out of a house with a confederate flag hanging from the porch & he chased us down the road calling us outside of all of our names & my buddy Derek said he swore he saw the man holding a shotgun & so we stuck to the fears of our own city from that point on & the second Defiance (band) album came out in 2006 & it was called The Great Depression & it nearly started an honest revolution in my little corner of heartbreak & I barely made it through 2006 cuz we had to bury Tyler & Marissa too & in the song "Condition 11:11," there are the lyrics "I remember in the kitchen when you told me your grandma died. That's when I realized it gets worse" & it does, oh it does & it is really something to really remember that you can actually be alone & so when Geoff sings "here's to this year I never thought I'd make it through" I put my arms around someone else who did make it & swayed along as the clock swung itself past midnight at the end of December & I saw Defiance (band) in another sweaty room in '07 & everyone there was sad & no one was into fighting that night & the band let the cello & the banjo strings sit thick & heavy in the air that night & no one seemed to mind & it's like if we all try hard enough in the same room, everyone can remember what it is to lose somebody at the same time & Defiance (town) is awash with heroin now & I see it on the news, a man nodding off in a car & two people overdosing in the same night & 27 people dragged to the town jail in a drug bust & it is the kind of town that will hold you under its tongue until it is ready to swallow you whole & they found the body of a kid who used to come up to Columbus for punk shows in an abandoned Defiance (town) apartment & his body was surrounded by spent lighters & he was at the Defiance (band) show where they played "Grandma Song" & everyone put up their cell phone lights but the true punks put up lighters & waved them when Ryan sang "Do you come from a dead people?" & Defiance (town) is dying off like all of Ohio's other towns that feed the bigger cities, in both food & those who escape & in the Defiance (town) paper I read a story about the heroin epidemic & the headline said "WE WILL NOT LET THIS DESTROY US" & above it is a picture of a mother pulling her young daughter's frail body close to her chest in front of a worn down house & in her eyes is a determination & in her eyes she is daring all the devils of hell to come & take what is hers & I thought about what it must be like to name yourself after a town that has become a ghost factory & play songs about surviving all manner of haunting & Defiance (band) hasn't made a record in six years & the last one sounded like they were trying to get out of each other's way & I heard they played in some Indiana dive last spring & I heard the pit was wicked & later that week there was another drug bust in Defiance (town) & there are times when destruction is not as much of a choice as we think it is & man, I barely made it out of 2006 alive & in the Defiance (band) song "Oh, Susquehanna!" the chorus that everyone sings goes "and I wonder / what do they do with the bodies / and I wonder / what do they do with the bodies / and I wonder."

*Hanif Abdurraqib is a poet, essayist, and cultural critic. Find more of his work online at http://www.abdurraqib.com.*

# 11

## A HEARTACHE NOT MY OWN

CAITLIN SEIDA
(THE PLAINS)

We could have been twins. We both took after our mother: brown hair, light eyes, and a penchant for mischief. I came from a stable home, something easily written off as privilege. Mom and Dad both in the house, never separated. Lower-middle-class suburban upbringing just outside Philadelphia.

As close as my little brother and I were, we were worlds apart. He was the outgoing one, the popular kid. His use of a wheelchair never seemed to matter. I was the blue-haired weirdo. Still, we had the same upbringing, same household, same values instilled in us. We went to the same schools and, being so close in age, had largely the same group of peers.

With just two years' difference, his generation was hard-hit by heroin: too many faces are crossed out of his yearbook, dead from an epidemic that would only get worse. And it didn't just impact the kids two years younger than me: it hit him. As best I can tell, my brother's addiction started with a supply similar to what so many white, suburban kids had: the medicine cabinet. And it ended with an arrest and rehabilitation. He's two years clean now. I won't pretend to know his whole story, and even if I did, that's his story to tell, not mine.

My story starts the week before I was to move to southeastern Ohio for school. I was ready for rolling hills and peace and quiet, and I wanted to get the hell out of suburban purgatory. That wanderlust wasn't lessened in the slightest by discovering my brother nearly unresponsive one night. My normally peaceful father, a strong but silent man with wrinkles of kindness around his eyes, hauled my brother into the shower to try to rouse him back to consciousness.

Over all the yelling and unprecedented violence, born of fear and a desire to see his youngest child live, the only thing that echoed in my head were my brother's words: "I don't know how I'm gonna live here without you, Cait." At the time I blamed myself. Maybe I still do a little bit. But ultimately I know his actions were his and his alone.

Still, it wasn't easy to figure out what was going on from 500 miles away. A friendly phone call from mom didn't exactly convey the realities of how my family was doing, and it was always a shock to see the changes during my annual visit home.

I met a local, married a local, and stayed local. I gave birth to my daughter, and I divorced local. Yet I stayed. Athens County is like nowhere else in the world. It's full of physical beauty and interesting characters. Life is a little slower here, and there's room to breathe. Ultimately, though, my decision to stay was a financial one: the cost of living is unbeatable. But the social cost is higher than I expected. In Athens County, everyone knows everything about everyone. The darker issues are right out in plain sight.

The veneer of physical beauty wears off for a while after you've lived here long enough. Soon those interesting town characters become people you'd just as soon avoid. Maybe you see them one day after they've picked their skin to the point of bleeding, or maybe they kept you up all night with shouts and screams about how they can't handle sobriety anymore. The pleasant backdrop of trees and rolling hills turns into a twisted funhouse maze of places and people to avoid because suddenly everything is dangerous: someone unpredictable is lurking behind that bush, someone eager to sell or buy is hanging out across the street. Suddenly you start noticing the detritus of addiction tossed away in flower beds and along roadsides.

Athens County is painted in poverty. The namesake city itself looks and feels cultured, educated, and full of resource and opportunity: one of the perks of housing a high-ranking university. But the further you migrate past city limits, the rougher the scenery seems to get. The setting mirrors the people you'll meet: peeling paint in bright colors on homes that were once loved and cared for but quickly fell into disrepair, sidewalks torn up and covered in crisscrossed lines, a jagged reminder of one careless moment or an event that left a mark. People doing their best to maintain their surroundings and themselves but never having enough money, time, or resources to quite make things right. As someone who has struggled with mental illness, I can appreciate it. I can even admire the county and its people as a thing of beauty. We're all doing the best we can with what we've got.

So it wasn't a hassle to pick up and dispose of used needles, burnt spoons, or Suboxone wrappers strewn around the streets. I may have grumbled and bemoaned people's carelessness, but I wasn't affronted by it. I wasn't even bothered too much by the high amount of traffic in my little trailer park neighborhood; the heroin dealer down the street was kind enough, but his clients were rude as hell.

I found myself getting madder and madder by every moment of my life being lived in the shadow of cleaning up after other people's addictions. I struggled very hard to remember that each person I saw was something to someone: a mother, a brother, a friend, and they were dealing with some pretty powerful demons. I tried to imagine my brother's face in each and every one of them: the stranger on his way to get a fix who ran down one of the feral cats I cared for, the woman who called me a nosy bitch for lingering outside too long with my dogs, the couple who left their children sleeping in a car in the middle of winter while they fed their demons.

I tried to maintain a sense of empathy, but it was tough. It was especially tough the day my daughter and her friend were playing outside and got a police escort to the door. The officer was fully outfitted in riot gear and sporting an assault weapon. I was told to keep them inside. They were raiding the neighborhood dealer's house.

For an hour we hid in the back room of a rundown little trailer whose walls all of a sudden seemed far too thin. I put on my best camp counselor routine and did everything I could to keep my daughter and her friend corralled in that room and as close to the floor as possible. We pretended to be turtles. We camped out under a blanket fort. We played "I Spy." We sang songs. Internally I was fuming, raging, and screaming. I didn't want them to see the harsh realities of life just yet, and I definitely didn't want them to become the victims of a stray bullet if things got violent. I was scared. They knew something was wrong: normally I'm not so cheerful.

It's hard to maintain a sense of empathy when you have to rush your daughter away from the harmful debris of someone else's struggle, to protect her from the pain of someone else's choices. It's a struggle I face every day when I have to explain why someone is passed out in the parking lot next door or why there are so many needles we pick up on our walks. I want to believe that people are doing the best they can, but it hurts my heart because it falls on the rest of the community to help and support without enabling—because I know what it's like to try to support someone going through a battle with addiction, even from afar.

My daughter knows what drugs are—I've had age-appropriate conversations with her. She knows people make mistakes, too, and the best way to handle them is to accept them with grace. She doesn't know that I sit and talk to some of my neighbors because I know they're fighting to stay clean and I'm the only sober person they know—and that one hour they sit and chat with me is one more hour they have behind them.

She doesn't know that I still cry sometimes, thinking of how life could have been had my brother not gotten help, and she doesn't know that I feel just as helpless as everyone else. To her, I'm mom and I can handle anything, but in my own mind I know I'm just one more person trying to do what I can to make the world—in particular, my neighborhood—a little kinder, a little gentler, a little easier for everyone, sober or addicted. It's the only thing I can think to do. Maybe it helps, maybe it doesn't, but in a small town where everyone is so close, you do what you can.

*Caitlin Seida has been a professional writer for over a decade. A single mother fueled by caffeine and sarcasm, she lives for and with her daughter and menagerie of pets.*

Brett and Travis. Credit: Vicki Scharbach.

# PART TWO

# PROCESSING LOSS

I T IS UNSURPRISING that so many contributors in a book about opioid addiction speak of loss. What is striking is the diversity in how they characterize loss and what it means to be actively working through loss on a day-to-day basis. Of course, given the danger of opioid addiction, we expected that many contributors would share stories about losing family or friends who died. But contributions in this section transcend this literal understanding of loss. Instead, contributors consider loss expansively—the loss of friendships and other relationships, perceived innocence, careers, confidence, and trust in institutions. For some Ohioans, opioids have contributed to the loss of social foundations such as empathy, hope, safety, and connectivity. From the clinical perspective, patients report losing access to medications, their physician's support, and their trust in medicine. Educators have lost students and students have lost what they once believed to be bright futures.

At the same time, readers will notice—most clearly in the section's opening selection, but in others as well—that some Ohioans have, in their coping and recovery, found tremendous hope in the face of loss. For many Ohioans, loss left them with no option but to try to locate something positive amid the grief. This isn't to say that the experience of loss is simply transformed into hope in any of these contributions. Rather, though our contributors are acutely aware of the many things that addiction can take from them, it is also true for some that writing can be a part of recovery—both literally and figuratively.

# 12

# WHAT ADDICTION GAVE ME

TONY ANDERS
(UPPER ARLINGTON)

Few things are as uplifting as an autumn drive through central Ohio. The foliage showcases a display of colorful brilliance that has many looking forward to those weeks in late October and early November. The drive from Columbus to Newark that November was unusually long and dreadful; the leaves were grayed-out, and the gleaming sun did not seem to draw attention to what is normally a joyous jaunt.

Typically, I am the driver behind the wheel. This time I was slouched in the passenger seat as my wife drove me in what was mostly a silent journey. The colors of fall were lost upon me as I peered through an opioid-dulled lens. The once-successful father, husband, and business owner had succumbed to the lies told to me by a daily consumption of pain pills. They promised that I could do anything as long as I fed the hunger. First I took the medicine; then it took me. Took me straight to Shepherd Hill—a behavioral health facility (a "rehab") in Newark.

Opioids lie. Opioids promise. They claim to take you to places where you will be free of pain, both physical and emotional. They give you a false sense of heightened performance. They tell you that you are a better parent. They tell you that you can work longer. Work harder. That you will have more confidence. That you can push through the pain. But then they call in their bets. They begin to take everything back. Then they take more.

As I was sitting on the edge of my bed in an unfamiliar place where I was separated from my family and comforts, I began to inventory what I had lost. Money? Of course. Lots. My business? The house of cards was falling. My relationships? My wife dropped me off at rehab like dropping a faulty car off at the shop. My daughter did not understand why I had to stay at the "doctor's" so long, and my four-year-old son thought I "was in heaven" since I was gone from the house. Along with all that came the loss of health, self-esteem, confidence, authenticity, and virtually everything else that opioids once promised in abundance.

I thought I was smarter than that. I thought I was better than that. I felt so foolish not to have seen it coming. The pills promised. They said they'd give, but they took. They took it all.

But did they?

One thing I did learn quickly was that addiction can give back. When one is steeped in a dynamic and active recovery process, the transformation one can undergo as a result can be extraordinary. Everyone loves a comeback. Comebacks are personal and hard and often need resources.

Ohio's opioid epidemic has shone a light on negative statistics, stigmas, and sad stories. However, I learned through my own journey that our state also has a vast network of recovery resources. My recovery gave me insight into the love and camaraderie of others willing to help me and plug me into various programs and resources to leverage my outcomes.

I was given fellowship. Early on, an isolating feeling of shame and being alone in my problem had hindered me from seeking help. My noble intentions had turned on me, and I felt alone in my brokenness. I met with others from around central Ohio who had been where I had been and were willing to share rather than shun. I learned about Alcoholics Anonymous and other twelve-step resources. I found there is no greater sign of strength than to say that I cannot handle something by myself.

Addiction gave me the opportunity to begin a practice of self-exploration. I found new ways to consider growing my own potential. I found that peering through my own narrow scope of reality often showed far fewer opportunities for growth than I actually had before me. Opioids like comfort, familiarity, and routine. Once I was taught the proper skills of self-exploration, I was able to see potential in myself, in others, and in situations far sooner than before. Addiction showed me that storms tell us where our proverbial leaks are. We must be proactive in restoring ourselves and plugging our leaks. We must learn from the challenges. Without learning the tenets of recovery, I would be a lesser man today.

I was given the gift of compassion. Although I had spent my life in service industries and considered myself "a compassionate guy," I did not have true compassion. I would point a finger of condemnation at others even as I did similar crimes to myself and my family. I found that in comparing outwardly, I was avoiding what was happening inwardly. I became enlightened to the fact that compassion must also start within. Opioids provided a false sense of warmth in the face of self-loathing. I was leading a deferred life where self-satisfaction and forgiveness were always on tomorrow's menu.

Humility was served up quickly in my recovery process. In my years, I had "dabbled" in a variety of recreations, yet none had ever burrowed to my core and changed who I was. Ego and fear kept me from seeking solutions. I always thought it was a battle of the will, a matter of "just stopping." Opioids proved otherwise. I had to humbly own my part as much as I had to learn about the brain chemistry of disease. Opioids proved to be a formidable opponent. I learned that there are things stronger than simple willpower and that I did not know myself as well as I thought I did.

Of the many things my addiction gave me, one of the greatest gifts was a career. I had spent twenty-five years in the beauty industry and thrived while doing so. I traveled the world and appeared in the media. The accolades fueled the facade. But I came to realize that I appreciated the human connection the most. I still craved the intimate connection and trust from others, and through my own recovery efforts and self-study, I returned to school.

I now serve central Ohio as a chemical dependency counselor working for a group of talented doctors who specialize in opioid addiction. I can turn what I once perceived as my greatest loss into a tool of hope to give to others. I have been given an opportunity to share contacts and resources to help others. I still get to enjoy my ability to speak and write, but now my focus is on what is going on inside a person's head as opposed to their outward appearance.

Nine years have passed since that solemn autumn day when I first went to Shepherd Hill in Newark. Recently, I attended a Gathering of Gratitude there. The vivid splendor of fall colors was not lost on me this time. A smile came across my face as I reflected on the changes that had occurred within and around me over the last decade. As I walked through the doors to share stories and smiles with those who were either in celebration or early in their own restoration, I felt restored. I was able to see clearly what addiction had given to me.

*Tony Anders enjoys the outdoors, cooking, martial arts, and being with friends and family. He continues to speak and write as well as coach and counsel people suffering from addiction.*

# 13

## THE STORIES MAKE IT REAL

### A Mayor in the Heart of the Opioid Epidemic

NAN WHALEY
(DAYTON)

Mornings with the Mayor is a program I started soon after I was sworn in as mayor of Dayton in 2014. On most Fridays, I hold open office hours at City Hall for anyone who would like to meet with me. Some of these meetings are scheduled and sometimes folks just show up. Sometimes we talk about neighborhood concerns or housing issues. Sometimes I hear complaints about city services, about potholes, or about trash pickup. Sometimes I meet with students working on school projects. On a fairly regular basis I perform weddings during these Friday Mornings. Too often, however, I also meet with surviving family members who tell me about the loved ones they have lost to addiction.

One conversation that will be etched in my mind forever was with a woman named Debra Hanby. At first I thought Debra was coming to see me about a new business idea. She was dressed professionally and carried a briefcase. When she placed her briefcase down next to her, she immediately began to tell me, without hesitation, the details of how her twenty-three-year-old son David had succumbed to a heroin addiction.

David had struggled with addiction since he was a teenager, when he was prescribed a painkiller for a slipped disc in his back. His mother sat in my office that Friday morning and told me about his caring personality. She shared with me his love for his family. And she shared his unsuccessful fight to come out of the shadows from what is a terrible, deadly disease.

We talked about how this epidemic is taking over our community and how it does not respect position or place. Regardless of income, regardless of race, regardless of whether you live in the urban center or the suburbs, anyone's child—anyone's family—could be the next to fall victim to this tragic nightmare.

Debra then had one request. She wanted to know how to go about raising money to support a sober living house that was being created in an East Dayton neighborhood. She talked about how $70,000 could not bring her son back, but how it could help provide others in our community with the long-term treatment they need. We spent the remainder of the meeting discussing what connections I might have that could help her reach this important goal.

I am a really organized person. At the end of every workday, I rarely leave a scrap of paper on my desk. But I still simply cannot file away the piece of paper Debra gave me that told the story of her son. The picture of a healthy David in high school sits on the right-hand corner of my desk staring back at me. It serves as a constant reminder of how personal this epidemic is for so many families in my city.

Many of the members of my staff who deal with this tragic issue on a daily basis work with it in terms of numbers. In 2017, the number of needles passed out in our harm-reduction syringe exchange program was over 125,000. The number of accidental overdose deaths in 2017 in Montgomery County—giving us the unenviable title of the most deaths per capita in the country—was 566. The number of public safety runs in the city topped 3,400, with police and fire services distributing 13,760 doses of Narcan last year on the streets of Dayton. The number of emergency department visits for overdoses in the region was 3,920. The amount our ADAMHS board spent on 2,500 people in 2016 for treatment of addiction to opioids was $10 million. Compare that to the 1,000 who were treated for alcoholism the same year. The number of children in foster care at our Montgomery County Children Services agency—children placed in foster care because everyone else in the family has an addiction or has died from an overdose—has increased 20 percent.

My staff tells me that they prefer to focus on the numbers because if they put a face and a name to each one, they are too overwhelmed to attack the problem. The magnitude of the pain caused by the stories makes them feel that it is an unsolvable crisis. The statistics are staggering, but they are measurable. They are actionable. They determine trends and track the severity of the challenge. The numbers help us determine best practices and direct us to implement those programs that work.

But as mayor, I can't get away from the stories. Nor do I want to. The stories make it real. The stories make it personal. For me, it got personal in 2008 when I learned that a young man whose family lived two streets away from me growing up, a young man whom I babysat when he was five and I was thirteen, died from a heroin overdose at the age of twenty-three.

I went back to Indiana to attend this young man's funeral, and for months I was inconsolable. "Who does heroin?" I thought. How did the person I knew as a little boy become so consumed with his addiction? In 2008 it seemed like such an outlier, such a mystery.

Unfortunately, this story was just the tip of the spear. The story of the young man I had babysat as a little boy quickly became the norm.

It got personal once again when I received a phone call last year telling me about a family friend who had overdosed twice in one week. This was a young man I had known for more than twenty years. A young man with a well-paying job. A young man who had served our nation in the armed forces and now had a family of his own. I remember him as a strong and healthy athlete in high school, his mom and dad filled with pride. It took four doses of Narcan to revive him when he was found unconscious inside his car.

It gets personal for me every time I have a heartbreaking conversation with family members and friends of those battling addiction who tell me how they struggle to get to the next day with their loved one still alive—or how they fight to move on after suffering a loss.

I think it is the stories of the people who have experienced, and are experiencing, this disease that are the most compelling force, demanding that we respond, making us take action. It is why Dayton was one of the first cities in Ohio to declare the opioid epidemic an emergency in 2014. It is why in June of 2017, Dayton was the first city in Ohio and fourth in the nation to file suit against the big drug companies, manufacturers, distributors, and doctors responsible for this crisis. To date, more than 650 communities nationwide have brought suits of their own.

More than 100 organizations in our community have been involved in addressing this public health crisis on a variety of fronts, and a recent report indicates that the number of overdose deaths in our county has dropped to its lowest level in three years. New Orleans Mayor Mitch Landrieu visited Dayton after this report was released to see for himself the work being done. Thanks to the close partnerships between Dayton Police and Fire, local nonprofits, and Public Health Dayton-Montgomery County, the programs we have put into place are beginning to make a difference. As president of the US Conference of Mayors, he hoped to learn some best practices on the ground to share with other cities around the country.

The community response we have witnessed and the results we are beginning to see offer a glimmer of hope that we may have turned a corner in dealing with this issue. The personal stories of so many who have been tragically impacted by this menace have pushed both public- and private-sector agencies to take aggressive steps to provide better solutions in terms of prevention, treatment, and recovery.

And it is the personal story of David and so many others that have moved families and friends to take action: raising money, hosting support groups, and advocating for more resources to be allocated to address this crisis. Debra, David's mom, continues to raise money for a sober living house, trying to find the partners and programs that would be the right fit. She refuses to give up.

After we learn how to treat addiction like the crippling disease that it really is, I think it will be stories such as these that will help us heal our communities.

*Nan Whaley is Mayor of Dayton.*

# 14

## JANE'S STORY

KERRI MONGENEL
(ASHTABULA)

Ohio is suffering. Ashtabula County is suffering even more. Not only do we struggle with the epidemic, but we struggle with resources. Ohioans are dying in droves. Every day more people overdose and are revived with Narcan.

I started a blog a while back to share my story and those of the families I work with and the children who have fallen victim to this crisis. This is a story of coming face-to-face with tragedy. This was likely one of the hardest days I've had, and it sits very strong in my memory.

Monday morning.

I arrive at work, and complete my regular tasks. Log in, check emails, listen to voice messages, make coffee. My teammates are bustling about and going in and out the door. I receive a call early in the morning from a screener saying the police are requesting assistance, and the worker they needed is busy on another case. I of course offer to go. She goes on to say all the information we have is a call from the police of an overdose, and there is an infant about six months old at the home. No names, no other info, just an address.

I grab one of my teammates. We grab a car seat and the agency van. Off we go. The sun is shining, the weather is warm. We pull into the driveway and of course there are the regular police cars, detective cars, and an ambulance. I enter the apartment and there are first responders everywhere. Social Work mode kicks in. I find the baby in the crib, smiling and cooing. An EMT stands near him. My teammate changes his diaper and gets him dressed. We gather formula, diapers, and clothing. The apartment is unusually clean and tidy for the clients we typically see. Suddenly, a smell fills my nose that I've never smelled before. I could not pinpoint what it was. It was warm, sour, and very off. I weave in and out of the police as they tell me the mother's name and what they think the baby's name is based on a crib card they found. No relatives were known at that time. I walk back through and glance to my side.

There she lies. Jane.

The baby's mother.

Pale, not breathing. She was still there. I had no idea. Usually they have taken the parent out of the home before I arrive. But there she was. And she was not coming back. Everything went into a spin. The police say a man was there who may be charged for giving her the drugs. I grab the baby and request custody, and off we go. My teammate and I start reliving what we just saw, and we can't believe it. A combined twenty years of this job between us and it was a first. A first we will never forget. We analyze, we break it down, we try to cope with what we just saw. We try not to cry.

Back at the office I found leads to relatives, including the father. I called the family members, and they did not know yet. Oh my God, I am the one telling them this happened. The coroner hadn't contacted them yet, but I needed a place to take this baby. I learn that Jane has another son, six years old, who was with his father. Her son is almost the same age as mine. My heart breaks in two pieces. Later in the day I meet with Dad, and the six-year-old cries because his dog died the day before, and today he lost his mommy. The grandparents cried. I met with the extended family and brought the baby to them. They mourn, cry, and scream "Why"? I have paperwork that I need to complete and I hate this. I hate that I have to be a social worker right now, when I just want to hug them and cry and say I'm so sorry. I do what I must do, and I leave.

The grandfather tells me later that the coroner determined she had passed away six hours before they found her. The man tried to put her in the bathtub to revive her. He was high. He did not call 911 because he was "afraid to get in trouble." So he waited. No Narcan, no revival, and her soul left, her baby in the crib. Her father says she's been sober for nine months. One relapse in nine months and she's gone.

My coworkers and supervisors asked my teammate and me if we were ok. Did we need to see a counselor, could they do anything? "No, I'm OK!" was my response. At the time I was. It was just another day in my crazy job that I love, right?

The day is almost over. I've completed everything for now, and it's settled down. An odd feeling comes over me and I need to leave. I ask my supervisor if I can leave a bit early and I run outside. I get in my car. I turn the key and pull out. I drive home and I start to cry. I can't stop. I get home and cannot console myself, but I did not want to be with anyone. Jane was not my sister, my mom, my friend. She was a stranger. She was dead, and I saw her. I'm a child welfare caseworker. We don't see dead bodies when we help children in need. This is what I told myself.

The next day a court hearing was held, and the father of Jane's baby was granted legal custody of the baby due to her death. I wished everyone luck, and we left the courthouse.

Case closed.

I thought that was the end of my part of story, but there was much more to come.

Months later, I had the chance to hug Jane's family and cry with them. I finally heard the story of Jane through her family's eyes and their path through her addiction to opioids. I then heard Jane's story in her own words, through letters she had left behind while in rehab.

I was contacted by a reporter from the *London Times* who was reporting on the opioid crisis. I told him of my day when I removed Jane's baby from the room next to her lifeless body. He asked me to set up a meeting with Jane's family for follow-up, which I was eager to do to gain insight and closure.

Another crisp but sunny afternoon, I entered the home of Jane's parents. The home was just as I remembered. Welcoming, warm, and cozy. The first thing I saw when I entered the home was the baby. He is two months older now and has doubled in size. Beautiful blonde hair and big blue eyes. Just like his mommy.

I met with the family. Jane's parents and brother. I hugged them and we smiled at how much the baby had grown. Then we sat on the same couch as before, and Jane spoke to us.

Her mom started with one of Jane's letters, which her mother read aloud. She couldn't finish reading it and asked me to finish reading it aloud. It captured her life story in a few short pages. The daughter of divorced parents, trips to Disney with her dad, stepparents, trials and tribulations. Abuse that no one knew about that she endured as a child. Feeling like an outcast as a teenager. And meeting a first love.

Through tears and heartache, I listened to her story. For two hours I ached, cried, and mourned this family. The day before, I met with a mother who after twelve overdoses in a two-year span said, "Heroin is the devil. But at this point, even my child is not enough. I know eventually I'm going to die." Such is the hold that this demonic drug has on the human brain. I talked about this with Jane's family and they confirmed it. In many ways they still cannot believe it, but they know now that heroin takes the person away long before they die.

Jane would write things in rehab and put them in columns. The last column she wrote said three things:

My boys
Jail
Death

She felt like these were the things she would inevitably lose or encounter—her only options in the depth of her addiction.

"We just didn't know." Through tears and heartache, it's what the families tell me. This is the common theme of families in middle-class America where heroin steals their family members. They think it's mental illness or the flu. They don't see it coming. They think it can't happen to them. Until it does.

When I returned to my desk after this emotional day, I sat and cried some more. Heroin and opioids have such a wide reach. The trauma and pain extend through every facet of a community. It starts with the addiction. It moves on through families, children, first responders, and more. It causes trauma to everyone around. Secondary trauma wreaks havoc on communities, and has done so in my small, "cozy" hometown. There is no prejudice. It can take hold of anyone. My hope is that someday we can find a cure for this problem and fight back. My colleagues and I fight the "good fight" every day for the lives of the children affected. We hope to pave a better future for these children. Hopefully Jane's story will change someone's life for the better. I hope that ultimately Jane's children will grow up strong and healthy. They deserve a good life, far away from the devil named heroin who stole their mommy much too soon.

*Kerri Mongenel is an Alternative Response Intake Caseworker for Ashtabula County Children Services. She maintains a blog (www.socialworksuperhero.blog) focusing primarily on the effects of opioids on children.*

# 15

## A COACH'S REGRETS

MATT DENNISON
(NEW PHILADELPHIA)

We are small town USA. We are proud of who we are and what we stand for. The sounds, sights, and smells of festivals occupy our summer days. Our kids play outside as we tend to our lawns. As autumn rolls in, so do Friday night lights. Our local New Philadelphia Quakers and The Ohio State Buckeyes dominate the coffee shop talk as everyone anticipates the upcoming games. Weekends of football bring us together to cheer on our kids and congregate with friends. When winter comes along, our downtown becomes a winter wonderland worthy of a Hallmark movie. Spring brings with it a rebirth, and the community comes alive again as we look forward to another year.

As the longtime head football coach at New Philadelphia High School, I look at our community with great pride. Our people are hardworking and blue-collar. There is a tight-knit feel to New Philadelphia. We stick together in times of need and rise up as a community when we are called to do so. As our society is changing, our community is desperately trying to cling to the culture that has been ours for generations. We have progressed to keep up with the times—for example, adding a Chipotle and Starbucks to our town—while still taking pride in the nostalgia of our downtown and our beautiful Tuscora Park. Increasingly, technology rules the town—our kids rarely look up from their screens.

As the progress of our times hit us, so have the struggles. Much of the business that made our town thrive has vanished. We have enough business to sustain ourselves, unlike other communities in eastern and southeastern Ohio. But our community has had its hardships. Our county leads Ohio in divorce rates, and poverty is rising. We hide this information because of our pride. We sell New Philadelphia as a middle-class community while we slide down the socioeconomic scale. In my almost two decades here, I have seen us fight, with great success, to thrive as a community, but I fear for our future. Our demographic is changing. We have fewer homeowners and more transient renters. We are losing families. Kids are not getting the guidance from adults like they should. Educators have felt this burden the most, as our role in our kids' lives has expanded tremendously. To more and more kids, we are the best adult leadership that they experience. Unfortunately, the increasing numbers of split families and the growing addiction rate have made things worse.

I see the rising drug epidemic as the biggest threat to our community. Now, I am not an expert by any means. I am simply a teacher and coach on the front lines. My grandfather left my dad without a father at the age of sixteen when he died in a car accident as a result of his alcohol abuse. My brother-in-law left two children fatherless as a result of his drug addiction. I have worked with many players who have had to grow up far too early because of their parents' addictions. I have seen students lose siblings. And I have lost players to addiction.

I don't know the difference between an opioid and other forms of drugs, but I do know it is the great enemy of our society. When I see the problems that plague society—like gun violence, physical abuse, and broken families—I see drug abuse as a root cause in more cases than not. It's the elephant in the room that no one wants to address. As a public servant who deals with people from all aspects of society, I find that this issue is easy to recognize—and I don't understand why we don't fight it more vehemently. Many educators choose not to see the issue because there is addiction in their own homes. Our kids have it tougher than we did growing up.

I have fought the addiction problem in our town more and more as I continue my career. Don't get me wrong: I don't seek out the kids in bad situations intentionally. I am not that noble. Because of my job I am presented with issues and I deal with them the best I can—which usually means that I get them working with the true heroes in our town.

My champions in this fight are Judy McGill (our school social worker) and Jim Borton (our team pastor—yes, we have a team pastor). These two, and several others in our community, see and work with the causes and effects of opioid and other drug addictions. They keep me and other teachers and coaches from feeling overwhelmed with the magnitude of problems that our young people face.

More often than not, unfortunately, it is a losing battle. I accepted the offer to contribute to this book because of the opioid addiction of one of my former players. I feel awful when kids whom I mentored as youngsters fight addiction. I feel a strong sense of responsibility and often think about what I could have done better that may have steered them in a different direction. I wonder what I missed in their development. However, I consider the addiction of one particular player as my biggest failure as a leader, a mentor, and a coach.

This young man was a great player and a little on the wild side. I mentored him throughout his young adulthood and stayed close to him. I worked with him when he was in college, and I knew that he was having issues with drugs. As he got older, I became proud of the man that he was becoming. His life seemed to be moving in the right direction. Then he hit some adversity and things spiraled out of control. I was on the front line of this battle with some great people. Thus far, it has been a defeat for everyone involved.

This young man's demons and addictions are winning. A young man of great promise is slipping away from us. I know that he wants to be better, but he can't break out. He seems to have given up, which is what keeps me up at night. I know he is a fighter, but he can't beat opioids and the spell they have on him. He was embarrassed by the person he had become, so he disappeared into the wind. I don't see him much anymore. I do know that he has gotten into trouble trying to get money for drugs. I have tried to find him on a few occasions when I heard he was back in town, but to no avail. His family is devastated. His friends are at a loss. I have a front-row seat to the effects of opioid addiction, and I feel helpless. I feel terrible for the loss of his great potential. I think of him and pray for him daily. I hope that he can win this battle he is fighting and see his own great potential.

My biggest hurdle as a teacher and coach, however, is dealing with those who have loved ones with addiction. While we have had some players who have dealt or currently deal with addiction issues, it rarely becomes a problem for our kids while they are in high school. Their addiction most often arises in their early adulthood after high school. Still, many addiction problems begin in high school—with marijuana, prescription drugs, and alcohol. I am no expert on this, but the addicts in our area don't jump into the heavy drugs. They seem to dabble with the gateway drugs and graduate to the harder stuff. The addicts are also our players' older siblings, aunts and uncles, and parents.

Identifying and helping the kids who are dealing with a family member's addiction is a great challenge as a teacher. I hear too many adults criticizing the actions of kids and not seeing the reasons for their actions. Unfortunately, many of our kids never complete homework or they come unprepared to class because their parents pay no attention to them. These kids are not always just lazy and going home to play video games. Some of our kids have bigger issues to deal with than the homework their teachers assign.

Several of the young men who played for me went through high school as couch jumpers. These kids are basically homeless because their parents don't or won't take care of them. These kids are experts at hiding the fact that they don't have a home to go to each night. They are proud kids who get embarrassed by their situation. Coaches are the people who usually uncover these situations, which are more prevalent than most people know. We coaches are with kids more often than regular teachers, and we develop closer relationships. When I don't know a young man's parents by the time they are a varsity player, it sends up a red flag, and we monitor that kid a little more than the others.

All coaches realize that the games and sports they coach are just vehicles to help kids grow into successful adults. The call to build successful adults becomes even more crucial with young people who deal with addiction in their lives. From our kids who jump from couch to couch at their friends' houses, to our kids who play football because we feed them dinners for three months of the year, to the kids we spend our personal money on to get them the necessities they need for life . . . high school coaches in today's society have a daunting job. Too many kids suffer from neglect, and it becomes our responsibility to help them.

Coaching in today's world is much different from when I began twenty-five years ago. The situations our kids come to us from are tougher than they were back then. Opioid addiction, in particular, is a cause of the struggles our teens face. Unfortunately, as coaches, we lose many battles in helping kids to strive to be successful in society. However, it is a fight worth fighting because for all the times we reach out to help someone but fail, the one time we make a difference makes it all worthwhile.

I am just a high school coach who sees and confronts the issues that our kids face. I am no different from most coaches. I do not do more for my players than other coaches do. I am just the guy writing because I was asked to write about it.

This issue is important to me because of my dad. Many people around the state of Ohio know my dad or know of him. He was a very successful college coach at the University of Akron and Walsh University. The list of coaches he mentored and players whose lives he touched is long. He has had an extremely successful life as a professional and as a father. However, if it weren't for a coach, he may have never had the impact on people that he has had. When my dad lost his father at age sixteen, his high school coach, Bill Barton, took him under his wing, got him to college, and gave him his first job. He is one of the few kids I have known to have risen from a home with addiction in it and use that experience to bring about positive change. That is why I do what I do when kids need help. But all coaches have their story as to why they do what they do.

I would venture to say that a large portion of our community doesn't even realize that the problem of opioids is on our doorstep. Though we may not admit it, we are not immune to the challenges that we face as a country. We battle addiction and its results in our community every day. Our police carry and use Narcan on a daily basis. And we are a strong and tight-knit community. This is a problem that transcends race, religion, and socioeconomic status. We are in this fight no matter where you live. Because we are a proud and caring community, we will work to keep and grow what makes us great.

*Matt Dennison is the head football coach of the New Philadelphia Quakers. He is a former president of the Ohio High School Football Coaches Association.*

# 16

## AN INDIVIDUAL'S ADDICTION, A FAMILY'S LOSS

AJ, JENNA, SHERIE, AND ALAN STEINBERGER
(HIGHLAND HEIGHTS)

### AWAITING TRANSFER TO FEDERAL PRISON
### (AJ)

I grew up in a normal household with a great childhood. No one in my family struggles with addiction. When I was a teenager I got involved with the wrong crowd of people and got introduced to drugs and a bad lifestyle. At first I thought smoking marijuana and drinking with friends was the normal thing to do. As time passed I went off to college and got introduced to pills and harder drugs. Eventually, when I was nineteen, I progressed to heroin and then fentanyl. I ended up dropping out of college because my heroin addiction got so bad. I had finished only about two years and had every intention of going back to finish the other two years.

Between the ages of nineteen and twenty-one, I went to rehab three times and always went right back. Opioids had me in shackles. I was very sick. My addiction got so bad that I would do anything to make money. Then an old friend reached out and said that if I let him send a couple packages to my house I would get money from him to pay for my heroin habit. I said OK, and a week later the FBI was raiding my house. They never took me to jail and said I would get indicted within two years. So I continued using, and a week after the raid, another package showed up and I opened it. I had no idea what it was, but I was so sick from withdrawal that I snorted the powder anyway. Later that day I realized it was fentanyl. I continued to use it for twenty-four hours and gave a good friend some because he called me asking for it. The next day at 5 a.m. he was found dead from an overdose of that fentanyl.

After this happened I went to rehab in Louisiana for roughly six months and got truly involved in Alcoholics and Narcotics Anonymous. After rehab I decided to live down there. For the first time I was happy and sober and had strong recovery in my everyday life. After I had been in Louisiana nearly seven months, the US Marshals picked me up for what had happened to my friend in Ohio the year before. Being sober really helped me deal both with my friend's death and with what came next with the legal system. After getting picked up on my indictment, I went to court several times. While I was waiting in the county jail, my fiancée continued to struggle with heroin. One day my dad came to visit me with bad news. My fiancée had overdosed and died. Just when I thought it couldn't get any worse, I lost the girl who had stuck by me through my addiction. This just goes to show how serious opioid addiction can be. It has affected my family and loved ones more than I could ever explain. I am now twenty-two and serving a twelve-year sentence for my friend's death. I am waiting to ride out to federal prison sometime in the next couple months. Today I focus on reading the Alcoholics Anonymous book and the Bible. I try to live by the Alcoholics Anonymous principles and better myself. Hopefully, I will get out by the time I'm thirty. And then I would like to be an addiction counselor.

## UPDATE FROM PRISON
### (AJ)

I am finally settled in at prison. It's not so bad when you keep a healthy mindset. Staying sober helps more than you can imagine. There are many activities here and plenty of opportunities to better yourself. I have taken a strong interest in drawing and art. I take classes in portrait drawing in which I'm learning about shading and other drawing techniques. Once the nice weather hits, I will be playing many different sports: softball, basketball, handball, and maybe a little bocce. I have been working hard to keep my body healthy. I exercise and eat as healthy as possible. I try each day to help someone. Many inmates are struggling, so I try my best to help at least one person a day. I still believe to this day that I am lucky to be alive—and lucky to have another opportunity at life. After all of this is over, I will be back home at approximately twenty-nine or thirty years old and I will be a new, reformed man. Prison has already taught me a lot about life and will give me an opportunity to grow up and mature—which is something I desperately need.

## PROGRESSION
### (AJ)

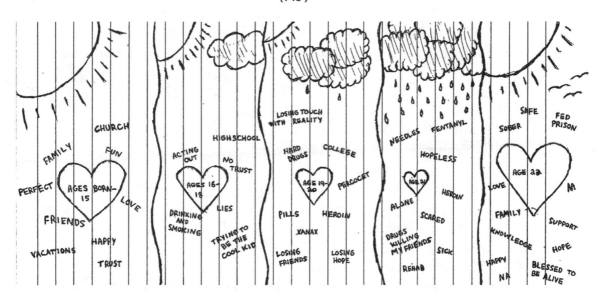

## SIBLING OF A HEROIN ADDICT: A TIMELINE
### (JENNA)

1998–2010

- Building forts, dunking on over-the-door basketball hoops, riding scooters, digging to China, lemonade stands, swimming lessons, sandcastles, Beanie Babies, building marble tracks

2011–12
- Wondering why the office doors are closed, playing catch with a baseball, having Nerf fights, why is Dad so mad, playing Horse and Around the World, why isn't my brother home very much

2013

- Brother: "Everyone does it it's really not that bad! Promise dude!"
- Sitting outside my bedroom door hiding in the hallway listening to why he's in trouble this time, sitting on the bottom of the stairs outside the closed office doors for hours
- Brother: "Let's hang out today!" which really meant come drive around with me as my cover so Mom and Dad don't get mad at me. Fighting.
- Text from Mom: "Where are you?"
- Brother: "You respond dude she will listen to you"
- Brother: "I'll be fine dude I would never do more than smoke weed. You don't have to worry everyone does it it's not a big deal"
- Brother: "If you don't tell I'll buy you ice cream and I won't tell on you."

2014

- Brother: "Can you lend me twenty dollars I swear I'll pay you back by tomorrow and don't tell Mom and Dad"
- Where is my cross? How come the money from my piggy bank is missing? What happened to all of our Wii games? Why isn't the Xbox at your apartment anymore? Who stole my tablet? When are you going to pay me back that twenty dollars?
- Basement ceiling full of bottles and cans
- "Fine I'll try it just this once"
- Sneaking out to drive around; "fine you can smoke but make sure I don't smell like it"
- Text to my best friend at 3:30 a.m.: "We just got a phone call. He's in jail. I don't know what to do. I'm freaking out we're going there now."
- Sitting in the living room with the TV volume all the way down so I can hear what's being said behind the closed office doors
- Police ringing the doorbell
- Crying in my bedroom
- Visiting rehabilitation centers for family day

2016–18
- Driving just to look over and see drugs being used in the car, screaming and swearing
- Police ringing the doorbell
- Missing my brother on holidays because he was in another state at a rehab center
- Text received during bio lab: "I tried calling your dad but he didn't answer, the cops just picked up your brother, I don't know what to do!" Heart pounding, sweating, ringing noise in my head, can't focus on the lab work in front of me
- Crying in my dorm room
- Attending court dates
- Reading Facebook comments from high school classmates about how he should "kill himself"

Current
- Visiting jail on the weekends
- Getting the best advice and keeping spirits positive
- Writing letters and creating an art account
- Having my best friend back
- Hope, happiness, laughter, smiles
- Time to breathe
- Brother: "You're the best sister ever. Thank you for being my best friend."

## ADDICT—MY SON
## (SHERIE AND ALAN)

These are the deep feelings that we endured through this journey of addiction with our son, from the time he was born to the present. Two things that never changed along the way were LOVE and HOPE. In fact, that is what got us through it.

# ADDICT - MY SON

son, sweet, joy, precious, happiness
preschool, fun, friends, babysister, love, FAMILY,
bicycle, scooter, sunday school, kind, loving, church, soccer
baseball, grandparents, video games, Cedar Point, fun, FAMILY,
Altar boy, youth group, metroparks, rapping judged, marijuana,
secrets, paranoid, lose trust, acquaintances, worry, constant,
everyone does it, cellphone, always a new number, endless texts
new friends, sneaking out, excuses, lies, police, no sleep, strangers over,
things missing, scared, consuming, constant, endless worry, angry,
sad, tears, fear, college, job, new job, new phone, new friends, drop-out
school, drop-out, struggling, school, drop-out, police, new apartment, new job
thin, pale, drugs, new drugs, secrets, lies, struggling, rehab, counselors,
$, texts, police, drugs, tough love, homeless, no sleep, trouble, scared
ER, terrified, friends dying, sadness, hoplessness, no sleep, $,
hates this life, hates heroin-the DEMON, almost gives up, scared,
tired, afraid, HELP, Rehab, fights it, sad, prays, talks, shares,
embraces it, HOPE, strength, working hard, 12 steps, accepts,
move forward, brave, grateful, arrested, court, sadness,
loses fiance-overdose, prays, prison, ACCEPTS,
thankful, chance, LIFE, healthy, reads, draws-an
artist, smart, college courses, funny, kind, thankful,
sleep, relief, help others, PURPOSE, future,
grateful, FAMILY, LOVE, ALWAYS, FOREVER
never alone, true friends, proud, new beginning,
Loved, my son
ALIVE
HOPE
LIFE

*AJ Steinberger* is currently serving a twelve-year sentence in federal prison for selling fentanyl to a friend who overdosed and died. *Jenna Steinberger* is AJ's sister. *Sherie* and *Alan Steinberger* are AJ's parents.

# 17

## THE PAIN OF WANTING TO HELP

ANONYMOUS

"I want to help people" is what most medical students say when asked why they want to be a physician. We want to fix, change, and help cure those whose paths we cross. I am no exception.

For as long as I can remember, I have wanted to join the medical profession and give back to the small, rural community in which I was raised. My community is a place where everyone knows everything about everyone and helping people is a way of life. I am proud and passionate about where I am from, so I was extremely grateful to be accepted to a medical school in Ohio where the medical education emphasized giving back to these specific communities. I was accepted and began school happy, eager, and ready to help. I then quickly learned the rigor of the work and the stress that medical school and life as a medical student entailed.

While I was busy learning the pathophysiology and pharmacology of the cardiovascular system, my brother was busy using heroin. Somewhere between his medical discharge from the military and reentry into civilian life, heroin became the answer to his problems. After the lies, stealing, and charges of operating a vehicle under the influence came to light, it was evident that his addiction was taking over his life. Incarcerations and overdoses followed. Remember the small community I'm from? Everyone knew. My family had to see his face plastered on the news and Facebook feeds. It was the talk of the town. This wasn't—couldn't be—my brother. I had no idea how someone I loved could be putting this much hurt on my family.

I was stressed. How do I balance hours and hours of studying, exercising, and eating healthfully with wondering every day if my brother was still alive? My daily routine generally included class, lunch, studying/meetings, dinner, work out, studying more, and calling my mom to talk about my brother, along with the twenty-four hours of worry. I am the calm and sensible one in my family, so I felt like I should be the backbone and support for my siblings and my mother. I was also the one in medical school. My job is to "help" people. This was my calling.

I started by talking to him every day. He answered the first few times but quickly hung up the phone after a few minutes of my talking about how he needed help. Then, each day, I began to send him encouraging texts. I let him know that we were behind him, that he could fight this, that we loved him. I never received replies. I sent him information about rehab facilities, which he did attend on several occasions but then quickly relapsed. Needless to say, I could not help.

How am I supposed to become a physician, to help others, when I can't even help my own brother? I failed. I failed my brother, my family, and even as a student doctor. Wasn't I accepted into medical school because someone saw that I had the potential to help others and be a good physician? They were wrong, I told myself. They have to be wrong because my brother, whom I grew up with and looked up to for twenty-four years, can't utilize the help I am giving. If I cannot help him, how will I be able to help and make an impact on a complete stranger's life?

Some days I wondered if I should be a physician and if I had chosen the right path. I had encounters with patients and clinical experiences where the only thing I could think was "I'm not making a difference in this person's life," "I am not aiding them in any way." I, like most medical students, do not like failure. I felt at this point that I was failing myself and my future. This wasn't me. I am strong-willed and have always known the medical profession was for me, so why was I second-guessing myself now?

One day as I was scrolling through old notes on my cell phone, I came across one of my favorite quotes by the graphic artist Mary Engelbreit: "If you don't like something, change it; if you can't change it, change the way you think about it." I didn't like that my brother was addicted to heroin, so I tried to change it. I couldn't change it, so I changed the way I thought about it. I needed to be resilient, to bounce back and get through it.

My brother and his disease knocked me down. But taking a step back and realizing where I was in life and the journey I was on helped me get through. I was pursuing my dreams to become a physician, with plans to practice in Ohio. Of course, I needed to try to help my brother, but I also needed to do this for myself. I will have the opportunity to help people the rest of my life. The battles I encountered with my brother will stay with me for the rest of my career. There are patients, try as you might, who do not want your help, are unable to act on your advice, or can't utilize the information you are giving. This does not mean that you should give up, or that you should look down at yourself—or even that you should explore different career paths. It means that you should change the way you are thinking about the situation. Help comes in many different forms. Something that you do not think helped a patient today may be that one little piece that the person uses five years down the line. It could save their life.

I wish my brother wasn't an addict, but his addiction has led me to explore paths in medicine that I would never have dreamed of. I became more involved with addiction services in medical school and learned how to communicate with and help addicts—no matter where I encounter them. Being resilient and learning from the situation will make me a better physician for all of my patients, not to mention a better person in general. As I write this piece, my brother is six months sober. I am proud of how far he has come. But he knows, and I still remind him, to be strong and that each day is a battle. Addiction can affect anyone, anywhere, from the wealthy county of Delaware to the poverty of Athens, from religious families to atheists. Addiction is a horrendous disease, but it has allowed me to find a way to help others.

*The author is an aspiring physician and native Ohioan.*

# 18

## MY REALITY AT THE BEDSIDE

HANK ROSSITER
(KIDRON)

When I started my nursing career in 1978, Demerol, morphine, and Talwin were the drugs of choice to control a patient's pain. Beginning in the 1990s I began to see more physicians prescribing Vicodin, Percocet, Percodan, and ultimately OxyContin for patients in the Intensive Care Unit. This was about the time that I began to see a slow increase in the number of "overdoses" admitted. I put "overdose" in scare quotes because these patients are not the ones who tried to commit suicide by taking an entire bottle of some medication. Today, it is rare that our twelve-bed unit does not have at least one "overdose" per week.

From my perspective, many of these "overdose" patients consider opioid "overdoses" just "partying" or "having a good time." Or they "just took too much." These patients are invariably difficult to handle, belligerent, sometimes aggressive, and never at fault. They often have no job and no insurance. Their families either want to have nothing to do with them or withdraw support in order not to enable their addiction. Neither I nor any of my coworkers want to take care of these patients.

I have taken care of patients who are lethargic and slurring their speech but still demand more opioids. This puts me in the middle of a demanding patient and an absent physician who hesitates to prescribe more narcotics—and rightfully so. Many physicians, especially in the acute setting of the Intensive Care Unit, just don't want the hassle, the recriminations, the yelling, the conflict. They have a lot of "real" patients to see and do not have time to spend with these addicted, self-destructive patients.

The increase in "overdoses" happened at the same time that pain was becoming known as the so-called Fifth Vital Sign. Soon enough, hospitals were being graded on how well the staff controlled a patient's pain. The goal was zero pain for our patients. All the area hospitals are now rated on how we treat and control pain. These ratings are then posted on social media, and if we don't have a great rating, patients will choose another hospital. Posters in each patient's room state that our goal in patient care is zero pain. Every room contains a visual aid for rating pain. There is a happy face for zero pain and, at the other extreme, a frowning/weeping face for a pain of ten. Immediately below this scale are the words: "Your one-hundred percent satisfaction is our goal." Satisfaction, in this case, means one-hundred percent pain control.

But this is unrealistic. We, the health care establishment, cut into flesh and bone and then promise a pain-free recovery. Could this be a marketing ploy in the competitive health care industry? I recently heard an NPR piece on the opioid "crisis" in which an orthopedic surgeon discusses his recent decision to start telling his patients they will have some pain. He and his staff will do their best, but there will be some pain. We'll see how that works out for their business.

I believe that the current situation is the culmination of a perfect storm of supply, demand, marketing, and culture. Our culture believes, and the health care establishment has reinforced, that to feel pain of any kind, and in any degree, is bad. There is a generational component to this as well. My seventy-to-ninety-year-old patients are hesitant to take large amounts of pain medication. "A little pain is part of life," they will say. Younger patients see it as their right to be totally pain free, even if it is detrimental to their recovery. Of note, I have had very few patients who tell me they got "hooked" on opioids after a surgery. Instead, they bought them on the street or got them from friends.

Sometimes I talk back to the radio when I hear the phrase "opioid crisis." Contracting influenza during an epidemic might be unavoidable. Taking opioids to stay buzzed all day is a choice. If this is a crisis, then it is a crisis driven by bad choices. This may sound harsh, and I fully understand the physically addictive nature of drug abuse. But not once has a patient told me they were tied down and forced to take opioids. In my opinion, better education, fewer prescriptions, alternative pain control methods, and more treatment facilities might begin to bring an end to this crisis. Having said that, I take care of multiple "repeaters" in the Intensive Care Unit—patients whom we have treated and sent to rehab programs but who return the next month with another "overdose."

————

There are also important cultural differences within this "crisis." In my career, I have not had one Amish patient admitted for an opioid ingestion. The drug of choice, especially among Ohio's Amish youth, seems to be alcohol, not opioids. Opioids are taboo within the Amish and conservative Mennonite communities, with whom I have experience working in Wayne, Stark, and Holmes counties. The community ethos of the Conservative Mennonite and Amish communities appears to help them avoid opioid addiction. The faith and cultural community sets the rules, mores, and boundaries for inclusion. As long as one stays within those boundaries, there is safety and support, especially after one joins the church. Go outside those boundaries, threaten the community bonds, and one is shunned until one repents and reforms, at which time one is welcomed back into the community. Addictions, which are seen as being part of the world and not simply in it, tear at the fabric of the community which sees itself as separate from the world. The Amish see pain and suffering as an inherent part of our humanness within the larger Kingdom of God. All of our lives are under God's will. This does not mean they do not avoid and treat pain, but that they do not expect a pain-free existence.

Faith communities may play a role in preventing and responding to addictions insofar as those communities set boundaries for communal behavior. In my own faith tradition, Anabaptist Mennonite, addictions are viewed as personally and communally destructive because they separate us from God, our Creator, and have the potential to bring conflict to the community. We belong to God and the faith community. We are not our own. Our bodies are created by God and are not to be abused. We are God's handiwork, created out of love, and addiction has the potential to create other gods that rule us. If someone in the faith community were to develop an addiction, the community would attempt to help that individual recover, offering spiritual, economic, and counseling resources. If someone entered the faith community from "outside," the same resources would be offered. But in both cases, the individual must make a choice: stay within the faith community and give and receive counsel and discipline, or leave the community. This may appear harsh in our malignantly individualistic culture, but faith communities cannot survive without clear and accepted behavioral boundaries. What we call the "English" (non-Amish) might see the Amish community as rigid and anachronistic in its reliance on and enforcement of rules (the *ordnung*). And yet upwards of 85 percent of Amish young people join the faith and remain in the community. They give up many of their individual rights for the security and promised assistance of the larger community. Likewise for Mennonites: being in such communities remains a personal choice. At their best, faith communities teach and model correct behaviors and offer reconciliation and healing within the framework of their shared communal life.

———

I will soon retire after nearly forty years as a bedside nurse. More and more of my younger colleagues are studying to be advanced practice nurses in order to continue to do what they love, but remove themselves from bedside nursing. The addition of opioid overdoses in the Intensive Care Unit has added greatly to the stress and frustration of nursing. On any given day, I may have a patient on a ventilator struggling with pneumonia or a patient in septic shock with multiple IV drips that must be constantly titrated. Then added to my patient load is the opioid overdose, a patient who is aggressive, belligerent, and restless. This individual chose to take a substance that put them in the hospital. To which patient should I give my limited time and energy? I was not trained as a detox/rehab nurse, nor do I want to be one. And yet here they are.

*Hank Rossiter, a Registered Nurse, practiced for thirty-nine years, recently retiring in 2018. His nursing experience has been almost exclusively in the intensive care unit at Affinity Medical Center in Massillon, but he has also practiced in California, Arizona, the Dominican Republic, and Liberia.*

# 19

## WHAT HAPPENS UNDER THE OVERPASS

NEIL CARPATHIOS
(PORTSMOUTH)

My friend who lived homeless for a year
tells me. You masturbate with your hand
or sometimes a cement pillar. You pick
lice out of your hair and pretend
they're licetronauts you flick
into orbit. You use an empty bottle
to shatter the skull of someone
who says suck me or else.
You urinate and watch the steam
cloud mushroom like a ghost.
You listen to cars and trucks
*voom* by above you like huge
metallic gods. You find a half-eaten Twinkie with ants dotting
the cream and you eat it,
licking your fingers. You read
the graffiti. You add a few pearls
of your own with a broken Bic.
You use a newspaper for a blanket.
You pick scabs on your legs
and create smeared jelly blood art.
You study the clouds shifting

as if they are symbols on a treasure
map. You hum to drown-out
your stomach's growling. You stare
down at your hands that are swollen
and empty and holding nothing,
the way you entered the world.


*Neil Carpathios is the author of five full-length poetry collections and editor of* Every River on Earth: Writing from Appalachian Ohio *(2015). The recipient of various fellowships and awards, he teaches creative writing and literature at Shawnee State University in Portsmouth.*

# 20

# COMMUNITY AND VULNERABILITY

BRIAN SCHWEITZER
(COLUMBUS)

*Brian Schweitzer is a Community Outreach Director at Advanced Recovery Systems, an integrated behavioral health care management company with national presence, including Ohio. Schweitzer, a recovering addict himself, is well-known throughout Columbus as an advocate for those struggling with addiction, with a particular focus on the Central Ohio LGBTQ community. Interview by Daniel Skinner.*

*Please tell me a little bit your journey and how it has shaped your thinking about addiction, generally, and opioid addiction in particular.*

I'm a person in long-term recovery and a member of the LGBTQ community. I knew I was different from a very early age, growing up in a small, rural town in Ohio.

I was bullied and abused by my peers from the fourth grade on. It made for an isolating life. I didn't realize how it had affected me until many years into recovery. I struggled to form friendships and relationships and communicate with my peers. I knew that I was different, and I struggled to understand who I was. I've used many different substances, including opioids, along the way—beginning as early as the fifth grade. Drugs gave me a sense of relief and being "right sized." I felt accepted, as if I was actually beginning to fit in with my peers. Despite this relief, I continued to struggle through school all the way up until graduation. After school, I felt a tremendous freedom in knowing I wouldn't have to see those people anymore. I focused on creating a new life for myself. I remained local for two years after graduation, working full-time and attending community college. I stayed busy and continued to hand-select my new friends.

When I moved at twenty years old from the small town to Columbus, my substance use took off. I was just coming into accepting myself—who I really was, who I wanted to be—but I still felt like I wasn't being completely honest with myself, much less with other people. Over the next seven years I worked for two Fortune 100 companies, obtained two undergraduate degrees at a local business college, and bought a house. From the outside many thought I had it all together. Instead, I was a high-functioning individual in the midst of a battle with a substance use disorder. That is, until Monday August 16, 2010, at 6:14 a.m., when I awoke in the midst of a complete mental breakdown.

In twelve-step programs, step 1 is "admit we are powerless over substances, and that our lives have become unmanageable." I knew for years that I had a problem with substances, but it wasn't until that moment of sheer terror that I realized how unmanageable my life had become. The material things that remained intact—my house, my job, my car—no longer mattered. The biggest thing I had lost was myself. I had become a dead man walking, a shell of a human being—barely struggling to survive. I was incredibly sick. My GI tract and other organs were affected, and it was obvious that I was not doing well from the years of substance abuse.

I began attending a twelve-step recovery program, working with a sponsor, doing everything I was advised to do to become active in my own recovery and become well again. Then, three years later, I was active in recovery and my life had improved dramatically, but I again became very sick. I saw a specialist, who referred me to an outpatient program (partial hospitalization program and an intensive outpatient program). I learned that there was a lot of anxiety and trauma that I'd been self-medicating for, dating back years.

From childhood isolation, issues with my sexuality, and, more recently, being the recipient of sexual harassment from two top executives at the large employer that I was working for, I had a lot of unresolved trauma. The harassment actually began when I entered recovery in August 2010. So this whole experience of still enduring trauma while entering recovery was rather profound to me. And all of this and more came out during treatment.

I worked the twelve steps and my life got better, but there was still so much left to be worked through. I learned how deeply rooted trauma and addiction can be. In the substance use disorder field it is referred to as "co-occurring": an individual who has a substance use disorder is also simultaneously experiencing a mental health disorder.

*While putting this book together I've spoken to a lot of parents about their kids. A common narrative is "We did everything right, we thought we were a good family, had good values, etcetera. And then our child ended up with this disease of opioid addiction. How did this happen?" I want to ask you, how should parents of LGBTQ children be thinking about the relationship between addiction and sexual orientation?*

Acceptance of your child, regardless of their sexual orientation, is key to helping kids avoid addiction and other unhealthy coping skills. Having a strong sense of community, a sense of love, to feel like someone understands—even if they don't fully "understand"—all of that is important. I have a friend who has a transgender son entering his adolescent years. She's a huge advocate for him, as is his father. The family really embraces Jim. I truly admire and appreciate her love, understanding, and willingness to understand what Jim is going through. And if he needs a therapist or support groups—like Kaleidoscope, a support group in central Ohio that works with LGBTQ youth—they make sure he has it. It's always nice to be around those who are similar to you. Nobody wants to feel different, right? Especially in one's formative adolescent years. The biggest thing that we can do is support our youth, our children, and keep those lines of communication open.

*So I'm talking to you on a Monday, after an affirming, positive weekend in Columbus, centered on Pride, where community was on full display. And I wonder if you can tell me a little bit about addiction and the LGBTQ community in Columbus.*

We're definitely in a pivotal moment in history. Behavioral health, as a whole, is changing rapidly. We have the opportunity to access resources that we've never had before. For example, Equitas Health, which has evolved over the years from several nonprofits serving mainly the LGBTQ community, now has centers with behavioral health resources popping up all over the state providing "care for all."

And if we build it, they will come, but we also have to create an awareness that makes people comfortable with the idea of coming to these centers to reach out and ask for help. Another big barrier is insurance. Too often, insurers refuse to pay for critical services, or they charge an astronomical amount for such services.

When working with these individuals, we have to understand that the diseases of addiction and behavioral health needs are deeply embedded in our families. These problems and areas of concern have existed for years, decades, and generations, so it will take time to shift this tide.

*You told me your story of feeling alienated. That's a narrative that's fairly well known with LGBTQ youth. But how does that narrative find itself in this current moment, when everybody is talking about opioids? The link to addiction—is it just a natural move that you just want to use to stop the pain and the drugs are there? Is it that simple? Or is there something more?*

Some of us are fearing for our lives. Some are afraid of rejection from our peers and/or our family. There are a lot of homeless LGBTQ youth. They get kicked out of their homes, so there's definitely a survival component.

So I think that it's definitely a method of survival for some folks. And it's a method of coping. The pain that LGBTQ people experience is in many ways unique, and, as a result, their relationship to opioids is unique. The mind, body, and spirit are not designed to be constantly in survival mode. Substances can give people relief from all that. While we're very fortunate to have amazing organizations in Central Ohio, areas outside of Columbus have fewer resources. Smaller towns are struggling. And in the area of LGBTQ youth and opioid addiction, I worry. In those places, the feeling of alienation and isolation are greater, which means that LGBTQ people—kids as well as adults—are more susceptible to opioid addiction. Opioids are readily available, so accessible. They are right there to help us "cope" in ways that non-LGBTQ people don't need in order to "cope."

*I find it interesting that when many people talk about opioid addiction, they tend to talk about things like Narcan, medication-assisted treatment, clinical interventions. But you focus on community.*

Well, there's power in numbers. No matter what program you're in, it's really hard to isolate yourself when you're sitting in a group of people talking about their struggles in life and how they overcame them.

In those spaces you find out just how alike you all are. As a sponsor once told me, "You'll find out just how different you are not." Hearing just how different I was not was critical for me. I was quick to point out the differences when I first came into recovery. Every time someone spoke up in a support group, I would point out the differences between us instead of going for the similarities.

But there are more things that make us similar than make us different. So community is incredibly important. You're bringing people together, people who have common concerns and common needs, and you are forming a group—there's something to be said about that. It really affects people, inspires changes, within individuals as well as within a collective group. I also understand that we all have the same "bucket" of feelings and emotions. My bucket is no different from that of anyone else on earth. While we may recognize or understand our feelings and emotions differently, in the end we all are pulling from the same bucket of feelings and emotions.

# 21

## REMAKING A FAMILY

CHRIS, ESTELLA, AND TYLER FERRELL
(MINFORD)

*We would like to share our story. We invite you to walk with us for a while, but please, remember that there are many stories like ours—and we are all human. It takes courage to reflect upon our journey, laying it bare for the world to see.*

### INTRODUCTION
### (ESTELLA)

Our family is from a small Appalachian town, nestled in the picturesque foothills where the Ohio and Scioto rivers meet. Abandoned shoe factories, railroads, and looming steel mill structures stand like giant metal ghosts. A booming port city during the turn of the century, it is now infamous for its newest major import and export—drugs. Our town has been featured in documentaries, articles from prestigious national newspapers, even books, both fiction and nonfiction, all attempting to tell our narrative.

Before the railroad, there were the rivers for transportation. Sitting on the levee, you can still see the almost graceful movement of the coal barges up and down the river. Coal, iron ore, lumber, and shoestrings provided for a booming economy—up until we lost the steel mills and major factories. With the major businesses closing shop, the small businesses followed. People moved, and those who stayed, or couldn't relocate, weren't left with much other than their land, low-wage employment, and each other.

Along with Portsmouth, Scioto County includes the suburbs of West Portsmouth (the West Side); Lucasville (where the Lucasville Penitentiary is, which is one source of the few "good jobs" in the area); Minford (Go Falcons!); South Webster (way out there); Wheelersburg (where the "rich" people live); Sciotoville (most famous for Highland Bend and its history with old-time gangsters); and, last but not least, New Boston (the only Walmart within thirty miles).

Chris and Tyler grew up in Minford; it is also the area where my children were provided some stability and sense of connection. It was there where I would drop them off at their grandparents' for days, even weeks—so that I could go use. Minford has two four-way stops. There is a gas station and a hot dog/ice cream stand. At the gas station you can get a tan, two pounds of Kentucky Border bologna, a loaf of bread. You can rent a movie and even buy a gun or knife on your way out. You know you are in Southeast Ohio when you can buy a gun and get a tan at the same place. Around the area, back roads run like snakes across large, hilly fields where you can see (and smell) the livestock. Addicts love these roads. You can avoid the cops and get out to pee, puke, or screw at your convenience.

## "I DREAMED OF MAKING A MILLION"
### (CHRIS)

I married young. My first wife, Sheila, and I had our son, Tyler. I dropped out of high school and tried a few low-paying jobs. We lived in low-income housing before moving out to the country. I began selling pills for money. My parents cared for Tyler most of the time. Sheila and I had problems, and she thought if she did drugs with me, we would be happy. Within two years, I found her dead in bed. This only propelled my addiction and, accordingly, the risks I was taking to sell and maintain my use—which had begun at fifteen.

It started with marijuana when I got suspended from school: a friend bought a joint, we smoked it, and we got caught. I would progress to hydrocodone within a year. It was pretty easy to get, especially since my parents struggled with health issues. The first time I tried OxyContin, it made me sick. But when I realized how much the pills were worth on the street, I started selling—even making up fake pain to get my own prescriptions. I was a "doctor shopper," going to several doctors (some of whom are in prison today) to get pills. I dreamed of making a million dollars, but I began snorting the product I was selling. At one point, I even sold crack cocaine. However, the more money I made, the more drugs I did. I tried OxyContin again. I started out using twenty milligrams; soon I was doing forty—then eighty. At my peak, I was doing up to ten OxyContin "eighties" per day to function—I needed four just to avoid withdrawals. I sold to sustain this pace, and I even involved my family in the wheeling and dealing. My parents lived close to me and said one day, "Just put a drive-through in because you have a lot of people at your house."

The first time my house got raided by the authorities, they did not find a lot. I was arrogant and thought I beat the law. I intensified my dealing. I got robbed, twice. The first time they used bear mace and beat my head with a metal bat. The second time, they shot at me and threatened to rape my wife.

Within a year, I was back in county jail. This time I was in serious trouble. I was sentenced to four years with a judicial release after two. I was inmate #489202. I was done; I surrendered.

I jumped into programs, going from one prison to another for treatment. It wasn't until I entered a program at Pickaway Correctional Institution that I got the treatment I needed. It changed my thinking. I also earned my GED and discovered that I wanted to help others like me.

When I got out I started my journey. I met my saving grace: Stella.

## A FATHER AND SON'S CONVERSATION
## (CHRIS AND TYLER)

TYLER: People say that adversity can make or break you. Count me in. I grew up in a world where I barely knew my biological parents. I saw them, I knew who they were, and I spent the night with them every once in a while. Thankfully, though, that's all I really experienced; since birth I was raised by my grandparents, who were amazing people.

CHRIS: At the time, I thought that I was being a good dad by giving you to my parents. Thinking back on it now, I just wanted to get high. I did not have time for a child.

TYLER: That's not to say my parents were bad people. It's just that when I was there, I was in an environment where you sold drugs and where Mom used drugs during her last few years on earth.

CHRIS: Tyler, at that point selling drugs was more important to me than raising a child. I thought I was destined to be a user and seller all my life. I quit school and thought I was going to make an easy life. It ended up causing me more problems in the end.

TYLER: You realized that it wasn't an environment you wanted me to be in and that was why you gave me to my grandparents. We'd have strangers coming and going and showing up at the house. You didn't even know their name.

CHRIS: That's how I made my living. Your mom was always trying to buy you stuff, and I didn't want to give her the money because it took money away from my drug selling and use.

TYLER: You weren't bad people, but you made bad decisions in a world where mistakes aren't easily forgiven and the prices are severe. I mean, you spent four years of your life in prison, and death took what remained of Mom's life.

CHRIS: I can still remember your face when you saw her in the hospital like it was yesterday. That was one of the hardest things, taking you in at seven-and-a-half years old and your seeing your mom dead. You cried so much that morning.

TYLER: My childhood wasn't hard. Things weren't easy, but they weren't impossibly difficult either. There was food, and if I wanted something within reason, I normally received it. The early adult years of my life were more difficult. There were more challenges and things to overcome. When you got out of prison, you tried your hardest to have a relationship with me, but by that time I had my own life and wanted to do my own things. It wasn't anger, I just wanted to play video games and sports like kids want to.

CHRIS: I know you said it was not out of anger, but I couldn't blame you if it was. I messed up. I don't know if you remember or not, but I told you when I got out of prison that "I am a changed man." You told me, "Actions are louder than words."

TYLER: Thankfully you met Stella, and she has helped you to stay on the straight and narrow path. She helped you through the hard times that I wasn't there for. Sadly, my grandparents' health started to decline. Every time I tried to connect with you, my grandparents would get angry. They thought I was trying to leave them.

CHRIS: I can understand why they felt like they did. They took care of you and you made their life worth living. They did not have their other grandchildren in their life very much. They didn't want to lose you too.

TYLER: It made it very difficult for me to establish a relationship with you and Stella. I was conflicted. I leaned on my girlfriend for support. My mindset was to never give up and to make the best out of what I have in life. I found motivation in the future I wanted with her. She and Papaw helped instill in me that I could get what I wanted as long as I worked hard and didn't give up.

CHRIS: I am glad you found inspiration in her. It takes a lot of people to break the cycle of addiction. I knew I couldn't use anymore. I knew that I had to be a better role model for you. I knew that losing Papaw was going to be hard on you. I had to step up and be the dad that I was supposed to be years ago. I hoped I was up to the challenge. I feel like we spent a lot of time together when Papaw was in hospice and even after he passed.

TYLER: Today I'm working hard in college. I admit, I'm scared for the future. No one's life is perfect, and I am thankful for what I have, and I believe that everything in my life has happened for a reason. I have a family who loves me and an amazing girlfriend who for some reason, which I can only explain as the grace of God or some kind of extraordinary luck, also loves me. I couldn't be happier with where I am and where life is going.

## MAKING A FAMILY
### (ESTELLA)

I was a bad parent. There, I said it. Anyone who sits in a meeting and says, "I took care of my kids," is most likely a liar. Your house may have been cleaner, your kids dressed nicer—but we all know. We are self-centered and selfish both in addiction and in recovery. It's always our children who are the last to recover.

I was in my third year of recovery when I moved back in with my father and stepmother. This was the third time I lived with them as an adult; it was the first time they actually asked me to. Chris lived with his parents and Tyler when he got out of prison. After about six months of dating, we decided to move in together.

———

Of course, it wasn't that simple. Starting a new relationship in early recovery is dangerous. A relapse waiting to happen. I had seen friends get high and even die from feelings of rejection, manipulation, or relapse because they associated with people they met "in the rooms" during treatment.

Chris and I met on a beautiful autumn afternoon. He was two years clean. I had just a few months more. He'd been out of prison for about three months and was frustrated by the lack of employment opportunities for a two-time felon, a frustration he shared with his peers at a twelve-step meeting. Someone gave him my number and told him to call me. I worked for a treatment facility in transitional services, where I helped recovering individuals with the "what next?" of their recovery. Thankfully, he did not become a client. Our first contact was a two-hour phone call. We talked about his feelings, his struggles, and his desire to help others. We talked about God and recovery. We shared how we had become addicts and when we bottomed out.

Our friendship grew and we became closer. Chris asked me out. I blew him off. I was scared. I was, after all, just learning how to have a relationship with my family, with myself, and with God. How was I supposed to know what a "healthy" relationship even was? The twelve steps had worked in all of my other relationships, and it was all I knew. To form our relationship, we began to use the one-liners found at meetings, things like "First Things First" (Remember our priorities), "Easy Does It" (Take it slow), and "Just for Today" (No projecting outcomes). This led to a relationship that has lasted for over nine years. We began speaking to each other in the evening, by phone. Once the kids were in bed, the work for the day was done, and we had put the day's happenings to rest—we talked. We started calling and saying hello throughout the day. "Just for Today" became a code—we wanted to get to know each other—no expectations, no worries. It was simple and honest. One night, after a particularly intimate conversation about how we felt, we realized we had talked late. It was almost midnight. We said our goodbyes thoughtfully.

As I lay there, thinking about this amazing person who had come into my life, I glanced at the clock. It was 12:01 a.m. Sheepishly, I grabbed the phone and dialed his number. When he groggily answered, I took a deep breath and quietly said,

"Hey, Just for Today. I just wanted you to know it was a new day."

He replied, "Well, yes . . . yes it is, isn't it?"

———

Though Chris and I decided to take it slow, we had other considerations in building a blended family. My daughter was not happy and felt, yet again, I was choosing a man over my kids. My oldest son was detached and really didn't care as long as he got internet and was able to hide in his room playing video games. My youngest son was just excited not to have to share a room with me. Tyler would not be moving in with us; we asked, but he declined.

Chris had enrolled in the local university. He would take his student loan disbursement and pay the rent for several months at a time, but I was the breadwinner. I would cover the bills, household items, and groceries. For almost two years, traditional roles were reversed. I went to work every day; Chris would take the kids to school, clean house, do laundry, and prepare dinner in between classes. I was parenting with a profound sense of shame. I was always trying to be everything to everyone—it was exhausting.

We spent time together as a family, taking vacations, camping, and going to the beach. We mourned the loss of loved ones. We welcomed the birth of the first grandchild. Tyler participated in some things; when he didn't, we felt rejected, even as we tried to understand. I was jealous of the relationship that Chris had with my own children. I had worked so hard to change, to rebuild our lives, and Chris seemed to have a close, effortless relationship with my children.

We still struggle, but we are trying to heal. Just because I set drugs down and walked away from them thirteen years ago didn't mean everything was fixed. Our children still carry histories born in large part of my addiction. As mine grew into adults, I witnessed their struggles and blamed myself for them. They say they have forgiven me . . . if I could only learn how to forgive myself.

# 22

## DEAR TRAVIS

### VICKI HAMILTON-SCHARBACH
### (OLMSTED FALLS)

I feel as if the universe chose me to be Travis's parent. I feel privileged to have been his mom. Travis had a sweet nature and was extremely sensitive—it was as if he had an understanding of others' feelings from an early age.

We first noticed Travis's obsessive compulsive disorder (OCD) when he was eleven—after he was caught in a tornado at a campground. He was quite traumatized, unable to leave the house, sitting paralyzed on the couch. His doctor suggested we put him on Paxil. I received quite a bit of criticism from friends and family, but two weeks after trying it, we had our Travis back. But eventually, at the ages of thirteen and fifteen, his disorder returned, and he began self-medicating.

I was not quite as prepared for the challenge I faced in trying to find mental health care treatment for Travis. His abuse of drugs and alcohol increased after he was prescribed opioids for wisdom teeth surgery; now he was addicted to pain meds. I knew from my research that Travis was "dual diagnosis," but his primary care physician was against using Suboxone for his addiction and wouldn't prescribe Paxil to alleviate Travis's OCD symptoms while he was abusing other drugs. Drinking and drugs became his means of self-medication.

Travis wanted to start Suboxone treatments, but his doctor suggested that he try detox instead. He made two attempts to detox at home, and, after fighting with doctors, psychiatrists, and ER departments, we set our sights on Suboxone. We finally found a doctor in Cleveland operating a Suboxone clinic. I was the last to find out, but somewhere in this journey to recovery Travis began using heroin.

*September 20, 2014*

Dear Travis,

I will never forget, as long as I live, the first time you called me from Stella's [Stella Maris Center, an addiction recovery facility in Cleveland] and I heard and recognized your sober voice on the other end of the phone. It was the voice I used to know as yours, but, more important, I heard raw emotion in your voice. Something I hadn't heard for quite a long time. Hearing your voice that day gave me hope, and when we hung up I cried my heart out and thanked my "Higher Power" on so many levels for your call. The next change I experienced was your appearance on my first visit to Stella's. I remember how excited, anxious, and nervous I was on my drive down there to Stella's. I had no idea what to expect; then I walked into the coffee shop and told someone I was there to see you and waited while they went to get you. My first reaction when I saw you was pure love and pride. You looked healthier, the color was back in your complexion, you were clean, and to me you looked absolutely wonderful—gone were those dark scary circles around your eyes. The difference in your appearance was so drastic, I forgot that your journey had just begun and you had so much further to go. I started to look so forward to our visits and even arranged my schedule at work to accommodate the hours. It gave me great pleasure to bring you all of your favorite snacks, articles of clothing, hygiene products, and cigarettes. The first time I was permitted to take you off campus to spend some time together, I was so excited when you wanted new shoes. It had been so long since you cared about how you looked or your hygiene, I was willing to buy you anything.

The first major change I noticed in you was the awakening of your charitable spirit. One of the best moments was when you told me not to bring you so much stuff on my next visit because there were guys at Stella's who came to rehab with nothing and no real family support. I was so proud of you at that moment, and your charitable heart continues to make me proud. I recall the times you gave others your cigarettes and snacks. There were times when you purchased bus passes for others with your last five dollars. You asked me to bring boots, shoes, and clothing down for others on my frequent trips. The more I visited, the more I became aware of your program and how it worked. You faced some challenges and were forced to meet them head-on. For the first time in your life since your father moved out of our house, you were asked to conform and follow house rules. The expectations of the program were nonnegotiable and difficult for you to meet. There were many times when your father and I thought, "This is it, he'll be asked to leave." It was at this point I realized I had to make it known to you that if you did not work your program and stay clean and sober, you could never come back to my home. If you were asked to leave Stella's, my home would not be your haven.

While attending group as a family at Stella's, I really became aware of your challenges and mine as well. I embraced the twelve-step program and was familiar with it because there were and still are alcoholics in our family. I myself attended Al Anon for two years, as you know. There were times when your honesty and things you admitted in group and to me in private tore me apart. I learned that your immaturity and irresponsibility were serious issues and something you would really have to change in order to succeed in life and in your sobriety. I also learned that you were deficient in many ways due to your excessive use of drugs and alcohol. Your memory was poor and you were selfish at times. Which brings me to your second biggest personal change, and that is selflessness. You are no longer selfish or self-centered and this makes me admire you and love you more. I witness you providing rides to other recovering individuals so that they have a better chance at sobriety through meetings and group support. Your contributions to our family have been numerous in the last twenty-one months, and I am thankful for the changes.

The best change of all that I witness every day in you is your spirituality and your relationship with your God (Higher Power). We've had conversations in which you have told me that the difference between the ones that make it and the ones who don't was that the ones who make it completely understand the steps and live them. Not just preaching them but living them, and I watch you live your program every day with all of your heart and convictions. The other significant difference was really learning to "let go and let God," realizing that there was a Higher Power and you were not in control. Your level of responsibility to your family and loved ones has truly elevated, and your willingness to learn financial responsibility and budgeting is commendable. I admire the fact that you now accept and acknowledge the role you play in every situation and relationship that takes place in your life. You have learned to look at yourself first and not analyze the actions of others. Your sobriety has also awakened your passion and love for animals, and this has demonstrated growth and responsibility while you voluntarily care for Sasha.

The areas in which I would still like to see you grow are accepting in life that there are many small things that seem insignificant that we must do whether we want to do them or not because they demonstrate character and responsibility for oneself; and becoming self-sufficient. I want you to take the appropriate steps and improve upon your ability to provide and care for yourself financially and take personal pride in your belongings. You definitely have improved on self-care by working out regularly and getting your teeth fixed. My hope for you is that you will care for your surroundings and personal belongings with the same intent that you care for yourself. I want to see you happy in your own home and begin saving for your future and retirement. I do not want you to struggle financially, as I have. It would be nice to have you pull into my driveway one day in a new car or truck.

I would like to close by saying how incredibly proud I am of you and your progress to this point. You continue to amaze me with your strength and courage to remain sober and demonstrate character. I know it is no small feat and you are to be commended for it. I wish you a life full of love, and please know that I will continue to be there for you and support you as long as you are living your best life. All my love and support, your Mom

*December 27, 2014*

Goodbye, my sweet sleeping prince. No more pain, no more struggles. You are at peace and serenity is yours. Today I buried my hero, Travis William Scharbach. Exactly two years to the day he entered into rehab and changed his life, the day he became a better man. R.I.P. Stella Fella.

*July 16, 2016*

Still have a hard time when I see parents embracing their young adult children. . . . I feel your journey was so incomplete and cut off way too soon. I will never know what would have been . . . but I do take peace in what you had become. . . . Even though you lost the battle, I loved the road and paths you took to change and improve your life when you were capable, and how you faced your challenges head-on. Most of us do not have the strength to succeed in some of these areas. We spend a lifetime trying. . . . Miss you. Love, your Mom

*December 15, 2016*

Getting closer to your Angelversary and I am really trying to hang in there . . . but the nights are rough. I decided I was going to post pics of you when you were happy and working your way into sobriety. These pics make me feel better, and I am going to share them on Facebook with friends and family. You were a beautiful baby and toddler and grew into a very handsome young man. I am celebrating you and your life. All my love, Mom.

*February 3, 2017*

It occurred to me last night you did not actually give up, my hero. . . . Your physical being gave up on you and decided "no more." I spent this evening and night missing you more than usual. Rough one. I love you and miss you, Mom.

*March 12, 2017*

It is Brett's thirty-sixth birthday. Our Higher Power knew what he was doing when he gave us Noah. I could have never imagined this feeling of overwhelming joy and love. After you left, I thought I was done and would simply grow old without you and never know joy again. Then along came Noah, Travis, and I realized my life was about to start anew . . . feeling so blessed and I know you are looking down on us just beaming with love for this little guy, words can't explain it . . . but you get it. Love always, Mom.

*April 3, 2017*

What I miss the most is the "future" I was supposed to share with you. Coming to terms (not accepting, because I can't) with you not being here and being part of my life gives me the opportunity to grieve over and over again when one of life's milestones presents itself. No wedding, no grandchildren, no watching you grow older and happier with time. I took such deep pride in the way you took on the challenge of rehab and recovery. As you became cleaner and clearer so did my life. Our relationship grew and I had my "Trav" back again. I will forever be thankful to have had those two years of sobriety with you before you departed. Make no mistake I try to be grateful in my life . . . but I really feel "cheated." I love you, always . . . Mom

*June 13, 2017*

I was watching a special on PBS this evening about Buddha. It occurred to me that there are those people in life who, when you meet them for the first time you know there is just something about them. . . . You get such a good feeling. Thankfully, in my life I have had that experience and knew right away there was something "special" about that person. One day you had said to me, "Mom, I wish there was one thing I was really good at." Well, guess what? That's it, that's the thing you were really good at and you didn't have to try. You just had to be you, this was your gift. People, kids, and animals especially loved you . . . and you know what they say about kids and dogs and their judgment of character. . . . I love "you" and miss that "you." I miss your soul being. Grief works like this . . . you never know what will bring on your sadness or pull forth your raw emotions. This was one of the many times I have experienced this type of moment. . . . I guess this is the path I take on my journey without you . . . your Mom.

*Vicki Hamilton-Scharbach currently works as a professional in the insurance industry. She devotes her free time to her grandson, Noah Travis, and his family, as well as educating the public about the importance of removing the stigma associated with addiction.*

# 23

## DESPAIR

GERALD E. GREENE
(DAYTON)

There is a place not far from me—
a place of despair.

Its poets tell of life within,
where hope is seldom found.

Its fruit of crime
adds pain to discouragement,
striking out where it lives,
revealing its presence,
and affecting those it loves most.

Its path leads to confrontation
with self and society,
driving its victims downward
in merciless surges,
like waves on ocean's shore,
pushed by nocturnal tide.

The young man wearing no shirt or shoes
stands on the stoop,

shouting at the driver
of a car parked at the curb.

Words of anger followed by retreat
into an apartment to retrieve the gun
frighten passers-by.

Neighbors hide in fear.

An hour later, all seems peaceful.

"How do I survive in a place
where heroin is easier to find than hope?"
a young girl asks the next day.

What should the preacher say?
Is she there for God's reason
or should she flee?

The opioids beckon with sweetness
and promise of relief.

All seem happy for the moment,
with despair's underside.
A counterfeit time sucking life
from the future, establishing its cycle.

Despair thrives in that place,
and I seek ways to help.

But answers elude.

So, I support my charity.

---

*Gerald Greene* is a retired businessman who enjoys volunteer work, from serving
as a spiritual coach to helping newly arrived refugee families relocate to Ohio. He is
active in the Dayton literary community.

Mythical Creature. Credit: Gabrielle Deacon.

# PART THREE
# MAKING SENSE

H OW DID WE get here? How did Ohio emerge as a national leader in opioid overdose deaths and neonatal abstinence syndrome? Were there warning signs, and, if so, how did we miss them? These and other questions frame the stories in this section, where contributors depict their own struggle to make sense of what is happening and find a way forward.

Along the way, these pieces move beyond cause to assess both responsibility and blame. Some contributors blame themselves, while others blame companies, government, cultures, economic decline, and their family lives. Most pieces reflect the complexity of the situation and acknowledge that responsibility is multiple. Yet the contributors are united in agreement that responsibility and blame are not merely forces of retrospection but are themselves important keys to being able to heal. There is, in other words, a regenerative dimension to this section, which concerns what it is like to live and grow in places devastated by opioids.

Ohioans have attempted to make sense of the opioid crisis in quite different ways, using different analytic lenses, narrative forms, types of media, and historical reference points. First-person accounts in this section look at data trends to show that while the statewide focus on the problem is quite new, the crisis actually developed over some time. Other pieces focus on existential questions, such as how they or their loved ones began using or distributing opioids. Some wrestle with the severity of opioid abuse and explore what, if anything, could begin to lead us out of this epidemic.

# 24

## A PREDICTABLE AND UTTERLY PREVENTABLE CATASTROPHE

MICHAEL HENSON
(CINCINNATI)

It is late afternoon of a late summer day. I stand at the corner of Gest Street and State Avenue in the Cincinnati neighborhood of Lower Price Hill, and I watch a young woman stumble out of a car. The driver is Hispanic this time, possibly from Chiapas or Guatemala, but if you watch long enough you might later see the woman stumble out of the car of a downtown businessman or a construction worker in from Adams County.

She stumbles, I say, and even as she rights herself, her body leans leftward like a bow, bent perhaps by the moons of heroin or the pressure of crack cocaine or by the distortions of her labor serving men in the cramped front seats of cars.

She is a small woman, not quite five feet tall, and perilously thin. The friends I work with know her, have known her since she was a child. She has a name tattooed at her neck like a shackle and there are random tattoos up and down her arms. Her teeth have gone clouded and gray, and there is something about her so twisted and damaged and childlike and holy that I cannot understand how any man would want to have her.

But the men do have her. Again and again, the men drive up to the corner where she waits. They pull to the curb and they roll down their windows and she leans toward them—these men from downtown or from the hills or from countries far to the south, who come to her because they are lonely or because she will give them something that they cannot get from the other women in their lives. They speak quickly and settle something between them; then she gets in the car and they drive her away. In a short time, they return her to the corner once again.

———————

Lower Price Hill is a mostly white Appalachian community in Cincinnati. In spite of its name, Lower Price Hill is not a hill at all. It is the floor of the Mill Creek Valley, the place where the Mill Creek flows into the Ohio River and where, in the mid-nineteenth century, a number of industries and a collection of working-class tenement buildings were cobbled together into a neighborhood.

Many of the tenements and most of the industries are gone now, and most of the open spaces thereby created are full of litter and rubble or, on the steep hillsides leading up to Price Hill proper, are thickly overgrown with honeysuckle and poplar. Gentrifiers have given the neighborhood the eye and, apparently, deemed Lower Price Hill not worth the trouble.

Somewhere in the 1950s, the original German and Italian residents moved out as migrants from the Southern Appalachians moved in. There are now a growing number of Hispanic and African American neighbors as well, but Lower Price Hill is still a largely Appalachian neighborhood where young people speak a mix of down-home and hip-hop and a group of us still put on an annual festival of traditional Appalachian music and culture.

Lower Price Hill was never your quiet, middle-class, tree-lined neighborhood. From the first, it was a hard-working, hard-drinking community, its environs hard-hit by the effluents of the local factories and, since the 1960s, the Metropolitan Sewer District's Mill Creek plant, an eighty-eight acre facility that adds its own fecal stench to the tang of volatile organic compounds.

In the 1980s and 1990s, residents concerned over the effects of all these pollutants on themselves and their children put up a stiff fight, and things have gotten better in some ways. For example, Queen City Barrel, a company that recycled steel drums in a plant that covered a full city block, was once one of the neighborhood's worst polluters. Persistent protests forced action, and the company installed technology to capture and burn off most of the fumes.

The plant caught fire one night in a spectacular blaze punctuated by the thud of exploding barrels, and the entire complex burned to the ground. The site has been cleared for what is supposed to be an industrial park to bring in jobs for the people of the neighborhood.

It's been several years now and those acres still stand idle.

But that's another story.

————

I came to Lower Price Hill in 2000 to work for the Urban Appalachian Council as a community organizer focusing on environmental justice issues. I had worked the previous seventeen years as a substance abuse counselor. Counseling was in many ways a wonderful job, one that worked tremendous personal changes in me and in which I had some success. In the path most people take, a person gets sober, then decides to work in the system. In my case, the job itself got me sober. I eventually became a mid-level supervisor; I was recognized as a trainer.

But at heart I was, and am, a writer. I realized long ago that writing was not going to pay the bills, and over the years I have worked as a schoolteacher, university adjunct, house painter, factory hand, and community organizer. But if I had to hold a job, I wanted it to be one in which I could help change the world, not just patch it up. I had worked for the Urban Appalachian Council before, and my work had brought me into contact with Lower Price Hill. I was ready to get back into what I felt was my true calling.

We built a community group called the Environmental Leadership Group dedicated to educating themselves and the community about environmental issues and holding the polluters accountable. The Environmental Leadership Group was able to elect a slate to the Community Council that brought a new, progressive, democratic voice to the neighborhood. We published results of a Children's Health Survey that documented issues of concern, and we began work on a health survey for women. Some of the worst pollution offenders, after incurring fines resulting from our work, took corrective measures.

But gradually things began to slow. Environmental Leadership Group members seemed distracted with family issues. Community Council attendance dwindled. We still had a core group, but they all wanted to talk about something else.

They wanted to talk about OxyContin.

————

The Arthur M. Sackler Wing of the Metropolitan Museum of Art in New York City is a beautiful place, a unique place, very stark and beautifully lit. Everything here is tasteful and uplifting, not at all cluttered or trafficked, as are the streets of Lower Price Hill. In the Sackler Wing, there is nothing even resembling the fetid air of the Metropolitan Sewer Division, and there are no young women on the corner bearing shackle tattoos.

To approach the Sackler Wing, you walk hundreds of yards, down long, quiet corridors of Asian and Egyptian art far removed from the hustle and glare of the streets outside. You enter the Sackler Wing through large glass doors. Immediately, to the right, you see a huge, slanting wall of glass that showers light down into a large, open room guarded by a pair of larger-than-life seated statues. Behind them, a reflecting pool shimmers. Toward the rear of the room stands the centerpiece of the Arthur M. Sackler Wing, the Temple of Dendur, an intricate and elegant stone edifice covered with bas relief figures who march in ritual procession along its walls.

The Arthur M. Sackler Wing was created with a $10 million grant from Dr. Arthur M. Sackler, who, as chief executive officer of the Purdue Pharma Company, developed the mass marketing strategy that most pharmaceutical companies use today. Sackler's use of that strategy turned Valium into a household name and—as an unfortunate by-product—generated a new era of addiction.

As a counselor and as a person in recovery, I have known many people who suffered through that wave of addiction.

Arthur M. Sackler died in 1987, but his legacy lives on—for Purdue Pharma, under the control of the secretive and well-lawyered Sackler family, later oversaw the creation, promotion, and mass distribution of the drug OxyContin, which led, by stages, to the sad plight of the lonely prostitute I can see almost daily at the corner of Gest and State in Lower Price Hill.

There are Sackler wings and institutes in museums, hospitals, and universities all over the world. The Sacklers are a very generous family.

But for me, the corner of Gest and State in Lower Price Hill will always remain Sackler's other wing.

————

The major innovation of OxyContin was its time-release mechanism. Had it worked as it was intended, the innovation would have meant that those suffering from chronic and debilitating pain—cancer patients, for example, or those suffering from mining injuries—could receive a dose of opioid pain relief without the concurrent danger of addiction which has been the curse of all earlier opioid pain relief. The idea was that a dose of OxyContin would slowly release over a period of twelve hours, providing a small, steady dose of opioid pain relief without the peaks and valleys, the constant shift from ecstasy to misery that traps an individual in addiction.

We know now that OxyContin did not work the way it was intended. And we know that the producers of OxyContin knew that from the start. We know that they drew conclusions regarding the safety of the drug based on the slimmest of evidence. We know that they ignored the actual evidence that their claims to OxyContin's safety could not be supported. And we know that they continued to promote OxyContin and to sell and collect millions of dollars on its sale as addiction rates soared and the suffering of desperate families was further compounded. Their complicity in the catastrophe that has become the opioid epidemic is well-documented.

Among other things, the history shows that Purdue Pharma

- used a limited study of a small group of patients in a controlled setting as "proof" that opioids prescribed for pain rarely induced addiction;
- ignored the growing evidence that OxyContin's pain relief was lasting only six or eight hours (and not the promised twelve), greatly increasing its addiction risk;
- ignored the growing evidence of diversion of the drugs from patients into the general population;
- ignored evidence that users seeking a high had discovered that the time-release mechanism was easily broken by crushing the pills, allowing for a powerful, immediate opioid rush;
- ignored evidence of highly suspect concentrations of sales to certain markets, by which millions of doses were being sold in sparsely populated communities;
- instructed their sales and promotion staff to falsify what they knew about the booming addiction rates and connection of OxyContin to it; and

- used their power and money to protect themselves from being held accountable.

The Sacklers and their minions were not alone. In fact, one of the stunning revelations in this whole sad story is the sheer number of supposedly responsible and respectable professionals, people who already lived comfortably and enjoyed a lifestyle their patients and clients could only dream of, professionals who were willing to put ethics, fiduciary responsibility, law, and common sense aside in order to make a dollar off the suffering of others.

An army of Purdue Pharma salespeople marched into the front lines. With brochures, gifts, "seminars," and paid vacations, they lulled the consciences of physicians, pharmacists, and other health workers who could prescribe and dispense the millions of doses of OxyContin that flooded certain areas of the country. Insurance companies, calculating that a pill was so much cheaper than holistic pain treatment, refused to pay for the massages, physical therapy, and counseling provided by pain clinics. In their place, "pain clinics," which came to be known as "pill mills," sprang up. Law enforcement did its part; top investigators and prosecutors whose job had been to bust the pill mills and rogue pharmacies found new, more profitable work defending the likes of the Sacklers. Not to be outdone, politicians figured out a way to profit. Having received a hefty campaign donation, a Republican congressman from a Pennsylvania district hard-hit by Oxy sponsored a bill that limits the ability of Drug Enforcement Agency agents to track concentrations of prescriptions.

We like to think of our drug dealers as thugs on street corners or as Mexican *narcotraficantes*. We don't think of them in lab coats or suits.

———

Demand for OxyContin–and addiction to it—quickly took hold in Appalachian communities from Maine to Alabama, and from there into the urban Appalachian migrant centers like Lower Price Hill. High rates of cancer and chronic injury in Appalachian communities meant that there was—and remains—a great need for pain relief. The perpetual economic and social crises of Appalachian communities, where unemployment is high and opportunities are few, also left these communities vulnerable. So when Purdue Pharma deployed the aggressive sales strategy that they inherited from Arthur M. Sackler, the army of salespeople found in Appalachia a target-rich environment.

Communities were transformed as people became desperate for the drug. Robberies, prostitution, and violence tore apart small towns and urban neighborhoods. Abandoned and neglected children overwhelmed social services networks.

OxyContin became known as "hillbilly heroin."

———

I am ashamed to admit it, but even the drug treatment profession has been tainted by the opioid scandal.

Word had gotten out about the OxyContin disaster. There were articles in the *New York Times* and other media. Communities raised hell, and supplies of OxyContin grew short. Purdue Pharma, in a desperate attempt to clean up its image, started a drug prevention campaign. (I attended one of the sessions they sponsored. It was laughable.) As physicians grew more reluctant to prescribe OxyContin, desperate addicts looked for alternatives.

One of these was methadone.

Methadone is a very effective aid to recovery when dosed properly and when combined with therapy. For years, Ohio has had a small but effective, well-organized, well-regulated network of methadone treatment centers

Indiana, not so much.

Cincinnati's methadone program was a short twenty-minute drive from Lower Price Hill, and a dose costs five dollars a day. But addicts in Lower Price Hill and other tristate communities figured out that the Indiana Treatment Center, a full hour away in Batesville, was willing to let them skip counseling and to take more than what they needed to control their cravings, at a cost of twelve dollars per day. With methadone, if an addict takes more than what they need to control cravings, that extra dosage will get them high. So addicts—cut off from OxyContin but not ready to get into recovery—had a cheap, legal high. A daily caravan left the neighborhood for the Indiana-Ohio border, and the troubles for the neighborhood continued. The OxyContin overdoses became methadone overdoses.

At least one overdose happened on the front step of Santa Maria Neighborhood Services, when an elderly woman nearly died after taking bootlegged methadone obtained from the Indiana Treatment Center.

So the community raised hell again, this time with the East Indiana Treatment Center, which responded by tightening its dosing policies. Methadone became scarce.

So the addicts shifted their tactics again. This time to heroin. Now, the OxyContin-overdoses-turned-methadone-overdoses became heroin overdoses.

Opioid addiction has now spread from Appalachian centers into the general population. A more-or-less localized problem has become a national disaster. We have ruined the nation of Mexico with it and fattened the bloody cartels.

A new generation of professionals now profits from the epidemic, as for-profit treatment centers blossom. The pharmaceutical industry is doing well with its sales of Suboxone, buprenorphine, and Narcan—drugs used to treat active addiction or revive individuals who have overdosed.

Pardon me if I sound cynical, but everybody seems to be doing well but the addicts, their families, and the people of Mexico.

———

Eventually, the funding ran out for my position as a community organizer, and I went back to working in treatment. For a time, I supervised counseling services for inmates in halfway houses, inmates who were leaving prison or living in homeless shelters. Later, I worked with a project providing housing to homeless alcoholics. In both positions, opioids complicated the work we were doing, and I lost several clients to overdoses. I have lost friends to overdose, and I have seen the children of friends succumb. My wife and I tried to help our neighbor, hopelessly addicted, but eventually he went back to prison

Now, in retirement, I read everything I can find. I write stories and I blog for an online magazine dedicated to addiction and recovery. I work with recovering addicts. I volunteer with a neighborhood group fighting addiction in the community where I live.

But the ironies continue to mount. Our president declares the opioid crisis a national emergency while presiding over a tax cut that is sure to undermine resources for treatment. The Oxy overdoses become methadone overdoses which become heroin overdoses which have now become fentanyl overdoses, and even buprenorphine overdoses. I used to live in the inner city where there was a drug dealer on the corner. But I moved out close to the suburbs where, you guessed it, there is now a drug dealer on the corner. When I walk my dog, I carry a plastic juice bottle for the needles I find. Overdose death rates continue to rise. Robberies, prostitution, and violence continue to tear communities apart. Abandoned and neglected children overwhelm social services at a time when we are cutting back on those very networks.

Need treatment? Can't afford it? Commit a crime. Our jails have become the most efficient gateway to the recovery system.

It really is insane.

None of this needed to happen. None of it would have happened if greed had not overruled common sense. But greed almost always does. And greed at the corporate level almost always escapes serious consequences. In some cases, the people who brought us this disaster have faced fines and civil suits. A few, very few, pill-mill operators mostly, have faced jail time, but no one at the corporate level, to my knowledge, has faced jail time or the loss of a loved one.

None of them, to my knowledge, has a daughter or a sister who stumbles in and out of men's cars, who stalks State Avenue with a marked and bent body, holy and sad, a tattoo like a shackle at her neck.

*Michael Henson* is a retired community organizer and substance abuse counselor whose writing on addiction has included the novella Tommy Perdue *(2012) and a collection of stories,* Maggie Boylan *(2018). He writes for The Fix's "Living Sober" blog and serves as a coeditor of* Pine Mountain Sand & Gravel, *the annual publication of the Southern Appalachian Writers Cooperative.*

# 25

## STANDING PROUD

ERIC UNGARO

(POLAND)

*Eric Ungaro has been a special education teacher and varsity football coach for the last twenty-eight years, serving in both inner-city and suburban school settings. He has been an elected official in Poland, Ohio, since 2012. Interview by Daniel Skinner.*

*Tell me a little bit about growing up in the Greater Youngstown area, in the Mahoning Valley, and how you saw the situation with opioid addiction developing over some years.*

Well, my father was mayor during a lot of the time when the crack/cocaine epidemic was going on. But we can even go back further when my mother had three brothers. Two of them ultimately died from substance abuse issues. So even at a young age, before we got into the political arena, I was living that every day, going over to my grandmother's house, seeing my uncles, and ultimately seeing them buried.

Then, after my father became mayor, I witnessed it from the inside out. There was a lot of corruption going on in our area with the gangs. We sent a number of prosecutors and judges to prison during that time. Guys were getting picked up with drugs and getting released on cheap bonds the next day. And that's when I started teaching and coaching in

112

Youngstown. So then I was dealing with those kids on a daily basis, witnessing what they were going through, feeling the trauma from losing their dads, their uncles. Then we got to the opioid situation.

My brother was part of the first wave of people in the mid-90s who started getting prescribed OxyContin for little surgeries. In his case it was a hernia surgery. That generation was prescribed those pills, and then they'd go down a road that they shouldn't go down, be it partying with the drugs a little bit, getting hooked on them, turning around, selling them to feed their habit, losing their jobs at General Motors, and then ultimately dying.

The kids I'm teaching now, in more of a suburban setting, they're the ones getting decimated by this, but in the late '80s, early '90s, it was more of the inner-city community. So I've pretty much lived the whole gamut. The sad part is that I've witnessed it from the inside out.

*What's unique about Youngstown when you compare it to other areas around the state?*

Corruption. Early on, it was the corruption. We've always had that stigma of "mobtown USA" or whatever. So I think the corruption led to the demise of a lot of inner-city families. And to be honest with you, right now, the opioid situation, I think it cuts through everything. Look, we lost a lot of steel jobs. So we're an area that numbs itself a little bit more with prescription pills. Many people are struggling with their financial situations, and the reality of it is, the epidemic of the pills, which leads to the heroin—the drugs are just too strong for people. They just weren't meant for people to take to numb their pain. I mean, they were basically made for people who were dying in a hospital bed somewhere. So those are the similarities in depression and economic distress.

*You wear a lot of hats. You're a father, a husband, brother, teacher, football coach; you're part of a well-known Youngstown political family, and a politician in your own right. Is there any one hat that gives you a unique lens that maybe the others don't, or is it all one 360-degree picture?*

No, they're all different. Obviously, the most traumatic is when I watched my brother. As a family member, starting grief groups with ladies in our community, starting Solace of the Valley [a nonprofit organization that provides support for those struggling with addiction], that's where you feel it. That's real stuff right there. That's talking to parents. On a weekly basis, I go meet with families that are asking me, "What could I do to help my daughter?" You're looking at this beautiful nineteen-year-old girl who has everything going for her. Money, the family's wealthy, and she's strung out on pills. So that family aspect is number one.

And the teaching part is number two because you're feeling their trauma too. These kids coming to school. "You know, my mom died last night." And being a special-ed teacher, you have a little bit more of a personal relationship with them because you're traditionally in a small group setting. So that will be the second part of actually feeling the trauma.

And then last, the political part. The good thing is I brought that passion to my role as an elected official. For example, I'm sympathetic to Narcan. We were one of the first townships in our area to start having our officers use Narcan. It's a suburban community, so it was a big step for our whole area. A little community that's predominately white, relatively wealthy. Their cops are using it, so we made it easy for everybody else to kind of jump on board. You just be strong and continue to have those initiatives even in the face of controversy of some of the people who aren't sympathetic to people who are struggling with addiction. You've just gotta stay strong and keep pushing away and just treat every human being's life as extremely valuable. It's what we all should be doing.

And I'm president of the Red Zone, which is former Ohio State football player Maurice Clarett's behavioral health agency in inner-city Youngstown. I'm also feeling their kind of struggle, more from a poverty standpoint.

But, again, actually losing a brother and being on the front line—it just gives you that passion to stand strong when anybody opens their mouth and acts ignorant like, "Oh, they're bums. You won't see them again." People can be ignorant. And then when the shit happens to their family (excuse my language), then they're all on board. So thank God I went through it at an early age and we've always been sympathetic to the struggles. And my father, even being mayor, was always open about my brother's addiction, and our family was a high-profile family. But everybody knew who the Ungaros were, not because we're rich, because we're a middle-class family in Youngstown, but because our dad was mayor.

*Obviously, losing a family member is a tragedy for any family. But when you're a family that's well-known in the area—what was that like?*

Well, I think number one, the grieving process is different for everyone. But they had my brother plastered on the front page when he would get picked up at a street corner with a needle in his arm. Back in 2012 and 2011, it wasn't cool to talk about this stuff. People thought they were garbage, pieces of crap, junkies. But we've come a long way in five years. I think our family's approach, even when it was hard and it wasn't popular, we always talked about recovery and trying to help people.

We used our influence to make great strides in our community and then ultimately some of these people die. That's when I just went crazy. I just said, "Hey, either I'm gonna sit around and drink every day and feel sorry for myself or I'm gonna get on the Mental Health & Recovery Board. We're gonna start Solace of the Valley. We're gonna start grief groups. We're gonna help the first responders and feed them spaghetti dinners because of what they do." So I kind of spun it into a positive. If not, I'd probably be dead too. The limelight that we were in, I just turned it into a positive the best I could. It still doesn't help my parents. They're still numb as hell. I still go to the cemetery every day.

*Your website makes clear that you're a person of faith, and I've seen you describe Sean's passing as part of God's plan. I wonder if you can just tell me a little bit about the faith component, how that's guided you through what your family's been through?*

I don't know. I guess . . . I went to a Catholic high school. Am I a church-goer every day? No. I'm kind of like one of those guys who lives by "the good you do today is forgotten tomorrow." You do good anyway. And there's really no other way to describe what has happened in my life.

I've beat myself up. I wasn't there with him the day he died. I traditionally would talk to him three, four times a day. I tried. Who knows what would've happened if things didn't end this way. Maybe he would've gotten in a wreck and killed some young kids, or maybe he would've started selling drugs and they would've come by and shot up my parents' house. I don't know. So I guess that's just how we're wired as a family. As long as you're doing good, the rest is going to be taken care of just through some kind of divine intervention.

*Since Sean's passing especially, you've been involved with a lot of different kinds of groups. You also said in 2011 or 2012, people in Ohio didn't think in such a nuanced way about people dealing with addiction, but I wonder if working with others to address this situation has changed your perspective?*

Absolutely. As you said, I wear a lot of hats. I can only grieve for so long. For a year, that's all I did. I called every drug dealer. I was convinced he was murdered. I played investigator for a year. I put my family in jeopardy. Here's one thing I do want to add. My dad being mayor, I'm not saying it contributed to my brother's situation, but it contributed to his sense of invincibility. A lot of the guys who were on the police force back then were guys I grew up with, who got hired under my father. So we would get a number of phone calls like, "Eric, look man. We picked Sean up down here. You gotta get . . . you gotta." Now again, contributing to it, no. But it contributed to his feeling of invincibility. Like, "I'm not gonna die. No one's gonna mess with me." So it's just kind of a sick way to look at it, but it is something that's always been on my mind.

But now, the ladies I work with, they keep my passion going. They lost their sons. They push me to stay involved. When I speak, I know I'm an asset because people know that I've always been on the forefront talking about it.

And people grieve in different ways. People drink. Some people take pills. Some people get active. Some people turn to the Lord. It's almost just like how you become a nonaddict. Everybody has their way of kind of coping with it. But in the end, my parents, they just shut down. They don't talk about it at all. Rarely does my dad get out in public and actually talk about what's going on or things like that. But, again, everybody's kind of different.

*Looking forward, what are your priorities with the opioid situation?*

I think number one, by far—it sounds simple, but it's not—is to be a strong voice for families that are dealing with this. Five years ago the stigma was still being broken down. Now, people are getting right to work. Another thing is that we've got to fight to make sure that insurance covers treatment and recovery. Those are just things you have to be a strong voice for. You've got to try to get to some kind of state plan where we have more beds available—instead of just throwing people in prison.

You know what, they always talk about "we're gonna sue the companies." I would just like to sue the companies just to have them pay for Narcan. Because then it takes that conversation away from "Oh, let 'em die . . . take that burden off the taxpayers."

When I talk about these issues, people listen a little bit more because I've had to live around this my whole life—from the inside out—and I know what's important. People need to detox. They need to be in a recovery house. They need to find a sober living house. They need to find employment. Education too.

So my mission is all intertwined in a sense, but number one, my goal is to just be a strong voice for families so that they can say, "Oh, you know that guy over there, his dad was mayor, he lost his brother. Lost a couple of uncles. He's standing strong. He's standing proud," because that's what people got to do—stand proud.

# 26

## UNCLE SUGAR

ANISI DANIELS-SMITH
(HIRAM)

Uncle Sugar was never really sweet. For as long as I could remember, his face showcased a scowl that dared anyone to transgress a set of rules that only he knew. I was convinced he maintained a low-level hatred for everyone, allowing his face to communicate what his attitude would not bother to do.

One day my father showed me a school picture of Uncle Sugar as a teen, posed in a starched pastel shirt with that same look as the star of the show. He'd spent part of his childhood in a small Ohio town whose economy depended heavily upon the Ohio River; then he and The Scowl matured in another steel-manufacturing city—about forty miles north of his childhood home. I wondered if the origin of his look rested primarily with genetics or with practicality. I knew nothing about his teenage years, but his adolescent face changed me. It asked me to know him.

The Scowl never budged when he smiled at me, but now I could see the love in his face. I still braced myself against accusation of some imagined infraction when he said "Hey girl" in the voice that was always too loud and sounded a bit too mean, but I opened myself to the possibility that he might have something to say that I needed and wanted to hear. That day came when we lost someone we loved, and we talked about the value of life. That conversation included what I had wanted to know for years: why did he sell drugs in the community he claimed to love, and to people he claimed to respect?

"I'm not going to no damn funeral. You all know I can't stand that kind of thing. When mom died . . . I'm telling you. There ain't nothing like seeing that casket close and knowing you'll never see that person on earth again." I sit quietly, watching his face darken in anguish. But I can't help myself. I need to know. "Uncle Sug. Do you worry about what happens when you die?" He looks away. "It's only so much worrying I can do. I don't know what's on the other side. But one thing I can say: I'll never kill myself. You go to hell for that. I don't care what happens or what kind or pain I'm in. I'll never kill myself. Life isn't ours to take." I knew that his deep religious roots were speaking, and I could nearly envision the grandmother I never knew nodding her approval at her son's stance. His sincerity silences, then confuses, then emboldens me. "Do you think you'll go to hell for selling drugs? You don't feel like you're killing people? They're dying from crack, heroin, and all kinds of things because they can't just walk away. It's not that easy, and you and I both know that. You don't think you're helping them to die a slow death?"

I was energized with curious indignation. I see a moment I'd once forgotten. Uncle Sugar had two houses. He lived in one and conducted business in the other. Both are in a rust belt city bearing the scars of manufacturing decline, labor outsourcing, and population loss. For as long as I could remember, my uncle made his living selling drugs in that city. Social stressors, increasing crime, and lack of viable economic opportunities provided a niche that my uncle filled to great "success." His sharp mathematical mind, emotional intelligence, and large stature qualified and sustained him where others failed. My brother and I spent many weekends in that city with our cousins, who felt more like siblings to us. They were the ones who taught me what to do when Uncle Sugar had visitors—say hello if they spoke and then leave. That way, we saw and knew nothing. We learned that the mention of our uncle's street moniker bought us a special brand of courtesy in stores, and we had unquestioned protection when we biked and walked the streets of the neighborhood after dark. The reputation remained as we grew older, and the houses were fixtures in the community. Visits to see Uncle Sugar became more infrequent as we grew into adults. But I made it my business to visit him every few months, following a refined protocol that remained with me from my childhood: I called, told him

I missed him, and asked which house I should visit. It was ingrained in me that minding my own business meant minding his too. I was never afraid when I visited either his home or the place where he often slept, held card games, drank with friends, and made his money. He always offered food and proud introductions of his niece. I laughed so hard and loved him so much that I would sometimes forget about the real purpose of the house.

Once, a young man came up the steps, peering into the screened-in porch. He knocked twice and then looked inside again. Nobody did that. I let him in. Grimy clothes covered a bony frame. Matted hair fell over his eyes and down into his collar. He scratched and held himself. He whispered a quick "Heyhowareya," and his eyes went elsewhere, obviously searching for my uncle. I regressed to the cousin lesson. I said hello, sat on the couch, and picked up my phone as if I had no interest in what was taking place. But this time, I broke the rule. I looked up. He was watching me, absently scratching crossed arms. I gave a close-lipped smile and he looked away, embarrassed. My uncle's heavy footfall hit the steps, so I excused myself to a bathroom I did not need. When I emerged, the visitor was gone. I said to my uncle, "That was unexpected. I'm more used to seeing people who look like us around here."

He told me it was a buyer's market, and "I got a little bit of everything now to take care of a little bit of everybody." I knew exactly what he meant. The epidemic I'd been reading and teaching about had become part of my uncle's diversification plan. He knew who he needed to reach and how to reach them. I wasn't the only one paying attention. Our venues and goals were different, but our awareness converged in that moment.

That shared awareness flooded back to me as I asked my uncle about hell and death, and whether he believed he was ushering anyone to either destination more quickly than they would otherwise arrive. His vehement response jolted me. "I might go to hell for selling drugs. But shit, people go to hell for lying, cheating other people, and all sorts of things. I'm not giving people something they don't want. I'm not forcing them. They come to me. I don't find them and make them take nothing I'm selling. Sometimes people need to escape. Life is harder than a motherfucker for a whole lot of people, and for a whole lot of reasons. You wouldn't believe the things I've seen that people go through. If they need a little something to help them make it or to keep them from hurting or killing somebody else, I don't see what the problem is. Yeah, I know some people get hurt. I used to be an addict myself. I remember crawling around on the ground, picking up rocks and pebbles thinking it might be crack I dropped. I thought I would never get clean. So I know what it's like. But I also know what it's like to not have hope for finding a job that pays your bills. You think men and women out here just don't want to take care of their kids or give their mamas or daddies or sisters or brothers a little something sometimes? Try to tell them that fast food or the nursing home is gonna give them everything they need. Tell them they'll get respect and a chance to own something of their own that way. With all that schooling, you know better than I do that if we don't give them something better, people are gonna do what works. Period. Even at the risk of going to jail or maybe sometimes people hurting themselves. I've been in this game so long, it's hard to see anything else. But one thing I know: I do this because I have to, not because I want to. I don't want to hurt people. I just want to live."

I nodded, hoping to communicate my understanding but not necessarily my assent. He was not expecting a response, and I know he didn't want one. It was time for me to head to the funeral. I hugged my uncle more tightly and held him longer than I ever had. He rested his chin on my head for a brief moment and said, "All right, Monster." He hadn't called me that in years. We both tended to our eyes and parted to grieve in our preferred ways. This man I'd always loved, whose goodbye usually included a request to pray as a family, sold illegal drugs to people. He was an active, guilty part of an epidemic that helped to sustain him while hurting others. Uncle Sugar, a pastiche of the upstanding businessman, cracked the door to a world that is easy to malign but harder to understand and change. He showed me that—whatever the issue—strength of conviction cannot replace depth of insight.

"I just want to live." Me too, Uncle Sug. They do too. In some way, we all just want to live.

*Born and raised in Ohio, **Anisi Daniels-Smith, PhD,** has taught sociology at Kent State, University of Mount Union, and Hiram College. She is a vice president of the Northeast Ohio Black Health Coalition.*

# 27

## POTENTIAL ENERGY

APRIL DEACON
(WHEELERSBURG)

As a high school art educator in Scioto County, I have seen the opioid epidemic from a unique perspective. When I arrived at my current school in 2007, three quarters of the student population qualified for free or reduced lunch. I knew from the start that my students faced many socioeconomic challenges that would impact classroom performance. A few years in, I began to see dramatically worsening conditions. Suddenly, I was learning of children who were homeless, parentless, food insecure, and worse—all due to the worsening drug epidemic. In 2011, the scope of the problem became clear as our county was ranked number one in prescription drug abuse. I was witnessing the impact upon the children of my community on a grand scale.

So I began to paint portraits of former high school students who had endured significant obstacles in their youth. I selected students who were strong, adaptable, intelligent, and talented; possessed social skills; and had extraordinary potential. I selected students who taught me something. I wanted them to see themselves as I saw them. I wanted them to know that their circumstances did not have to define them. It wasn't until I looked back at the students whose portraits I had painted that I realized nearly all of them had been impacted by the opioid epidemic.

I created the student portraits using acrylic, enamel, and gouache. The different surface texture that these mediums provide creates variety.

The images are painted on doors, chosen as a symbol of opportunity. I worked from photographs and added either text or graphic shapes to the imagery. Both the words and the brightly colored shapes serve as a reminder that we are all universally worthy of life's gifts. The portraits are a celebration of possibility. (See plates 1–4 at the end of this essay.)

I'm concerned for the next generation of children who were born in the apex of the opioid battle. They have just begun their educational journey. Today in our elementary school, nearly all of our students qualify for free or reduced lunch. Things just seem to be getting worse. Our children are resilient and so are our educators, but the challenges are immense. It is exceedingly difficult to convince a child who does not have their basic needs met that they are capable of greatness. But still, we try.

*Since earning her MA in art and design from Marshall University in 2007,* **April Deacon** *has been the high school art instructor at Portsmouth High School. Deacon lives with her husband and two daughters.*

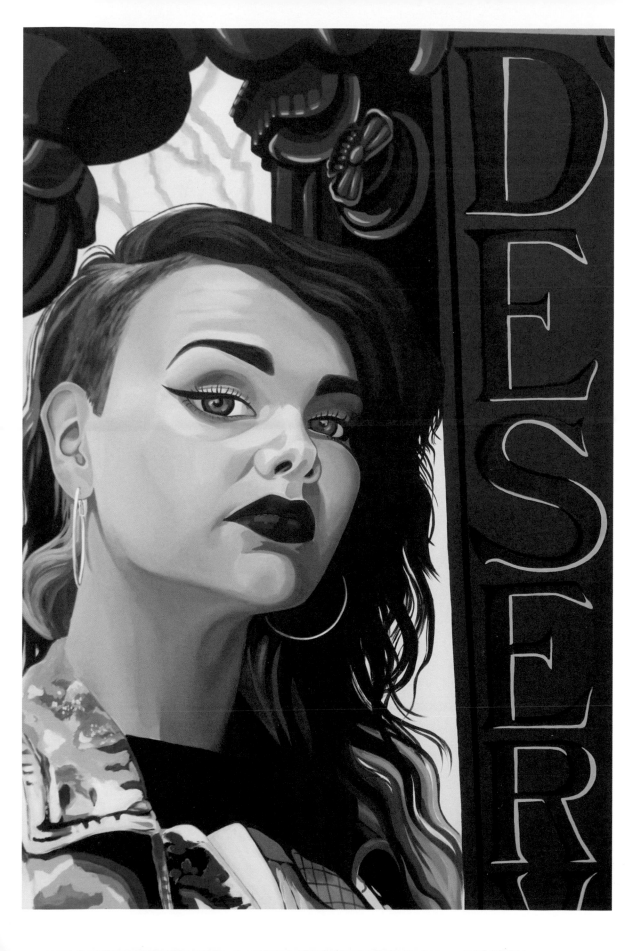

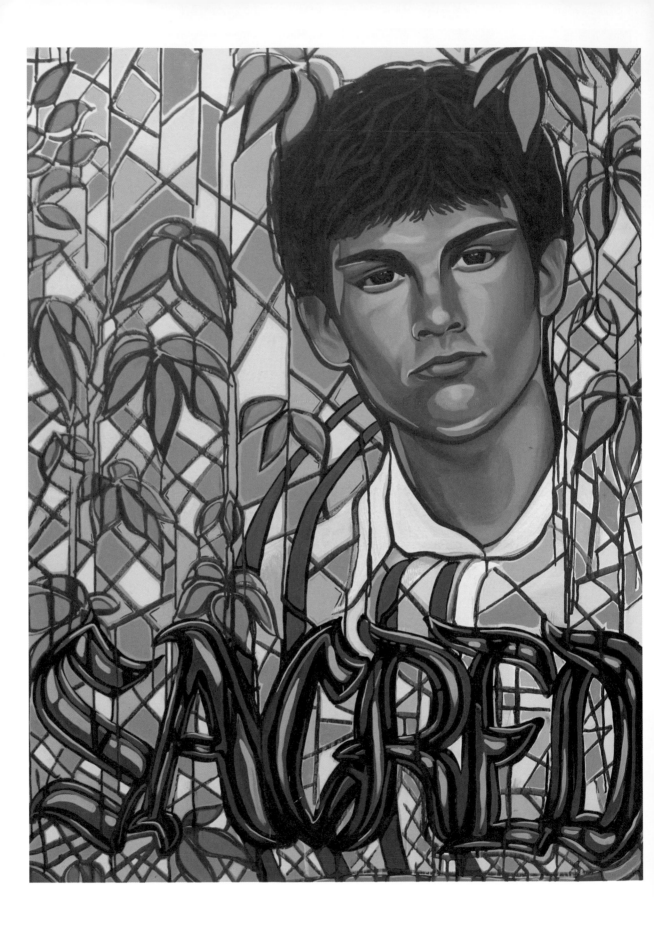

# 28

## THE ROAD TO RECOVERY

ALEX DRIEHAUS
(ATHENS)

Whitney Johnson and Jeremy Rhoades hold each other in the parking
lot outside of First Baptist Church in Logan, Ohio, before Celebrate
Recovery, a Christ-based support group for recovering addicts.

Whitney smirks as she talks to Jeremy during a Celebrate Recovery meeting. Jeremy was under house arrest at the time, and the meeting was the first time the couple had seen each other since Jeremy moved into the sober house.

Whitney Johnson and Jeremy Rhoades are well known in Logan, Ohio. Whitney says they were "the worst of the worst" when it came to the addicts in town, but right now they're both clean and trying to stay that way.

I met Whitney and Jeremy while working on my senior capstone project in 2017. I spent three months photographing them and getting to know their stories. They welcomed me into their lives without hesitation because they wanted to share their experiences and hoped that they could have an impact on other addicts. I feel lucky to have been a part of their lives, and I hope I've done their story justice. They certainly had an impact on me, and I'm excited to pass that on to other people.

Whitney is the kind of person who can't walk down the street without stopping to talk to someone she knows. She's loud and charming, and her catchphrases spread like wildfire. Jeremy is more reserved and quiet. He's deeply empathetic, and he's loyal to a fault when it comes to the people he loves.

No one ever expected that Whitney and Jeremy would get together, but they found solace in each other when they started their recovery. Whitney likes to point out the irony in the fact that Jeremy, her partner in sobriety, was the first person to sell her heroin.

Like many other addicts, Whitney and Jeremy were driven to get clean partly out of fear. Not fear of jail time, which they say barely feels like a punishment at this point, but fear of death. Opioid overdose deaths have risen drastically over the past few years, tripling in Ohio in the last five years alone, according to the Ohio Department of Health. "People are dying, and I didn't want to die, so I got clean," Whitney said.

Whitney and Jeremy weren't motivated entirely by fear, however. They each have discovered a deep faith in God, which they say has given them strength and hope. "If you have spirituality in your life and you really believe in God, that's the one that's going to help you the most," Jeremy said.

Whitney and Jeremy both found their faith in somewhat unusual ways. Jeremy had just gotten back from a stint in jail, and he found himself slipping back into old patterns, smoking weed and getting high on Suboxone. One night he did a shot of meth, and it kept him up for over forty-eight hours. "The second night, or maybe even the third night I was up, I had an epiphany. Like Jesus actually talked to me," Jeremy said. "I know a lot of people . . . are gonna say it's because I was up on meth and I was delirious, but no, it wasn't, and ever since that day I've been determined to be with God and to be clean."

Whitney says she found her faith in "the hole" when she was in jail. "Best place ever. I miss it sometimes," Whitney said. During her incarceration, Larry Swart, a pastor, visited her regularly as part of a jail ministry program. She wasn't sold at first, but when she was put in solitary confinement and all her books were taken away, she fought to keep her Bible. When she rejoined the rest of the inmates, she felt like a new person, and she started spending her time preaching to anyone who would listen. Larry and Whitney formed a strong bond through the jail ministry, and when she finally was released, Larry and his wife Karen took her in for a while. Whitney became a part of the family and even got baptized in the river behind their property. That spot is special to her, and when Jeremy was ready to get baptized in October, she let him use it. She's made it clear that's not something she would do for just anyone.

Whitney hugs Jeremy after his baptism by Pastor Bruce Livingston (left) and Whitney's adoptive father, Larry Swart (right). Jeremy has known Pastor Livingston since he was a child and sees him as a sort of father figure.

Whitney and Jeremy hold hands during a church service. Both credit God's support as a driving force in their recovery and look to Him when they need strength.

Whitney and her friend Chelsea carry Jeremy's daughter Paisley into the house in her stroller after going to watch the Logan Christmas parade. Whitney and Jeremy each have four children, none of whom live with them. Whitney is unable to visit with her children, and has taken up a maternal role with Jeremy's kids.

Jeremy's baptism was important to him, not only because he was committing his life to God, but also because all four of his children were able to be there for it, which is something that rarely happens. Though he would like to, Jeremy doesn't have custody of any of his children. He likes to think that he's a good dad to them when he's around, but he doesn't feel like it's enough. "They deserve better," Jeremy said. "They deserve a dad that's not getting high."

Both Jeremy and Whitney dream of having a family. Whitney talks constantly about getting her kids back, but for now she tries to treat Jeremy's kids like they're her own when they come to visit.

Recovery hasn't been easy for Whitney and Jeremy. Whitney had trouble getting off of the Suboxone that she had been addicted to for nearly a decade, and she started using meth to help get through the month-long dope sickness that she experienced. Then she had trouble getting off of the meth.

Paisley rolls around on the couch, trying to get attention from Whitney and her friend Melissa.

Jeremy's recovery is monitored by the Vivitrol program that he attends through Hocking County Municipal Court. A few months into his recovery, he got caught with Neurontin in his system and was ordered to move out of Whitney's house and into a sober house for thirty days. Jeremy says he was lying to himself and claiming he was clean while still taking Neurontin because it's technically a non-narcotic, even though it can get you high if taken in large quantities.

Whitney was angry when Jeremy had to leave. She felt abandoned, like she was being punished for something he did wrong. Initially Jeremy was put on house arrest and wasn't allowed to have visitors, which Whitney thought was completely unreasonable, and she was frustrated that he didn't stand up for himself with the judge. Most of Jeremy's restrictions were eventually lifted, but it was a difficult period in Whitney and Jeremy's relationship. "Messing up and going to a recovery house . . . did have a toll on our relationship," Jeremy said. "Hopefully we can get it back. We're doing a lot better now."

A note from Jeremy's daughter Vada hangs on the fridge.

Jeremy kisses his daughter Paisley after putting her hair up in a ponytail. Paisley is Jeremy's youngest, and he sees her the most because she often stays with his mother.

For the first few months of recovery, Whitney and Jeremy had little to do outside of attending court, church, and support groups. Time during the day that had once been filled by a constant drive to fuel addiction gave way to an almost overwhelming sense of listlessness. Whitney and Jeremy have had to find new ways to fill their time, and both have started working. Jeremy applied for multiple jobs while living at the sober house and is now working at Wendy's. Whitney is helping to fix up JR's Transmission, a mom-and-pop mechanic shop that is owned by another recovering addict.

Whitney doesn't plan to stay in Logan much longer because she's constantly surrounded by addicts and reminders of her old life. "I don't think it's conducive to my recovery whatsoever," she said.

"I really felt drawn to help addicts, and that's what tripped me up." She has big dreams of moving down the road to Nelsonville and taking care of Larry and Karen's property. "I'm gonna have to go somewhere else and have a fresh start, because I deserve that too," Whitney said.

While Whitney likes to look toward the future, Jeremy tries to stay grounded in the present. Of course, he has hopes of one day marrying Whitney and raising their kids together, but for now he tries to keep his mind from straying too far. "I'm trying to take it one day at a time, for real," he said.

Jeremy is moving back into the sober house soon, but this time it's his choice. He's not sure what it might mean for his relationship with Whitney, but she agrees that it's probably best for his recovery, and he says he's sure of how he feels. "You're not supposed to be in a relationship the first year you're clean, you're just supposed to work on you," Jeremy said. "But I really feel like she's my soulmate, and I'm gonna fight 'til I can't fight no more."

FACING: Whitney hugs her adoptive sister, Angel, at their family's property off of old route 33 near Nelsonville. When Whitney moved away from the Swarts' house she returned to an abusive husband, and her relationship with her adoptive family became strained. After getting clean and starting a new relationship she was able to return to her adoptive family's home to visit for the first time in months.

Sunday morning light hits the garage in front of Whitney's apartment. Whitney feels like staying in Logan is keeping her trapped in her old life, and she hopes to move away soon.

Whitney and Jeremy hold hands as they talk by the river after Jeremy's baptism. Recovery hasn't been easy for either of them, but they're taking it one day at a time.

*Alex Driehaus is a graduate of Ohio University with a Bachelor of Science in Visual Communication. She enjoys working on documentary projects because they allow time for forming genuine connections with the people she photographs.*

# 29

## FROM FELON
## TO LAW ENFORCEMENT
### A Retrospective

BRANDY E. MORRIS-HAFNER
(CHILLICOTHE)

In the small town of Frankfort lived a little girl with big aspirations; she was the youngest of three siblings with two working parents. I was that little girl. We were the typical American family. We were a bit dysfunctional, but I believe all families are a bit dysfunctional. My dad liked to drink, but he was a weekend drinker. However, when he did drink, he got mean. Violence in our house was a normal part of everyday life, a lot of fighting between brother and sister, sister and mom, mom and dad. I always felt like I was on the outside looking in. I lived in constant fear of that violence turning toward me. I stayed out of it as much as I could. I focused on school and horses; school was my sanctuary, and my horse was my escape. I was a straight-A student and a cheerleader, and I excelled at everything I did. Fortunately, or unfortunately, depending on how you look at it, my family was too caught up in their dysfunction to even notice me. That dysfunction eventually got to be too much for my mom, and she filed for divorce. In a small town back in the early 1990s it was taboo to divorce. So not only did I get to deal with the public shame of it, but I was forced to deal with the emotional side of it on my own because my parents had checked out mentally and my brother and sister had already moved out of the house.

I started looking for comfort and attention in any way I could. I joined a gang and started hanging out with people from the city who were in similar situations. When the divorce was made final, my dad was ordered out of the house by the courts, and my mom was reinventing herself. She met this guy whom she would continue to date for the next fourteen years. At first she would stay the weekend with him, then some days through the week, and then all the time. I was about sixteen or seventeen at this time. She was still paying the house bills and still buying me groceries, but she wasn't there. My mom and her boyfriend came to the house one night and called me into the kitchen—on the table were an ounce of weed, scales, and rolling papers. He said, "I'm going to show you how to make money so you can start taking care of yourself. Your mom is going to stay with me from now on." I have to admit, I was intrigued. He showed me how to make bags of weed to sell, dime bags, half quarters, quarters, and he showed me how to roll a joint and put a price on each so I would know what to charge. I guess you could say I got a crash course in the art of being a drug dealer, and all this happened on the kitchen table that my family used to eat dinner at. So I started selling drugs in order to pay the bills, eat, and buy clothes for school. Yes, I still went to school, but barely. I just lived a different life than my friends from school did. While they were putting in college applications, I was putting in work, or hustling as some might call it. They're mapping out their future, and I'm mapping out the best way to bring back ten pounds of marijuana from California. I gave in. I just figured that this was my life now. I excelled at everything else—might as well excel at this too.

I was first arrested at eighteen years old. I had an ounce of weed and scales on me—my normal accessories. I was pulled over for speeding and was searched. This would be my first trip to jail, and, honestly, it didn't scare me—I thought it was exciting. Here I was, a girl from a small town getting all this attention, and that feeling of neglect I felt for so many years briefly went away. This arrest that should have scared me unfortunately just made me love the life even more. I continued to sell weed and cocaine and I continued to use both socially. A couple of years later I was arrested again for driving under suspension. I was stuck in the county jail for a weekend, and that time I hated it! I hated it because I had two young kids and I had never been away from them. I wasn't a full-blown addict—not just yet. I would go out on the weekends; I hated being drunk, so instead of not drinking as much, I thought it would be cooler to snort cocaine. Little did I know what it would turn into in the coming years.

As I continued to sell dope, my "enterprise" got a little bigger. In 2002 I got raided because I sold to an undercover narcotics detective. I had been selling pretty much everything, but mostly cocaine and Oxy-Contin. Around this time is when I truly became an addict. I was taking forty milligrams of Oxy eight times a day just so I didn't feel sick—I would take more when I wanted to be high. While going through the court process, I had stopped selling drugs, but I still had a drug problem. My husband introduced me to heroin. It was more powerful, lasted longer, and was cheaper—to an addict, that's a no-brainer. I started off snorting it and eventually started shooting it. But I still had these felony charges to face. I thought "I'm a first-time offender, I'll just get probation"—I was sentenced to two years.

When I got out of prison, I actually joked about it. To me it was another notch on my belt that made my street cred that much stronger. I still had my family and friends who visited me and sent me clothes, money, and food. Honestly, I was taken care of so well that prison was just a messed-up vacation from my life of paying bills and being the caretaker for everyone around me. I didn't learn my lesson, so I wasn't scared to go back to that life. If anything, I learned a few tricks on how not to get caught. I got out with a lot of hopes and dreams of staying clean and living a productive lifestyle, but things weren't as easy in real life as I had envisioned they would be. I did get my kids back the day I got out, but I had to live with my father, who lived in the country which made it hard to get places that I needed to. My record and lack of transportation prevented me from working—well, that was my excuse anyway. So three months later I started doing dope again. Not opioids though. I started shooting cocaine. I was off to the races. This is when things started to slowly go downhill. I was bouncing back and forth from my dad's house and my mom's house while both of them helped me take care of my girls—in my mind they owed me that. I started selling crack and powder cocaine and was dating an abusive drug dealer whose name I got tattooed in four-inch letters across my throat. The tattoo wasn't a sign of loyalty to him; it was a sign of what I chalked my life up to being. I was a drug dealer, had no ambition, and felt completely empty and forever hopeless. I soon started down a path that took everything from me, and did so in a short time.

I went years without being arrested, but from 2007 on, I got arrested every couple of months due to my heroin addiction. I started selling it so that I could have it around constantly. I was a drug dealer, but I was

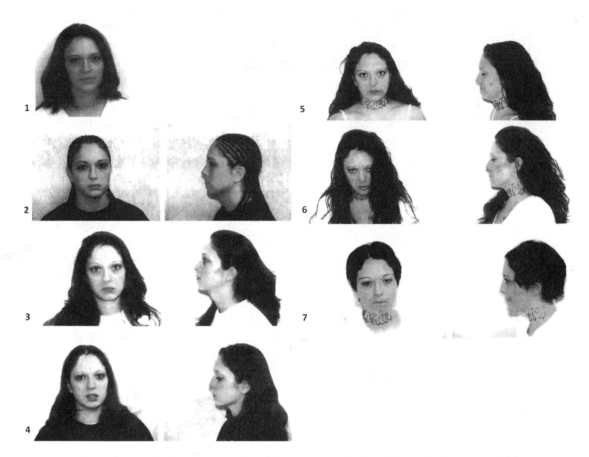

Brandy Morris. Ross County Sherriff's Department Mug Shots. (1) October 2000, (2) February 2004, (3) October 2005, (4) January 2006, (5) August 2007, (6) October 2007, (7) March 2009. Courtesy of Brandy Morris-Hafner.

more of a user. I would stay up for days in the vicious cycle of heroin and crack. I would shoot heroin and get too high, so then I would smoke crack to wake up, but it takes the opioids out of your system, so then you have to shoot heroin again and it just keeps going and going. I was staying away from my kids so that they wouldn't see me like that. I eventually wound up putting them with my sister. It was supposed to be temporary until I could get my life together, but that was the drug lying to me. I visited them for the first six months, but then my sister cut me off altogether—and that's when my addiction really went downhill.

The one good thing in my life was gone—I wanted to die! The guilt and shame of being a junkie ran my life. Instead of doing something about it, I just did more drugs. I started getting sores on my face. This is what happens when you get too high and you think things are crawling on you, or you are seeing acne on your face that isn't really there—so you pick and pick. My teeth were rotting out and I probably only weighed a little over one hundred pounds. In March of 2008 I was raided at the trap house [a place where drugs are sold] for selling heroin. In true Brandy fashion, I never showed up to my sentencing date and went on the run. Then one day the city police caught me coming out of a crack house and ran my name. I was put in jail, where I soon detoxed. I remember lying on my bed and asking God to take this power of addiction from me.

I truly believe that a miracle happened right then and there. I say "miracle" instead of "healing" because a miracle is instantaneous, but a healing happens over time. My body, my mind, and my emotional self were still healing, but my addiction was miraculously gone. I finished out my sentence, and while things were not ideal when I came home, I didn't make excuses. I didn't take no for an answer, and I stayed away from everyone who I did drugs or committed crimes with. As of March 2018 I have been sober for ten years. I am a summa cum laude graduate of Ohio Christian University where I majored in substance abuse counseling and minored in business management. After graduating, I became a Licensed Chemical Dependency Counselor.

When I first began my journey of recovery, I started by being the night monitor at a local shelter. I then became the executive director of the women and children's homeless shelter and mentoring program in Ross County—the Daughters of Ruth. In 2011, I started in the correctional field as a case manager with The EXIT Program, specializing in placement of sex offenders and other male felony offenders in Chillicothe. I then went on to Community Corrections at Alvis, a halfway house for female and male felony offenders. While at Alvis, I continuously climbed the ladder, starting off as a case manager and then advancing to cognitive behavioral specialist, treatment manager, operations manager, and finally substance abuse counselor.

In 2012 I met a wonderful man who has supported me tremendously through all of my craziness and whom I went on to marry. In 2013 I regained custody of my girls, and shortly after I bought a house for all of us. Today, I am working at the Ross County Sheriff's Office as the Program Director for the Day Reporting Program located at the Terry Collins Re-Entry Center. I am the first convicted felon to be sworn in as a deputy in the history of the Ross County Sheriff's Office. It just goes to show that no matter if you have tattoos or a felony number behind your name, if you work hard and prove yourself, you can change your life. But you have to take responsibility, you have to be humble, and most importantly you have to stay clean, which in some cases means staying away from your own family members. Recovery needs to be individualized and selfish because there's only one person in this fight who can make a difference: you! Life offers all of us choices. Do you want your choices to be rewards or consequences? Today I'm choosing rewards.

*Brandy Morris-Hafner is a wife, mother of two young ladies and a feisty but cute wiener dog, and a grandmother to an amazing baby boy. She is also the Program Director for the Ross County Sheriff's Office Day Reporting Program.*

# 30

# A LITTLE TOO CLOSE TO HOME

KEITH F. DURKIN

(ADA)

By now, most people know that the opioid epidemic has hit Ohio hard. Not many seem to know, however, that things have been particularly bad in our state's rural areas. As part of my work as a professor at a university in one of these rural areas, Hardin County, I have been involved with the local court, providing program evaluation and quality assurance services. I am responsible for calculating the relevant statistics and measuring the effectiveness of court programs. I work extensively with the data for two dockets that involve opioid users: the Hardin County Juvenile Drug Court and the Hardin County Family Recovery Court.

In 2011, I began my work as the program evaluator for the Juvenile Drug Court. The court had received a $1.2 million grant to establish a juvenile drug court to attempt to address the growing problem of criminal and antisocial behavior among youth in the community. The drug court model, which is used by the Hardin County Juvenile Court, seeks to treat rather than to punish offenders. Participants are provided with services such as substance abuse and mental health treatment. At that time, I did not know that my involvement with these court programs would bring me to the epicenter of the opioid epidemic. When I first started with the court, the drug of choice among juveniles was marijuana, and there was a growing problem with kids using similar synthetic drugs such as K2 or Spice. By the end of 2013, we were seeing our first cases of juveniles using prescription opioids for nonmedical purposes. Today about 25 percent of cases involve kids who have a history of nonmedical use of opioids.

I have always been an active researcher because I have a natural curiosity about human behavior. At the time I got involved with the Juvenile Drug Court, I was doing research projects related to internet crime. However, the fact that kids in the drug court were now abusing opioids was terribly concerning to me. I shelved my other research projects and decided to focus exclusively on the growing opioid epidemic in my community. I was tremendously concerned when I first saw data indicating that kids were experimenting with prescription opioids. These kids aren't numbers: they are human beings who are children, grandchildren, sisters, or brothers. In my mind, self-reporting the misuse of prescription opioids is the first indicator that a young person is headed down a dangerous path that all too often ends up with heroin addiction and premature death. Examining data related to juveniles in the drug court who abused prescription opioids, I discovered that those youths also had serious psychological challenges. The vast majority had symptoms of psychological disorders such as attention deficit disorder or a conduct disorder. Approximately two-thirds of youths who have abused prescription pain pills have symptoms of a mood disorder, traumatic stress disorder, or general anxiety disorder. Their mental health challenges are typically complex, with about two-thirds having symptoms of more than one mental disorder. Juvenile opioid abusers also report high levels of mental distress, fear, and anxiety and tend to self-medicate, usually with drugs and alcohol, to forget things from the past.

After learning about the psychological challenges facing youth, I wanted to know more about what other factors might be related to the abuse of prescription opioids among young people involved with the court. I found a fairly strong association between peer drug use and the misuse of prescription opioids. Youths who report they have friends who have recently used drugs—any kind of drugs—are more likely than other youths to engage in this behavior. I also found that the abuse of opioids by these juveniles was often related to family problems, such as poor supervision, frequent household conflicts, and parents who are experiencing problems such as criminal offending, substance use, or mental illness. The fact that young people are spending much more time with peers than with their families is concerning because peer influence is the primary cause for the nonmedical use of prescription opioids. Family problems can also cause or further aggravate the symptoms of mental illness.

In addition to working with kids, I lead evaluation efforts for the Hardin County Family Recovery Court, a specialty docket established in 2011 to provide collaborative evaluation and treatment services for substance-abusing parents who have either lost, or are at risk of losing, custody of their children due to neglect, abuse, or dependency. More than two-thirds of the parents involved with the court have a history of heroin abuse. Because so many of these parents are here as a result of heroin use, I decided it was important to study these forty-nine parents to understand why heroin use has increased so much in rural Ohio. I view heroin-using parents as an example of how this epidemic impacts more than just the drug users—kids are growing up without parents; grandparents, often in failing health, are forced to raise their grandchildren; and our social service system is stretched beyond its capacity. Simply put, our entire community is affected.

These heroin-using parents encapsulate the epidemic in rural Ohio. The vast majority are white females who have never been married. Approximately three-quarters are under the age of thirty. Most have multiple children. These heroin-using parents epitomize economic deprivation: 80 percent are unemployed, and 34 percent did not complete high school or earn a GED. Similar to the findings among youth, a large percentage of these heroin-using parents show symptoms of one or more serious mental disorders.

Our court's staff experience a number of challenges in serving heroin-using parents. One obstacle is that opioid addiction is extremely overpowering and seemingly controls the program participants. As a researcher, I am frustrated because many parents seem to lack any motivation to recover, even with regaining custody of their children as an incentive. Participants often seek ways to game the system, such as attempting to beat a drug screen by taking other substances to alter test results, using someone else's urine, or even resorting to extreme measures like reverse catheterization. Some search for ways to continue to get high from opioids despite the medically assisted therapies included in the program, such as skipping their medications for the sole reason of wanting to experience an opioid high. Others use a drug in addition to opioids to continue to get high. We are seeing some of these parents turn to cocaine and methamphetamine for this specific purpose.

A second obstacle is created by the terms of the Adoption and Safe Families Act, which allows one year for reunifying children with their parents, with some possible extensions to a total of two years. Since opioid-using parents often do not enter into the court's family dependency treatment court program until months after their children have been removed from their homes, the window of opportunity is very tight. As a result, the length of treatment necessary to address opioid addiction makes it difficult for parents to regain custody of their children.

Years of studying opioid abuse have shown me that we need to pay more attention to the relationship between mental health and opioid abuse, for both juvenile and adult opioid abusers. Opioid abuse and mental illness need to be seen as co-occurring problems, not separate issues. Individuals who are being screened for opioid abuse should also be screened for mental illness, and vice versa. If mental illness is left untreated, individuals who are receiving treatment for opioid addiction are at a high risk of relapse because the underlying cause of their substance abuse has not been addressed. Furthermore, this situation is complicated in rural counties such as Hardin because organizations with treatment services for both addiction and mental illness are scarcer than in suburban or metropolitan areas. This disparity in service availability needs to be addressed to better combat this epidemic.

Economic deprivation plays a supporting role in the opioid epidemic in Hardin County. We know that socioeconomic factors such as poverty, low education, and a decline in manufacturing jobs may be linked to the demand for opioids. The slow climb out of the Great Recession in rural areas contributes to making the opioid epidemic worse. As a sociologist, I am especially interested in how people perceive their economic situation. Hardin County is certainly economically disadvantaged relative to its urban and suburban peers, with a per capita income that is significantly lower than the state average. However, many residents have come to believe that their economic situation is hopeless, which further demoralizes them. With little hope in their minds for a better future, they may turn to opioids as a reprieve from their fatalistic despair. Tragically, this temporary reprieve turns into a life-threatening addiction.

Researching opioid abuse has been challenging on a professional level. The immediate obstacle confronting academics who may want to study this phenomenon is the fact that the contemporary opioid epidemic is a fairly new phenomenon. It takes hundreds of hours to review the relevant literature to understand why opioid use developed in the first place, why it became an epidemic that continues to grow, and what methods work for helping children and adults through recovery. The epidemic is also multifaceted, affecting individuals and communities physically, psychologically, and socially. We can learn about opioid abuse from a diverse array of academic disciplines, including medicine, public health, neuroscience, criminal justice, sociology, psychology, forensic toxicology, and social work. Understanding all of this is a large task for the individual researcher. And much of what we know about opioid abuse does not come from academics, but from individuals on the ground, such as criminal justice and social service professionals. So much essential information can be learned from these professional practitioners.

Although I have engaged the opioid epidemic through my professional work as a researcher, this experience has also affected me personally. The town of Ada and the neighboring communities in Hardin County are relatively small. The people generally know one another, and news, whether good or bad, spreads rather rapidly. Living in a community so heavily impacted by this epidemic, one is going to know people who are directly impacted. For instance, very recently a couple I know lost their eighteen-year-old daughter to an overdose. Apparently, she had recently begun using heroin and unknowingly used a dose that was tainted with fentanyl. I've also had friends of my teenage children tell them about how their parents struggle with opioid addiction. For about ten years I coached youth wrestling and football in Ada, and I'm now starting to see young people I personally know abusing opioids. It is heartbreaking to me as a person. As a researcher, it frustrates me that I can't develop better explanatory models more quickly that will lead to more effective solutions.

*Keith F. Durkin, PhD, is Professor of Sociology at Ohio Northern University.*

# 31

## DELUDED

MARTY HELMS
(CINCINNATI)

*Marty Helms is a former laboratory researcher with a degenerative bone disease. She contacted us in mid-2017, concerned that efforts around Ohio to combat addiction were going to result in her losing something that she needed to live. Some months later, she was cut off from her opioid regimen during a time when physicians' prescribing practices were being watched more closely. While the transition was not easy, Marty recounts her story of getting off opioids and changing her perspective on pain management. Interview by Daniel Skinner.*

*Please tell me how you began to interact with opioids.*

In 1997 I was in college and had a three-year-old daughter. Most days I had to carry her and my book bag to school and her daycare. That's when my back pain started. It was so low in my back and down my leg that I had no idea what it was. Then I noticed that if I bent forward, I wasn't able to stand up without physically pushing myself up. I decided to see my primary care doctor about it. In 1999 I had a procedure called a discectomy. A fragmented part of my disc was pushing on the nerve that was interrupting my movement. That was removed, and that was it. The doctor assured me that it would be years before I would need any help again. "Oh, we won't see you for years," he said. "You have a lot left in that disc." Two years later, I had my first fusion, and then it just went on from there, from a first fusion to a second, to a third, to a fourth, and then the fifth one. They took all that hardware out, and they just put new hardware spacers in. So my whole lumbar spine is hardware.

*Is this a problem that's common in the family, or is this unique to your story?*

No, many people in my family have degenerative joint disease. Your shoulders will mess up, your knees, your back, my neck is starting right now, but I guess it is what it is. We all seem to carry this gene. We have five kids in our family. I think all but one have it. Two grandchildren have it as well.

*What's it like to live with chronic pain?*

It's depressing. I just keep thinking of when I was younger, I could do anything. I could do anything. Nothing would stop me from doing what I wanted to do, and now I can barely do anything. I walk at an angle, a forward angle that is pretty severe. I can't lift anything. My shoulder hurts all the time. It feels like it catches. When I go to reach for things, it feels just terrible.

I'm an optimistic person, so I always think I can get better. I always have that in my head: "Maybe if I get better," and my husband says, "Stop, just stop saying it. You're going to depress yourself." I do take antidepressants because I cried about it one day to my doctor and they gave me antidepressants. I should be allowed to cry about this. It's bad.

For a while, my left leg would just give out. I'd be walking down the stairs and my leg would give out. Thank God I always hang on to something. I always use the railings. One time I got up to answer the phone and my leg just went out. I fell down. So they tried to fix that in my last back surgery, but it's not all the way fixed. Living with this is depressing. Even for an optimistic person.

*When you first had this experience, was your inclination to think of it as a medical issue? Did you think of it as something you could take care of on your own?*

Considering I didn't know anything about back pain, I thought at first I had some sort of strain issue, so I tried to be more considerate of my back. It was no big deal. I didn't see a doctor until I had the issue with bending over and not being able to stand up. My body would not go back up unless I pushed it. That's what sent me to the doctor. I thought that was a medical issue.

*When you had your discectomy, did that come with pain medicine?*

No, not at all. It was a Band-Aid surgery. They gave me aspirin for it. It was nothing.

*But you described your doctor's optimism, and he said, "I won't see you for a long time." But then you were back for a fusion shortly thereafter.*

In less than two years.

*When does the part of the story that interacts with pain medication start? Is it the second surgery, or is it further along?*

Pain meds became full-time between my first and second fusions, between 2001 and 2007. Prior to that, I wasn't on anything daily.

*After you took them for a while, did your view of the pills change?*

No, not at that point. At that point, my regular doctor said, "You have to see a pain management guy, because I can't just keep prescribing pain medication for you." He didn't have, I guess, the ability to give you a variety of things . . . to try things out . . . so he sent me to a pain management guy in 2005 and that's what started that.

They started me off mildly, real mildly. They gave me methadone or something like that, and then when that stopped working, they went up to a low dose of Percocet. I tried to resist by saying that Percocet made me ill. The doc keep telling me that the illness would go away, and it did. After that didn't work anymore, they gave me a higher dose of Percocet, and I stayed there the whole time.

*When opioids became a daily part of your life, that was when you were working with the pain specialist?*

I started pain management between 2005 and 2006. Opioid use became daily after my 2007 fusion. I still didn't like them and wanted to be off at some point. I told my doc that I was getting surgery and probably wouldn't be back. His exact words were, "He won't take care of you long-term." I didn't think anything of it. My 2007 fusion was a disaster! It created more issues than it fixed. That's when they became a daily part of my life until this year.

*When we first spoke some months ago, you were concerned that you were going to lose access to drugs that you really felt you needed, which is the opposite of the way a lot of policy makers think about the problem. Tell me a little bit about the transition you've gone through, even in the few months since you and I've been talking.*

That's what I thought. I'm like, yes, I have to have these pills. You don't understand. People like me who have chronic pain have to depend on something. Otherwise, we'll just be miserable and life would not be worth living. It wouldn't. But then, as I was going through this, my step-dad died, and we were at the hospital for hours and hours, because they'd keep calling you to come in. They think that's his last breath, the final moment, and you have to be here.

We were there one day for eight hours, and I didn't have any of my medication with me because I left it at home. They called me at 1:30 in the morning. I was sitting there forever. My husband had to go to work and I'm like, "I have to have some of my pills. I have to have one." He's like, "All I have is tramadol. I don't have time to go home and get you another one, just take that."

Five days after that, I went to my doctor and I tested positive for a minute amount of tramadol. That's not good. They get mad at you for that.

They cut my medication in half and I thought, "Oh my God, I'm going to die, this isn't going to be enough. I know what I know about it," and I started to feel better without it. I did. I still do. I haven't taken any in a couple of weeks. I don't believe that stuff . . . you should not be taking that medicine for twelve years like me.

*What was that feeling like?*

If I would sit on a couch for a length of time to watch a movie, and I got up, I would have these tearing feelings in my hips. It felt like the flesh was being torn from my bones, if you can imagine what that feels like. It's this terrible feeling, my stride was so little and I was just in pain, just real pain, to where the only thing I thought would make it go away would be another pill. It did sometimes, but what I wasn't realizing is that the pills keep your pain receptors alive so that I guess you need more pills to satisfy that.

I feel better now. I don't have those pains in my hips when I sit. I don't have all these cramps. . . . I still take muscle relaxers, so that's not, the cramps have nothing to do with it, but I just feel less achy, less tearing pain. I feel more alert, so I don't know. I guess that's it. I just started to be less dependent.

*So the dependence has gone away, but not the pain?*

Yeah. Sometimes, but not the way I did before. I felt incredible pain, a lot of the time. My husband always held my pills for me because otherwise I would just take them whenever I need or wanted one. He would only give me whatever I was supposed to have that day. He was my conscience.

*Do you do anything else to deal with your pain? Have any of your habits or practices changed?*

No. I still do some therapy exercises when I can. I've tried to do that a lot lately, but it's not because I stopped taking pills. I did it before that too.

*How do you narrate the role of your doctors in your history with all of this? Do you think that they did the right thing by you? Are there things that you think they should've done differently?*

Yes, of course, but hindsight is 20/20, and I'm not a doctor. The back surgeons that I went to . . . the first back surgeon I went to, he's good and I just loved him. He did my first two back surgeries. I thought if I ever needed another one, he would be there and I'd be able to use him. He always explained everything, and I was getting to the point in 2006 where I needed him again, but he was gone.

He had gotten a patent on a replacement disc and he quit doing surgery. I had to go to somebody in that office, another guy, and that was a horrific surgery. My third one turned into my fourth one, when one of the screws just totally came out. The material that they screwed in between those two vertebrae went up under the nerve of my armpit, and I was screaming. It was horrible. It was the most horrible pain I've ever had in my life.

*So around the time that you switched doctors to the one that you regard as being a really bad experience, that's really when you started to need more of these pain medications?*

Yes. All surgery can fail, or you may not respond to surgery, I realize that. Everybody isn't the same, so I think surgeons are like mechanics. I think they just go in and fix what they can and they get out—that's it. Some are better than others, and I don't know what happened in my surgery. I don't know if he let his assistant operate on me or what, but that doctor did not do a good surgery, and yes, that's what started my everyday pain medicine.

*Can you tell me a little bit about working with the pain management physician too? How do you describe that relationship and how do you reflect on it?*

He's a nice person and he didn't cut me off when I failed a drug test. The thing that he said was, "If I cut you off, nobody else will pick you up. I'm just going to keep you."

He's a nice guy, but I don't think he knows how to deal with this issue. He's not a policeman, he's an anesthesiologist. All he knows to do is those types of shots, and he would say, "I'm a spine guy. I do shots for the nerves in your back. I don't do anything else." I noticed that every specialist is so fragmented away from a primary care doc, it's not funny. You can't even ask that guy a question. He's like, "I don't know, you'll have to ask a surgeon." They seem to only know one thing, and I just think that's weird.

*Do you think that your pain specialist should've cut you off earlier?*

I don't know. As far as I knew, I needed them all the time. I just did. The way I walk and my legs and the pain in my legs, heck yeah, I felt

I needed them all the time. You would be taking away the thing that made it possible for me to live. If you were there routinely, you go in and see a doctor or a nurse practitioner for five minutes while they ask you where your pain is. "Are you in pain here, are you in pain here," and they touch your back so lightly. "Do you feel this," "No," and then you're out of there.

It's kind of like a Dr. Feelgood kind of place. That place is packed. I don't know if people are going there to get drugs or if they really are in pain like me. I don't care about that. I'm worried about me. But I understand why people want to deal with this problem.

*In hindsight, do you feel that you might have had a problem?*

Of course. That's why I said I was so wrong. I've never been so wrong about anything in my life. I just can't believe it. I really needed those pills at the time, but how can I go from one dosage to half that dosage and feel okay, and even feel a little better?

*Drawing on your experience, do doctors have an obligation to reduce patients' pain?*

I think they need to treat you if you're having an issue. I don't know how they would be able to tell how much pain you're actually in. I have so much scar tissue and stuff, and so much stenosis that there's no way of knowing what's going on with me. They would have to just prescribe me something, but I don't think that's a real cure. I think you should take people off for a little while or at least reduce their dosages for a while, like me right now, just to see if they can manage on their own.

*I wonder if there would've been a difference if your doctor had refused to prescribe you, let's say, ten years ago, as opposed to 2017. What would you have done if your doctor cut you off some years ago?*

Started taking nerve pills probably, like Neurontin or something. For a while, I took this drug called Topamax. It's an antiseizure medicine, but it's supposed to reduce your pain, which it did. It did reduce my pain. I didn't have that pain in my legs that I always had, and that always woke me up.

When I sleep at night, or I used to, if I laid on my right side, just a pain would start up. It would make me move. It would wake me up. It was working great. It made me lose weight because I was never hungry. It was awesome, but my husband said it made me the worst-tempered person on earth. He was like, "If you ever take that again, I'm leaving you." I was so mean. I didn't even notice and everybody around me said, "Yeah, you're horribly mean." It made me paranoid.

*Your need for opioids seems to have been intensified by depression. Would you say that depression and pain need to be problematized together?*

Well, of course if you're in pain all the time, it's going to wear on you. When I first had all this, up until 2009, so, ten years after I started getting back surgery is when I started taking antidepressants. So, no.

*What would you say to policy makers and others in Ohio who are trying to address this situation? What can they learn from what you've been through?*

If there were a program or some way of finding out when you're just taking pills to be taking pills and not realize it, that would be a great tool. There's got to be a way to figure out that your pain isn't really that bad anymore, like when you just psychologically think you need these pills, and once you take half the dosage, you're okay after a couple of days.

That would be helpful, because I'm sure there's people that are just like me, that are in pain and think they need it. I would say those pain pills were more debilitating than my pain because they made me stay in pain.

That's the weirdness of these drugs. Why can't they come up with a drug that's non-narcotic and won't tear up your stomach? It's ridiculous.

*So somebody in your position doesn't really have many options, and more options would allow you to make better choices?*

During my whole time, the only thing that was really presented to me was to get surgery. They were like, "Yes, you need it. Get the surgery." Giving those drugs to people that aren't seriously in pain is not a good idea. Maybe that's why those people turn to other drugs. There is more of a mental kind of dependence. I promise, I really thought I needed those pills. I wasn't in denial. I really thought I did. Now I got half the dosage, I'm like, "Oh hey, this works just as good and I feel better."

Not everyone wants to take the drug. There are people who will just suffer. There are people that will exercise, and if they tighten up correctly, they don't need it. I have been on medication since I was a little kid, and I think that started a behavior where I think a pill will take care of it.

My mom had me on drugs my whole life because I had ADHD and I had a real unstable life, so I was always sick to my stomach. She gave me this stuff called Paregoric. I don't even know what that is, really, some kind of narcotic, and then when I was fifteen, I was overweight, so she took me to a doctor that gave me amphetamines. I've literally been taking pills my whole life, taking another one isn't going to bother me. I have had issues with Kroger, Walgreens, and CVS when it came to filling my pain med prescriptions. My sister has the same issue. I think that they arc told that everyone is a drug addict, and they act accordingly. But it's not our fault the drug companies haven't come out with better therapies for it, and honestly to God, the people at CVS, look at you like you're crazy. You would get these looks and glares if you decided you want to fill it a day early. They would freak out and look at me like I was a major drug addict, like, "What is wrong with you? You don't need it until tomorrow." My paranoia isn't there anymore.

# 32

## OPIOID ENCOUNTERS

### Fragments from Training and Practice

JENNY ZAMOR
(COLUMBUS)

I have practiced medicine for over a decade in Ohio. I was trained here and have seen patients all over: in rural areas, the inner city, small towns, suburban areas, and college towns. Throughout my training and practice in obstetrics and gynecology, I have encountered substance abuse continually, often within the context of other issues, such as chronic pelvic pain. As I was going through training and in my early career, I kept journals to help process my experience and development as a physician. I've reworked these entries into short stories. I've removed real names or any other information that would violate patient privacy. These excerpts testify to the saying that "experience is the best teacher." The challenges of caring for the opioid-addicted population during my education and progression to becoming a fully board-certified obstetrician-gynecologist were as invaluable to my professional development as salt is to a good meal.

### OB-GYN RESIDENCY IN ATHENS AND PORTSMOUTH, 2000–2004

#### The Runaway

As a resident, I arrived in the ER thinking it was the usual consult. I read her chart to familiarize myself with her condition and background before entering the room. She seemed startled to see me despite the fact that she had said "come in" after hearing my knock on the door. The teenage girl had just experienced a miscarriage and turned away when I tried to make eye contact. She was shy, thin, and in the process of wiping remnants of badly applied makeup off her face. Her female friend was with her but left the room to respect her privacy during my visit. During my fact-gathering questions, she admitted that she ran away from home three years ago because she was sick of her stepfather making sure she was "his other wife" when her mom wasn't home. I discussed her recent loss and lab results. She showed no real remorse. She said she was always careful not to get pregnant, but the kid is lucky to be gone. After obtaining permission and with a nurse in the room, I examined her and noticed the needle marks on her arms. I asked about them and she said, "I ain't an addict. This is how I can forget things so I can stay alive, Doctor." I registered what she meant and admitted her for pain control so that maybe I could get her help in the morning. A man came to visit her while she was in the ER, and by the morning she had left (against medical advice) when she pretended she was going outside to smoke a cigarette. She ran away from help. She did not have to hide or go back to her misery. She did not have to go back to whatever she had to do to "stay alive" and "forget things." I cried because I wondered if I should have thought of a different way to handle her case with the hospital team. She was eighteen . . . an adult. "Age ain't nothing but a number" in this case. I still wonder, Whatever happened to that runaway?

## The Broken Teacher

Doctors in training look for role models to develop professionally and say, "I want to be like that when I am done with my training." You expect certain behavior out of your attending and put a certain amount of trust in their hands when receiving your education from them. "Attending physician" is the title given to a doctor who has made it to the big leagues and can now train us "little people." Due to the level of seniority and spotless reputation, my attending's sudden subtle changes in behavior went unnoticed and unchecked. When I learned that a doctor teaching me was suspended—and that it was related to prescription opioid abuse—I was in shock. When I filled out the DEA registration application, it was a serious day. I fully realized the power, and the responsibility, of prescribing medicine. There are rules, not just to keep the public safe, but to keep myself from being liable as well. I never thought of the temptation, let alone the potential, of being part of opioid abuse.

I prayed for the successful rehabilitation of that attending physician because they are humans before they are teachers. Everyone makes mistakes and a career should not be thrown away over this tough lesson.

## PRACTICE, 2010–2017, ST. MARYS, FREMONT, ASHTABULA, AND TOLEDO
### Things That Make You Go "Hmm"

I was headed to a new assignment in Ashtabula, a small town outside the city limits of Cleveland. Billboards populated the highways and small roads with the same messages: "You are not alone. We can help with your fight against opioid abuse and addiction. Call xxx-xxx-xxxx." And so the journey began . . . drug seekers in the ER, OB triage visits populated with mothers who had colorful histories of use, abuse, and addictions. The complications—especially preterm labor and drug withdrawals—were too common.

Being a temporary doctor, I needed to have a serious conversation with the permanent doctors I came to relieve on the weekends. I needed to know what resources were available and how they were handling these patients so I could follow suit. One doctor absolutely refused to care for any patient who tested positive for any substance. I questioned that stance because then the mother would burden the ER and be triaged without established care. The response was "You are new here. These patients don't care and are noncompliant. She doesn't take responsibility for her actions, so how do you expect me to do that? I am an OB-GYN, not a rehab doctor." My mouth dropped to the floor—but my thoughts ran in circles.

### The Interior Decorator

I was the new doctor in town and eager for business. Word of mouth travels fast. My new patient arrived on time. Body language told me that she was a lady on a mission. She presented per her primary care physician for evaluation of chronic pelvic pain. After the usual exam, I gave her an order for a pelvic ultrasound and then a prescription for Motrin.

Sucking her teeth, she took the piece of paper and I led her to the front to make her follow-up appointment and get her scheduled for imaging. I moved on to the next patient. Hours later there was a big commotion in the lobby. My receptionist looked terrified, texting me that the lady had returned demanding a script for "Percs." I quickly had my current patient leave through the back door and called 911 after hospital security let me know that they don't handle "this sort of thing." She had turned over all the chairs in the lobby and was banging on the counter. She was "rearranging my lobby." As we awaited the cops, my staff pacified her by stating, "The doctor will see you soon." That seemed to work, so I called my staff in the back to wait. When the two dispatched officers arrived in full uniform, we emerged and I attempted to hand her a dismissal from the practice letter. But I had to hand it to the officer since her escalation of anger led to her being placed in handcuffs. "So y'all called the cops on me?" Before leaving the office, her dismissal letter accompanying her to the precinct, she expressed herself using colorful street jargon not worthy of quotation. I will never forget that mean face with the deep knife scar across her left cheek. Whew, that was close.

*Jenny Zamor, DO, FACOOG, is a board-certified obstetrician-gynecologist and Assistant Clinical Professor of Osteopathic Manipulative Medicine at Ohio University, Heritage College of Osteopathic Medicine, at the Dublin campus.*

# 33

# AN AWAKENING

JOE GAY
(ATHENS)

It's not really that we were asleep. Treatment professionals like myself, in Appalachia and other rural areas, were very much awake and alert to the problem—we just thought it was alcoholism. I'm a recovering alcoholic, so I was intimately familiar with problems related to alcohol. Between 1988 and 1999, as Clinical Director of Health Recovery Services, I had personally supervised the outpatient treatment of several thousand individuals. Most had alcohol problems, about one-fifth struggled with marijuana, and even fewer used harder drugs. I knew a bit about heroin from the crazy days of my youth, when I hung out in a folk music scene where heroin use was common. I had watched people shoot up. I had seen lives ruined and tremendous talent wasted. What I saw scared the hell out of me. Thirty years later, living the life of a licensed psychologist and director of a treatment agency, I was relieved we were not handling heroin cases.

In my eleven years as a supervisor, I came across only a few clients who misused prescription opioids. Usually they had started with a legitimate prescription and then began misusing the drug. Heroin use was extremely rare. Invariably, these heroin users had moved into the area with the habit; they were not homegrown. It seemed that in Appalachia there was some cultural barrier to heroin use, and I didn't expect it to change.

Then, late in the fall of 2007, a counselor from another county asked if my agency was seeing an increase in heroin use. Based on my experience, it seemed like a ridiculous question, but I agreed to ask my front-line clinicians. They told me they were mostly seeing pills but had seen a few cases of heroin. Then, just three months later, they said, "You jinxed us. We're seeing heroin all the time."

Now, I'm a numbers guy, so I went to the data to help depict what was going on. We saw that opioid use was skyrocketing among our clients. A third were using some form of opioid, and two-thirds of those clients were using heroin. Use by injection was growing, which only increased the danger of a blood-borne disease outbreak. For me the emotional impact was like hearing that a friend had cancer.

The years 2008 and 2009 were dark days in the field. The state was cutting treatment funding at the same time opioid use was increasing. We had to turn away roughly a third of potential admissions because we simply did not have the resources to treat everyone. We prioritized individuals who were already injecting heroin, but we knew that many people we turned away would eventually progress to injecting heroin.

To make matters worse, we were having little success in treating heroin users. More than half dropped out of treatment. For alcoholics and prescription opioid abusers, the dropout rate was about half that. Heroin users had enormous difficulty stopping. They said being without heroin felt like being held underwater—they were as desperate to get drugs as you would be to get air if you were drowning.

Fortunately, we shared a few clients with a physician at Ohio University who had begun treating patients with Suboxone. These clients seemed to improve. The scientific literature made clear that medication-assisted treatment (MAT) was the way to go. Soon after beginning to integrate Suboxone into our treatment regimen, our results were comparable to those reported in the research publications. Luckily, this turn toward MAT was accompanied by positive changes in policies and priorities at the state and federal levels. We went on a binge of grant writing and gradually began receiving support for some of the things we needed to do, including training for our counselors, particularly around evidence-based practices, and we managed to provide some expansion of MAT services. This provided momentum for taking advantage of the most impactful change involving treatment availability, which was the expansion of Medicaid eligibility at the beginning of 2014. The biggest changes that occurred were our ability to serve more clients, essentially all of those seeking and needing treatment, and the expansion of MAT services. Although the general model of treatment remained the same as before, we focused more on topics that seemed to be at the heart of dependence: shame and dealing with urges and triggers. With MAT and the additional training and experience in place, our counselors became more skillful in treating patients with opioid problems.

Working with those addicted to opioids, particularly heroin, is demanding for clinicians, and I found that my role as executive director changed in response to the opioid crisis. Previously, I had been primarily involved with administrative matters. With the surge of opioid use, I found that one of my most important jobs was to provide moral support to the counselors. It was important to let them know I understood how hard their jobs were. Sometimes I was able to provide consultation on specific issues, facilitate communication among team members, or reduce bureaucratic barriers to efficient care.

A counselor, recalling the period when individuals addicted to opioids first began to seek treatment in large numbers, said that withdrawal was "the biggest problem" and was excruciating for both the patients and the counselors. Our heroin users experience significant shame. Consequently, it is much harder to get heroin addicts to talk, which makes counseling more difficult. Injecting is particularly stigmatizing. We have had clients tell us that they had been too ashamed and fearful to seek medical treatment for things like injection-site infection. Failing to seek treatment for infections can lead to complications, including amputations, but we managed to avoid this outcome among our clients through close monitoring by our physicians and nurses.

Opioid users often also lack social support. Stigma, shame, and secretiveness make it difficult for opioid addicts to reach out for more than just medical help. The family and friends of heroin addicts may not be supportive, since the users have often manipulated, alienated, and sometimes stolen from them. Intergenerational trauma—trauma that spans several generations—is common in these families.

In addition to these challenges many users resist treatment. Sometimes, our counselors feel as though they are working harder than their clients. We have to be patient in developing an approach that not only effectively treats opioid addiction but also prevents counselor burnout. What drives counselors and others working in these settings is the first signs of change, when good things begin to happen to their patients. Seeing a client finish school, acquire a certification, or get a job is reason for celebration. As one counselor said, "For the client who wants to change, it means the world to them that you care and that you are not judging them."

Developing models of care for opioid abuse was new territory for us, and we were grateful to find others to collaborate in this work. In 2009, I became aware of work at the Ohio Department of Health, which was and remains an unsung hero of the opioid epidemic. Here was the first place I found a group of people as worried about opioids as I was. The work they were doing was important, but it is impossible to make it sound exciting. It was meetings and committees, phone calls, memos, and reports. Hours spent looking at spreadsheets. We worked hard and produced recommendations for meaningful prevention approaches, particularly through better regulation of prescribing practices, and for expanding access to treatment, especially medication-assisted treatment.

Progress in addressing the opioid crisis was slow at first, but this began to change when groups formed around the state, mainly composed of people who had lost family members to opioid addiction. The group Surviving Our Loss and Continuing Everyday (SOLACE) in Scioto County was one of the first to form. The poignancy of their stories touched state leaders and prompted real action. The passion for change at the state level and within local communities came from these family groups. The blueprint for the change came from professionals working through various committees and work groups.

From my perspective, gathering data and statistics played an important role in recognizing the scope and trajectory of the problem, as well as planning to address it. Early on, health department data had provided a rude awakening for me. Hard-hit Ohio counties lost three or four per 10,000 people each year to overdoses. Fentanyl was largely responsible for the increase in deaths, causing more than half of all overdoses in Ohio during 2016. These deaths were devastating to family members and friends, but the deaths were not necessarily noticed in their communities. It was only through health department tracking that the trends really became evident.

Local input was very important, but data also helped guide what actions needed to be taken and where. For example, overdose death rates in Southern Ohio were the highest in the state. Then data verified that certain physicians in so-called clinics were dispensing huge amounts of opioids. The collection of data led to changes in legislation, rules, and law enforcement actions. Eventually these pill mills began to be shut down.

Overprescription was a problem across the entire state. Closer analysis showed problematic prescribing patterns and problems such as individuals obtaining opioid prescriptions from multiple physicians, referred to as "doctor shopping." Targeted changes in regulations addressed these problems, and now the number of deaths from prescription drug overdoses has begun to fall.

Working intensively in the field of opioid treatment for a decade, I had occasion to have many, practically daily, conversations regarding opioids. Questions were posed in many of these conversations that helped shape my conceptualization of the problem. One of the most frequent questions was "Why would a person even use heroin or other opioids in the first place?" Again, statistics provided a background for the answer, with the National Survey of Drug Use and Health having been a particularly important source of data.

Most Americans try alcohol at least once, and roughly half of adults have tried marijuana. Thus it is no surprise that almost all of our opioid users had begun doing the "normal" thing of using alcohol and marijuana. Many of them in fact had progressed to having some problem with these substances. Many started using at younger ages, in their early to mid-teens, which statistically is a risk factor for problem use later. Many tell us that their parents and extended families had drug and alcohol problems, suggesting a vulnerability based on genetics. Those individuals who eventually became our clients had also gravitated to peer groups who abuse substances. Within these groups "pills" were regularly available—and weren't considered dangerous.

The data were important—pivotal, even—but so were the firsthand accounts of our clients and the stories of friends in recovery. Experimentation with opioids produced a novel and intense pleasure. Many in treatment or in recovery described a vivid recall of that moment. I also noticed that many other people I talked to either did not like the experience or saw the danger in a substance that leaves you with nothing to worry about. They were people who understood a little pain and knew that some aspirin was a better alternative. Such sound reasoning is not so available to some people.

The decision not to use is harder when all your friends use too. It's more likely that someone will keep using if their life is stressful and complicated. This can happen if a person already has problems related to depression, anxiety, or mental illness. Those who have experienced loss or trauma are at risk as well.

It's not always pills at a party that get the ball rolling. Some people we treated received prescriptions for legitimate physical problems or injuries and, already being at risk for any of the reasons mentioned, began misusing their prescriptions and eventually seeking the drugs without a prescription. It seemed to me that otherwise "normal" teenagers with sports injuries or procedures such as having wisdom teeth removed and who were given opioids to prevent pain were particularly at risk.

For the vulnerable, prescription opioids are highly addictive. To continue to experience pleasurable effects requires taking higher and higher doses. Discontinuing use will produce withdrawal. There are limitations to the supply of prescription opioids, and the cost is higher than that of heroin. When people are on the brink of withdrawal, the fear that inhibits most of them from using heroin is no longer a factor. Some heroin addicts move on to other highly addictive drugs. In Southeast Ohio, problems with methamphetamines are on the increase, and this increase seems connected to the opioid-using population.

For more than fifty years, I've also been a volunteer firefighter. Over those years I've noticed that the best firefighters sought out the busiest stations, the most action, and the biggest fires. So, too, many addiction professionals have risen to the challenge of opioids. There is satisfaction in taking on challenges. Of course, addiction was a major problem before opioids became so prominent, but opioids have increased the visibility of addiction and the intensity of the work. The pain and the stress experienced by those who use impact the helpers too—those who experience what's called "secondary trauma."

There are many lessons yet to be learned. There is a need to monitor trends in substance abuse at the state and local levels so that changes in services are responsive to changes in substance use trends. This may involve training and adding new services at the local level. At the state level, coordination between divisions of government is important. The Ohio Department of Health conscientiously counted the dead for several years before there was much change in the systems that needed to be addressing the crisis. Also, as a preventive measure, there needs to be a continued focus on opioid prescribing practices. Though we still have work to do, I believe Ohio did a better job than many states in handling the problem.

We have a long road ahead of us. The effects of today's opioid epidemic will be with us for a long time. There is hope, however. People who are addicted do recover and lead useful lives. There are means of reducing the number of people who become addicted if there is public support for doing so. We hope for the best.

*A Licensed Independent Chemical Dependency Counselor, Joe Gay, PhD, has worked in the field for more than three decades. He was Executive Director of Health Recovery Services for eighteen years.*

Reconnecting. Credit: Flying Horse Farms, 2016.

# PART FOUR

# DEVISING SOLUTIONS

SINCE OUR STATE began to come to emotional terms with the effects of widespread opioid addiction, many individuals and organizations have set about building the resources and networks that are needed to meet Ohioans' needs. Many of these solutions are aimed at building capacities that could have positive and meaningful long-term effects. Several of the contributors in this section are individuals who have come through the hell of addiction and its effects and who now plan to become agents of change in our state. Others, realizing the complexity of the problem, have turned to creative and sometimes surprising solutions.

In some cases, contributors report coming to terms with their own roles in enabling the crisis; they seek to change their professional or personal habits to be a force for good. Others have set about rethinking the role that institutions such as law enforcement or religion could play. Each of these contributors challenges us to consider how people, collectively and as individuals, stand to impact opioid addiction and the long-term consequences that have affected families and communities. They remind us that although many economic, historical, and societal factors are outside our control, we all have choices to make and a role to play moving forward.

It would be cliché to say that solutions are necessary. What these pieces make clear, however, is that the most impassioned solutions grow

out of specific contexts and in response to firsthand personal or professional experiences. Yet, while we may be building capacity throughout
our state, there is still a sense that we have only scratched the surface.
Our contributors reveal the real vulnerabilities that set us up for widespread addiction. A series of entrenched social currents—economic and
social inequality; industrial collapse; alienation intensified through race-,
gender-, and sexual-orientation-based discrimination; and stigma—
have made neighborhoods across the state less socially cohesive than
they need to be to promote healthy development and living. This section describes solutions that not only stand to play an important role in
addressing this particular moment, but could make Ohio's communities
stronger and more dynamic going forward.

# 34

## THIS IS NOT THE MEDICINE I WANT TO PRACTICE

### One Physician's Journey to Heal, Not Harm

KATY KROPF

(ATHENS)

These are edited excerpts of my journal starting in 2015 when I began a soul-searching process about my role in prescribing opioid pain medications. Through reflection and journaling, I found increased clarity, and I began advocating for myself and my colleagues in family medicine to decrease our prescribing of opioid pain medications for nonmalignant chronic pain. I wrote these journals as a way to process my feelings and deal with the conflict, both internal and external, that I was experiencing.

*July 2, 2015*

I am on the cusp of a bold, courageous move.

But I'm actually not convinced it is either bold or courageous. I feel scared. And I'm doing it anyway. So it must at least be a bit courageous. I am not surrounded by many who have done the same. So I guess it is a little bold.

I am confused. Afraid. What is the right thing to do? And right for whom? Who am I, not having lived through horrific, unbearable pain, to say that I will not offer you this thing that is so powerful that it makes people beg?

Because it controls you. I have seen it control you.
It does not allow you to live your life.
Your vital, creative, intelligent life. It numbs and constipates you. It becomes the only thing that matters when you come to see me.

Are there exceptions? Yes, of course.
Some people appear to do quite well.
But how do I know when what I offer is helping and when it is harming? Where do I draw the line?
Today I have chosen to draw the line on the safe side of accidental overdose.

*July 26, 2015*

Exciting news! We have met as a practice group twice now. After the first meeting we had consensus that we are prescribing too many narcotics. We are going to get everyone's dosage down to no more than the equivalent of 80 milligrams of morphine per day*—that's our starting point—and to work on tapering others down and off as well. (*80 milligrams morphine = 80 milligrams hydrocodone = approximately 55 milligrams OxyCodone).

We are going to draft a letter to patients who are on narcotics, outlining the risks and harms of being on long-term opioids. We are going to give them some alternative resources and ideas about how to manage pain. We are going to back each other up.

*September 6, 2015*

We had our third meeting on prescribing opioids. One doctor started with clarifying the terminology. Opioids. Not narcotics, not opiates (which are naturally derived from the opium poppy plant).

Another doctor was saying, "It's not possible for me to stop prescribing totally." I had to jump in with an insistent "Yes, it's possible. We always have a choice!"

I've practiced medicine in Ecuador, El Salvador, Guatemala. I've talked with people who have farmed for their livelihood for years, farming steep hillsides with hand tools of hoes and shovels, walking miles daily to and from their fields and their homes. Yes, they have back pain. They have never had a narcotic in their life, and yet they still farm. It is out of necessity. They would be grateful to have access to some ibuprofen or acetaminophen, but there is no CVS or Walgreens anywhere to buy it.

There is pain in being alive. Are there ways we can embrace pain instead of completely shutting it down with opioids? Perhaps "embrace" is not the right word—rather, to "accept" pain as part of life. To live with it, listen to it when needed, not let it control us. The goal of eliminating pain is a dangerous one. Pain is a driver of change.

A patient has been on high-dose narcotics for years. I sent her to pain management, and something in that interaction led her to say, "I want off this OxyContin." She is tired of how she feels on it. She has stopped it completely. She is struggling. She keeps some leftover OxyContin in her safe, reassured to know it is there. She has gone to her safe many times to possibly take it out, but so far has gotten herself to turn away.

We have spent several hours over the past few weeks discussing her symptoms: some from physical withdrawal, but mostly from psychological withdrawal and the fears associated with decreasing these dosages. I had her talk with our behavioral health consultant, and she is going to start talking with a counselor. I am thrilled. I've tried to get her to do that for years.

Her partner is very controlling, and rarely lets her out of her sight for thirty minutes (trips to the doctor being one of the times). She has had many tragic experiences in her life, including physical abuse at the hands of a former partner. The changes with the medications may be the force she needed to look at some deeper issues around self-love and self-care.

*October 7, 2015*

All the materials are ready:

1. A letter for the patients about the risks of chronic opioids.
2. A bifold pamphlet that talks about what we are doing, why we are doing it, and how the patients can have support.
3. A list of alternative options for treating pain.
4. Examples of a taper.
5. An office protocol of not prescribing more than 80 milligrams of morphine equivalents per day—not starting new chronic opi-

oids—and not prescribing medications to help with withdrawal symptoms.

We plan to go live next week.

But all these tools, papers, and letters are nothing compared to the face-to-face conversation with patients. It is terrifying to sit across from someone and begin the conversation about their well-being and their opioid use. Opioid use that perhaps I started or escalated, or opioid prescriptions that perhaps I inherited from a former provider.

How do you know who will thrive when they are off opioids? And who will shrivel? For some people I think it will worsen their quality of life. For most of them at first it will.

I'm trying to figure out how to make this a more mutual decision and action. But the reality is that I have made the decision. I have a clearer vision of the health and healing that are available to them. Right now, they see the fear, the pain, the withdrawal.

One guy said, "I just want to be left alone," as I handed him the letter about the risks of chronic opioids. He has always said that when he retired, he'd be able to get off methadone. His job was intensive and physically demanding. But now that he is retired, he is cutting up some big trees in his yard, and this too is intensive and physically demanding work, and he needs the pain medicine for his back.

I took him a step (a couple of steps?) too far that visit. Seeing the potential for health and well-being—my version, anyway—that he was not ready to see. His triglycerides are through the roof, and I began a discussion about sugar and refined carbs in his diet.

"Yes, I drink a lot of pop and I'm not changing," he quickly said to me. "I know you care about that stuff, but frankly, I just want quality of life, not quantity. I just want to be left alone."

How do we move forward? I clearly want more for him, but he will settle for ten years of pop drinking and taking methadone. This is not the medicine I want to practice.


*October 8, 2015*

A patient I saw yesterday already had tears in her eyes and a tight face as I entered the room. She was the last patient of the day, so I experienced both a sense of ease that I could take the time I needed and the sense of fatigue that comes with carrying the stories, concerns, and diagnoses of the ten people before her.

Over the past month, we had tapered her opioid dosage considerably—10 percent decrease for two weeks, then another 10 percent for two weeks, then a 20-percent drop. Clearly she was not happy. She is scared that her pain will increase, she'll lose function, and she'll be "back in the chair." To her, opioids had meant freedom from her wheelchair.

As we talked, her face relaxed a bit and some of her anger dissipated. Toward the end of the visit, she could even offer that her thinking is clearer and she's less drowsy. But the fear of being "back in the chair" has her scared, and that trumps all.

In each of these interactions, there are moments of panic. How am I going to get through this without reversing my plan or feeling like a jerk? Patients are asking me—and when it comes to opioids, often begging and pleading—how I will fix them. I take a breath and remind myself that it is not my job to fix these hurts that have existed a long time.

I feel the tightness in my face relax a bit.

Somehow I figure out how to steer us toward talking about alternatives. I pull out the sheet of paper with pain management options. Together we work toward some ideas. She agrees to see one of the docs who does Osteopathic Manipulative Medicine full-time. I had referred her months ago, but now her motivation to see this doctor is greater.

Progress. Softer faces, fewer tears, still fears. But we are moving forward, both of us a little more confident in the other than when we started.

*December 2, 2016*

What is your passion? What is your calling? If you are busy dealing with drug seekers, having your energy drained by difficult conversations, there's no room left for developing and pursuing your calling. Your calling as a healer is your greatest gift for your patients. How can you best help?

When I joined University Medical Associates in 2008, I would leave clinic some days crying and crying. So frustrated, so torn, so confused about what I was doing with people coming in practically begging for pain meds. Now I've seen the other side—people who have gotten clean—and

I can see how their erratic, distressed, chaotic, demanding behavior was a symptom of their drug addiction. They can see it now as well, but couldn't at the time, or at least they wouldn't admit it. I am very empathetic. I know that life gets shitty sometimes and people resort to desperate things to cope. I know about "harm reduction"—sometimes someone uses a lesser harm to avoid a greater harm (cutting oneself in lieu of suicide; vaping in lieu of picking up cigarettes again).

Name what is really going on. Someone is coming in with a chaotic life and with destructive behaviors, demanding treatment for their pain. The problem likely isn't a physical pain but a psychological one. Perhaps of addiction or of a hurt so deep and profound they don't know how to get through the day unless they are numb. You don't have to throw your empathy out the window just because you feel manipulated. The patient is still clearly sick—just not with the disease that they are telling you they have or that they think they have. You can tell them that you are concerned that they are hurting. You can offer a different kind of support. They may not be in the place to hear that, but you won't be one of many doctors just getting mad at them and throwing them out. In a different moment, they may be able to hear what you said.

*August 2017*

Since I first started my own soul searching several years ago about prescribing opioids, a lot has shifted. While just a few years ago the opioid epidemic was amazingly tolerated under the premise of "we must treat pain," now we have an opioid crisis, and there are more national and state guidelines, protocols, and morphine-equivalent limits, and more threats to prescribers and retail pharmacy dispensers who don't follow the ever-evolving rules.

It is no small thing that the culture has shifted, and I have more support and imperatives to help me say no to opioid prescribing. But a guideline on paper is just that—paper thin—when it comes to sitting in the office across from someone face-to-face, someone who is suffering, whether from physical pain or some form of psychological pain. Controlled substance management is emotionally exhausting and time-consuming. I am still faced with the daily questions of how and when to prescribe opioids and benzos. Many questions and quandaries remain. A patient who was able to taper off opioids has a new injury and requests opioids again. What do I do? A patient with end-stage COPD still has pain from degenerative disk disease and is anxious from both having a difficult life and not being able to breathe. Where do I draw the line between prescribing opioids and benzos for palliation and risking an overdose? A provider inherits a retired provider's patient panel and finds herself faced with hundreds of patients on controlled substances. What do these providers do? How do they face angry, frustrated patients visit after visit?

Doctors are not so different from other people: we want to have pleasant human interactions, we want people to like us, we don't want to feel threatened. We want to enjoy our jobs and have time and emotional energy to focus on the aspects of medicine we love.

I am still a work in progress. I am doing this for selfish reasons—I want to focus on the aspects of medicine that inspire me. I hope that in the process I am a better doctor who causes less harm and does more good.

*Katy Kropf, DO, is Assistant Professor of Family Medicine at the Heritage College of Osteopathic Medicine and a family medicine physician with the OhioHealth Physician Group Heritage College Primary Care in Athens.*

# 35

## PROBLEM-SOLVING IN COLERAIN TOWNSHIP

DANIEL MELOY

(CINCINNATI)

In early 2014, I was asked to speak about heroin at an event in a neighboring community. I was last on the agenda, following a state representative, the local coroner, and victims and family members of persons who were suffering with, or were lost to, addiction. I was new to the fight. I had just been appointed Director of Public Safety by the Colerain Township Board of Trustees. My previous experience as Chief of Police involved leading an agency that regularly arrested suspects for trafficking and possession. In 2010, the township experienced a transition in the type of drugs that our officers were seizing from arrestees. In 2009, cocaine, crack cocaine, LSD, marijuana, and prescription medications led the list of categories. By 2010, the list was composed almost exclusively of heroin and marijuana.

Firefighters and paramedics were responding to an increasing number of overdoses. The Colerain community was aware that heroin was a problem, but that night I heard many people speak about the importance of doing something more than responding. The new partnership between all public safety departments that I now directed devised a proactive problem-solving effort. The opioid epidemic had become such everyday business for our public safety agencies that it was difficult to imagine that solutions were even possible. But the community expected their leaders to do something. It was time to engage.

I worked to see the epidemic from the perspective of the victims and their families. I met inspiring people like Carol Baden and her husband, Peter, who launched the Community Recovery Project to provide information about resources to anyone who asked. I also met Alec Sheiring, a firefighter who was injured while serving—and became addicted to the pain medication prescribed as part of his recovery from his injury. I met Nan Franks, CEO of the Cincinnati Addiction Services Council, who later authorized their partnership with Colerain's Quick Response Team (QRT) model.

I learned that emergency rooms were struggling. I learned that when families requested treatment resource information, agency phone numbers were often out-of-date or out of service. In August 2014, Colerain Fire and EMS began to provide resource recovery packets to families and victims of an overdose. The packets provided up-to-date resources for people who had no idea whom to contact or trust with the care of a loved one. When I first took the job, I didn't think this is what I'd be doing, but police and fire personnel are often called upon to be the problem-solvers. It only made sense to us that we would be able to help.

Providing our first responders with these resources allowed our personnel to actually *do* something. This ability was important because when people in need seek the help of police and firefighters, and when these providers have no good answer, it hurts all involved—including the officers and firefighters who often want to do more but are unable to do so.

First responders were not required to distribute the packets. Making this optional was important to the fire department's EMS captain, Will Mueller, who, along with me and the public safety chiefs, Frank Cook and Mark Denney, believed that for this to work, we needed true buy-in. We had to win over officers' and firefighters' hearts and minds. If we had just issued a directive, they would be distributing the packets not because it was the right thing to do, but because we had told them to. In our first year of distribution, the rate of distribution of the packets exceeded 100 percent. Captain Mueller asked, How could we be distributing more packets than the number of overdose incidents? What he found impressed us. We learned that besides providing packets to overdose victims, responders were leaving packets at every interaction where they learned a person had a history of drug or alcohol abuse. At that point, we knew that the Colerain police and fire departments were fully on board.

Before becoming director, I presented at the October 2013 International Chiefs of Police Conference. At the conference, I attended a presentation on the unique response to the Aurora, Colorado, theater shooting. An emergency physician explained how one decision made during that tragedy positively impacted the number of lives saved, and I left with ideas for establishing a partnership of Colerain police, fire, and EMS. In 2013, Colerain fire and EMS introduced the concept of Tactical Medics—paramedics partnering with police during critical incidents.

I worked with the chiefs and other township leaders to provide a First Emergency First response model as a tool to proactively address varying service demands of Colerain's two public safety agencies. As 2015 began, the QRT model was becoming more of a reality. There were, however, challenges. The most difficult step in the creation of the team involved patient privacy. We could not use EMS records to conduct our follow-ups, but without that data we couldn't get our officers in contact with those who had overdosed. After several months of discussions and legal reviews, the police and fire departments changed their approaches so that we could differentiate heroin/opioid overdoses from others. In July of 2015 our QRT effort was off the ground—we finally had a sustainable approach.

The team went door-to-door to distribute an educational brochure titled "What Is a Heroin Overdose?" with information on the twenty-four-hour hotline run by the council. Three local media outlets covered the team's first day and helped distribute the brochures to more than 200 homes. The police department also developed a "Drug Box." We learned that sometimes when families lose an elderly loved one, they have a large amount of leftover prescription medications. The Drug Box allows the families to safely dispose of these medications. As a result of that effort, five persons or their families contacted the team requesting assistance with locating treatment services.

Since that first day, the team has grown to four members. The QRT continues to positively impact the epidemic for the Colerain Township community, working two days per week trying to reach each victim within three to five days of the overdose—which many believe to be a critical window. Of 350 follow-ups, close to 80 percent of survivors reach treatment. Our community is showing what's possible when you stand up to do something. Together, with a display of compassion and empathy, officers and medics present "community" to those who feel alone in the battle against this powerful disease. We learned early on that when officers and medics extend their hands and heart to those in need, people who aren't expecting this kind of demonstration of humanity are often surprised.

Just four years later, QRT teams are operating in six states. It is humbling that our idea has made such an impact on so many people and communities. I learned that "doing something" was the right decision. Too many lives are still lost each day to the opioid epidemic. Communities need to ask questions and then demand accountability. We cannot allow others to use the "crisis" as an excuse for not doing something. Community leaders, like public safety personnel, make courageous decisions all the time, and they must use this courage to act—to make a difference. Luckily, Colerain's leaders were not afraid to act.

*Daniel Meloy has served Colerain Township for more than twenty-eight years as a police officer, the Chief of Police, and eventually the Director of Public Safety. He was honored in 2012 and 2017 as Public Administrator of the Year by the American Society for Public Administration for "Excellence in Innovation."*

# 36

## THE BUCK FIFTY

DAVE HUGGINS, CHRIS SCOTT, AND ANGIE FERGUSON
(CHILLICOTHE)

*The Buck Fifty is a 150-mile relay race where teams of runners wind through the hills of Ross County. The race supports eight Drug Free Clubs of America school chapters where students pledge to be held accountable for staying drug free throughout high school. When we first heard about this race, we were interested in understanding how a group of community members from Chillicothe came together to build the race and the student programs. We sat down at Bob Evans in Chillicothe on a Sunday morning to learn more about the chapter founders' experience and how opioid abuse has inspired local communities to find new ways to work together. **Dave Huggins** serves as Race Director for The Buck Fifty. **Chris Scott** serves as Branch Chair for the Ross County Drug Free Clubs of America chapters. **Angie Ferguson** has been with Drug Free Clubs of America since its inception in 2005, becoming Executive Director in 2012. Interview by Jane Balbo and Berkeley Franz.*

*How did you get involved with Drug Free Clubs of America?*

DAVE: In the summer of 2015, I was the Rotary Club president for First Capital Rotary, and my term was winding down. Each member of the club is responsible for bringing in a speaker, and Chief Deputy Hollis from the Ross County Sheriff's Department came and told this story about these two guys who were robbing farmhouses. The sheriff's department received a tip that they were driving down the road, and a few cruisers were dispatched.

The deputies followed these guys to a farmhouse. The two men went inside to rob the place while the deputies moved into position. When the guy comes out, the deputy says, "Did you not see us following you for the last five miles?" The man says, "Sir, with all due respect, I need drugs. This is the way I need to get it. I'm not saying this is right, but I can't see twenty feet in front of my face right now. This is what I have to do." It was a gripping story. The drug had them in such a way that they knew they were doing things that were wrong, but they believed they didn't have any other option. So that was my first epiphany.

A few weeks later on Thursday, July 30, 2015, the real magic happened. We met with Wayne Campbell, founder of Tyler's Light. Wayne told us all about the opioid epidemic and his son Tyler who played football at the University of Akron. I'm a football guy, and Wayne explained that his son took these pills to stay on the field to cover up a painful injury. I can buy into every single line of that with wanting to be on the field to play football with your team. Wayne talked about how his son became addicted, and then I found out his son had passed away from an overdose. I thought, "Holy crap! What do we do?" It brought me back to the guys robbing the farmhouses. Wayne's explaining the messiness of the problem and how it can happen anywhere, you know, Pickerington, Ohio, . . . so what do we do?

That's when he first introduced us to the Drug Free Clubs of America program. We quickly wanted to understand how the program worked. The concept made sense because I could imagine a teenager being in a car on a Friday night with friends. One of them has a substance they shouldn't have. They offer it to someone else and say, "Try it." How will that teen respond? How will that decision affect their life?

With Drug Free Clubs in the picture, we now have a situation where drugs get offered, and the kid can say, "No, I can't; I might get tested." Every person in that car knows that's a real thing because they have seen them get rewards in school. This is not a "mom and dad finding out" thing. This is "You could roll into school on Monday and get popped for a drug test, and now you're busted." So that's where I feel like this thing has really created a culture change in our high schools. There are a whole bunch of dead kids in this world because they were the ones who were not supposed to try drugs, but peer pressure got to them. The reality of drug testing helps them have a backup.

*What is unique about the Drug Free Clubs of America model?*

CHRIS: It is student led. We pulled a bunch of kids together from the beginning and figured out what the kids wanted as rewards for participating in the program and passing drug tests. I'm also a car dealer, so before that, I was thinking "new car." I'm thinking iPads and material things, so we met with the kids, and we did some brainstorming and flowcharts. We sat down with them and just took notes. Heck, they already had iPads. They also didn't want a car. They were like, "Oh, we need a lunch pass, can we go to lunch early, can we go outside for lunch?" That stuff was cool; preferred parking at the school was cool. It was all these things that didn't cost taxpayers or the school anything. And if we hadn't listened to the kids, we wouldn't have known.

The other item we focused on was trying to provide them an experience. Events or activities that would bring them together as one. What if we had a concert and a rally they'll remember for the rest of their life? They won't remember that one person in their class who won a prize or a scholarship. But every single kid will remember the moment in November when we had them in downtown Chillicothe. They'll remember that day the rest of their life. There are a lot of kids who have never been to a concert before. We brought Shane Runion in—a local artist from Portsmouth. He's got a song that's called "I'm Proud of Where I'm From." So we had him sing that one song at the courthouse, and we had the kids speak about why DFCA was important to them or how DFCA has helped them. It was an amazing experience for everyone who was there that day.

DAVE: One problem, adults being adults, is they try to influence things and make it go the way they think it should go. We decided to let the kids recruit the kids because that's the way the DFCA program is intended to operate and they are experts at this.

ANGIE: That's part of establishing your branch. At the beginning, one of the first things you do is appoint student officers or just gather the students and say, "All right, here's the concept." Ask them what's meaningful as a reward and what isn't, both at school and in the community, because I might work really hard to get a discount somewhere and the kids say, "We never go there." It is surprising what a challenge that can be. Administrators are often so used to just getting things done that to find out and follow a teenager's thoughts instead of their own is hard. The process can be challenging, but it makes all the difference in the world when the teens drive their own club.

One of the biggest strengths of the strategy is that this reaches so many parts of the student body. On drug test day, it's just crazy to see that standing in line you've got the guy in the jersey, the kid carrying the super-heavy backpack, the girl in the black lipstick, and the one in the corner who's not really talking, who's standing next to the class clown getting all the attention. They're all there. That's missing in so many programs.

*Did you have success enrolling students in the club?*

ANGIE: Our average participation in schools at that time was 18 percent. But we had never had an entire county of this size launch all their schools at the same time before.

CHRIS: We were going to do cool things like have the band Maroon 5 on the football field at Adena High School, or take all these kids up to the spring game at Ohio State. Experiences. These kids are passionate about not wanting drugs in their future. When you can sit in a room full of kids and go, "Raise your hand if you know someone that's OD'd," and the whole room raises their hand. And then you go, "Keep them up if it's somebody in your family," and 75 percent of them still have their hand up because it's a family member. I've never drilled down further. Those kids are passionate because they're tired of it. They are starving for a positive environment. They have known challenge and adversity and negativity a good portion of their lives. They've seen this struggle, but they haven't seen anything positive on the topic. So when a school takes on the program and builds that culture inside the school and they tell them, "We're proud of you for staying drug free," they've probably never heard that before.

DAVE: So one of the most difficult things with high school kids is getting parents engaged too. When Angie suggested collecting money with students' applications to help pay for the program, we initially resisted. And then she explained to us the philosophy of it. That is, if I go home with a paper and I say, "Mom, sign this," Mom signs it, doesn't read it, hands it back to me. When they go home and ask for money, it starts a conversation. We have a really strong focus on bringing the parents back into the conversation. We're constantly making them aware that drug testing happened today. Because even if they intend to talk to their child about drugs, the moments can pass. A week becomes a month, and a month becomes a quarter, and a quarter becomes a year, and you haven't talked about it once. You can say, "This is how you talk to your child about drugs," and there are a thousand brochures out there like that. But when do they do that? Not necessarily just how, but when?

*What have been the biggest challenges with sustaining the Drug Free Clubs of America chapters?*

DAVE: Back in 2012, I ran in a race called the Bourbon Chase, a 200-mile relay along the Kentucky Bourbon Trail, with twelve people on a team where each runner runs three different times. I came back from that and thought, "Man, that would be a cool event to have in Ross County." But I didn't yet have a reason to do it.

But then Chris let me know that we needed a strategy to cover the $67 student fee. That's when I thought we could build a race to sustain this program. We could sell sponsorships, have runner entry fees, and build a machine to help fund these kids. We started planning right away in September 2015. We thought we were getting into a game of raising about $50,000 to support 700 or 800 kids in our first year.

I remember the first time I was talking to Chris in the fall of 2016, and I'm like, "How many kids do we have?" He's like, "I don't know exactly. I know by the school." I'm like, "Well, what are they by school?" I'm at my daughter's soccer practice, and he's rattling them off. "I've got 150 here. There's 200 here," and I'm adding them up, and I'm like, "Chris, holy cow, man. We've got like 1,500 kids." I got really excited but also realized that we were going to have to do things differently than we had planned to raise the money it would take to support these teens.

We wanted a race that lasted around twenty-four hours. We wanted it to kick off on a Friday afternoon and end Saturday night before dark. I spent over 100 hours mapping the course. I did some work online and would then go out and drive it. I remember one day being out in Tar Hollow State Park going down what I thought was a road that went from asphalt to bumpy asphalt to gravel to dirt to briars on both sides. I was in my wife's Honda. It's snowing, and I think this is maybe not a good idea. I remember it snowing like crazy; I had no cell service, so it was time to get out of there. It was a memorable day during those early planning stages. After exploring the county, we built this 150-mile track, and that's how we came up with the name, "The Buck Fifty."

ANGIE: There are some crazy people out there who love a good challenge.

DAVE: In our first year we had thirty-eight teams, and we netted $85,000. We missed our goal by 15 percent in fundraising for our first year, but Chris doubled his goal in recruiting students. I had never written a $70,000 check before, so it was rewarding for our team to contribute so much to something we truly believe in with Drug Free Clubs. The kids kept enrolling in droves, and now, in our second year with DFCA, we have 2,300 kids, which means we'll need to raise $200,000. I've had moments where I have doubts about how our team can do this, but the kids are the real motivation, and God has helped us find a way to support them. We've just got so many different people from so many walks of life helping both as volunteers and financially. Our race volunteers who work the twenty-nine checkpoints during the race have crushed it, and they blew the doors off of everyone's expectations. Of the thirty-eight teams, I would say 80 percent personally reached out to me and sent me a text, an email, a phone call. "We have no idea how you did this, but this is the greatest thing we've ever been a part of."

*Can you tell us about the course?*

DAVE: Our start and finish lines are at Ohio University-Chillicothe. So we start there, and we work our way out to Frankfort and Adena High School. Then we work our way up into Clarksburg, come across the top of the county, and we go into Kingston. We run down to Great Seal State Park to begin some great trail runs. We have twenty-three miles of trail runs on the course, and the Great Seal section is at night. It's fantastic terrain, and one of the highest points in Ross County. Some people get their hind ends handed to them in this thing because it's such a challenging course with 8,800 feet of elevation gain. They will run some great back country roads over into Tar Hollow State Park about the time the sun is coming up. Then they come down to Southeastern High School and down Old 35. One of the favorite checkpoints, #21, is hosted by Huntington High School (which has 87 percent enrollment in their Drug Free Club) before they start on the Buckeye Trail into Scioto Trails State Park for some insane trail runs. The last twenty miles is in historic Chillicothe and it's a real beauty. A lot of these legs have names to them that I named after people or things. For example, Leg Five we call Chasing the Light. It's dedicated to people we know who have lost their battle with addiction, and it gets emotional for us.

*What motivated you to get involved in this work on a volunteer basis?*

DAVE: I felt like the negative story being told about Ross County nationally needed to be changed. I knew our teens needed a brighter future, and as a father of two, I had to do something to help. We knew that to support our eight Drug Free Clubs of America chapters we needed a sustainable funding source. The Buck Fifty could help us do that. We barely got by in the first year. Year two was equally challenging, but our team would not back down from this challenge. We felt like we weren't going to sit around and we're not going to ask for anyone's permission. We went to the schools, and they said they needed DFCA. That was the only thing we needed to know, that we've got to figure out how to do this. Every dollar invested in prevention saves seven dollars in rehabilitation and criminal system costs.

CHRIS: The things we've done have heightened awareness in the community, and for all ages. I know two people, including my father-in-law, who just had surgery but did not want to take opioids because of the heightened awareness. Now, four years ago in this community, if a doctor said to take it, I'd just take it. I was in Portsmouth when the things happened that Sam Quinones wrote about in *Dreamland*. My ex-wife worked at a doctor's office in Portsmouth. I watched all the food, the vacations, everything that was going on with the doc at that time, and I'm going, "Something's not right." Then a long time after that, you know I had watched Procter get busted down there. It's in the book. I was there. Well, lo and behold, my ex-wife who worked in this office, she was an addict. I didn't know it. She was taking thirty Percocet or whatever a day. Until I found prescription bottles with my name, her dad's name, her mom's name, and this all comes to a head. I got out. I tried to get her in rehab, work with her and everything. Years later she died. My friend's son, a nineteen-year-old pizza delivery driver in Portsmouth, ended up getting murdered in a $100 drug deal. Those things fueled my passion.

DAVE: I'm 100 percent Chris's opposite on this. I have no addiction in my family. None. I fight because it's wicked and I don't want it to hurt more people. I've seen how awful it is. Just looking around the room right now at Bob Evans in Chillicothe, I see someone my daughter's age sitting over here—he's one of the kids I want to protect. That whole family over there is important to me. I went to high school with her. Their son is one of our first Drug Free Club ambassadors. Their younger son is a member now. We're tied up in this community now. We want to end it.

Here's what Chris and I think: If we're the only ones doing this, and obviously we're not, but if we don't get every community doing this, the battle is never going to end and it's never going to go away. But if there's no one buying drugs because we're raising youth who are empowered to stay drug free, there's no one to sell drugs to. If we could save one kid's life, it would be worth it. When we're selling sponsorships for the program, it's $67 per kid. What's one kid's life worth to you?

CHRIS: Sixty-seven dollars is a pittance, but it's still been a real challenge to sustain this club year to year.

DAVE: It is a challenge. But even knowing that now, I would still have embraced it.

# 37

## PLANS AFTER PRISON

JONATHAN BECKER

(AKRON)

People tend to talk about the opioid epidemic as a whole, as though it is one giant problem. It is this, of course. But it is also hundreds of thousands of individual problems—individual people united by similar problems that make up the nationwide problem of addiction. This means that addiction can't be tackled as a whole. It needs to be tackled person by person, individually. Every person is different.

The answer to the question of how or why someone would start using opioids is different for everybody. For me, looking back, it started with addiction. Since the age of seventeen, I had a problem, whether it was drinking, smoking, or pills. By the time I was twenty-one, coke and pills were my main drugs.

I suppose heroin use was bound to happen. As an addict you just keep looking for that next high, and you can only keep trying so many things before you end up there. The first time I tried heroin, I was hooked. I asked how I could get more and my "friend" said, "Get in the car." Ohio is an awful state for addiction.

We drove to a parking lot off Kenmore Trail and got another bag off some guy posted up on the corner. It was as easy as that. I had never met him before, but he sold it with a smile. Believe me when I say that whether it's Akron, Barberton, Kenmore, and I'm sure every other city in Ohio—it's that easy. You just have to know how to ask, know the slang, and have the look of heroin. Sober people may not know the look, but dealers and users do. You just know.

Availability fuels the epidemic. Once you want it, you can get it. A lot of young adults abuse opioids simply because it is so easy to get, whether it be from a doctor or the corner. Doctors give out "percs" and then when those aren't good enough, you can get heroin on any corner. You'll try to find pills because of the addiction, and then you can't. Then someone will tell you heroin is basically the same, but cheaper.

It is a strange thing. Once you start using opioids, next thing you know you're hanging out with other users and you wonder why. You start to know every other opioid user, and dealers know that you're a user. They want you to use and to sell to you. Not all users are bad. It's the drug that makes you bad, the addiction. Once you're hooked you'll do anything for that feeling, that escape from reality.

Once you start using, other addicts somehow just find out, along with the dealers. That is how I started using with Alex and her friend. One day they both texted me asking for help getting them some dope. I did just that and we became using buddies from there. This went on for a while. When you use you hide it very well. We all did.

One night, Alex texted me to split some dope. I already had some, so I told her to come over. We were chilling, doing the dope, and then she asked for the rest of the bag. I said, "Sure, I am going to bed anyway." She told me she was going to lay down in the living room for a while and let herself out. I said ok.

I think about that night over and over again. What happened? The only thing I can think is when she went in the living room by herself, she did too much and nobody was around to save her. We were all asleep. The next morning we found her dead, the worst day of my life. The week after her death, I was numb to the world. It didn't hit me till a month or so after I was arrested. I had to be sober to fully understand and feel it. Do I think about it every day? Yes. Would I give anything to take back what happened? Yes. Do I regret it? Yes. The thing is: people are who they are. She was an addict like me. Our roles could have been reversed. But they weren't, so I have to try to make something positive out of this. Try and just reach and save one person. Tell one person what happened, and maybe it won't be in vain.

I got charged with her death—involuntary manslaughter and drug trafficking—and sent to prison. Since I've been to prison, I've gotten sober. Life in prison is what you make of it. I've decided to be proactive, go to meetings, get vocational training (CNC [computer numeric controlled] machinist for me). I've signed up for programs to help me change my thinking, things of that nature. There is, of course, another route you can take. There's gangs, there's violence, and drugs everywhere you look. Honestly, prison is either a solution or your introduction to hell. Getting sober here of all places takes willpower. Mine comes from wanting to help others. Not letting my friend's death be in vain. But trust me when I say this: if you don't really want sobriety, this place will eat you alive.

When I get out, I plan on using what happened to help people, to try to save a life, or to get someone sober. I plan to help people upon my release, which is scheduled for June 2021. But most important, I've found out I have a son, Jackson. When I get out, all I plan on doing is helping addicts and being the best father I can be. To live a life worth living. I've made mistakes and hurt people, but I can use my past to help people now, save people. Most importantly though: be a father.

My experience is preparing me well to help others. Addicts don't want to have someone just read from a medical book or get advice from some kid with a college degree who's never been through this. To reach them, they need—they want—someone who has been through addiction and loss. That's something I can share with people like me, addicts. I hope to help them by relating and humanizing what happened, explaining what can happen. Because it did happen to me.

*Jonathan Becker was convicted in 2016 for selling carfentanil to a friend who ultimately died from an overdose. He is scheduled to be released from prison in 2021.*

# 38

# AVOIDING THE ABYSS

SHARON PARSONS
(BEXLEY)

I wish that I had known more about the disease of addiction from the beginning. Maybe things would have turned out differently—but probably not. My son, Sean, hurt himself during finals week in his junior year of college. He had told me that he was going to ride dirt bikes with a friend at his farm. I told him that it was a bad idea—he could hurt himself and would not be able to take finals. He did it anyway and, of course, he hurt himself. He did not want me to know what he had done, so he didn't go to urgent care or the emergency room. Instead, he accepted some pills—OxyContin—from a neighbor. They worked, he liked them, and he went back for more.

That was the beginning of the end. At first, I just noticed that he didn't seem to be quite himself. He was half a step behind in his actions and responses. When I asked, he would reply that he was just tired. After a while it became clear that something more was going on. At my urging, he went to rehab. He did learn lots of positive skills while there. Unfortunately, he also learned that heroin is the same thing as OxyContin—and pennies on the dollar. He tried to stay clean, but it didn't last long. Soon he was addicted to heroin.

Sean became extremely adept at lying and stealing to get what he needed. After stealing from me one too many times, I threw him out of the house at the urging of my ex-husband and younger son. He moved to Georgia, where a friend was living. As it turned out, this friend was also an addict. While there, Sean did the recovery waltz—steps one, two, three—until he hit what I thought was rock bottom. Broke, unemployed, and hungry, he entered a rehab program there. At the time, I credited it with saving his life.

He got a job, started living a fairly conventional life, and then relapsed yet again. At this point, his father brought him home and paid for him to go back to college, where he got his degree. He lived with his father during this period, with strict rules which helped to keep him clean, but he probably had episodes of relapse. He did get a job and was regularly attending Narcotics Anonymous meetings and actually got a sponsor. He was fairly happy but told me that it was still a daily struggle. While on a Narcotics Anonymous–sponsored trip to go whitewater rafting and camping, he hurt himself and had to have ankle surgery. We tried to keep the pain management from throwing him back into using, but it probably played a role. At this time he found a girlfriend and we were hopeful that he was on the road to recovery. However, instead of her lifting him up, she became addicted. She had a young child, and the three of them eventually moved in with her father after her mother died. Her father is a physician and became an enabler not only to his daughter but to my son as well. For the next couple of years Sean got clean several times but would continue to relapse. The relationship with the girlfriend was toxic, and his mental state deteriorated.

He went to North Carolina to stay with my sister, who offered to help him get clean. She had been actively using drugs when much younger. I had urged him to do this, thinking that maybe this was finally the answer. My sister and her husband live in a remote area in the mountains and Sean loved the outdoors. It did work as far as him trying to be clean and spending lots of time hiking and being active. However, Sean called to tell me that my sister and her husband were encouraging him to drink and smoke pot. He said that this is how they stopped using drugs. Disillusioned, he called the girlfriend, who drove down and got him. He quickly moved back to his old ways staying at her father's home.

After reaching a point of desperation, he confided to me that he wanted to get clean and start a new life. He claimed that he had been detoxing and was interviewing for a new job. He had passed the drug test and begged me to let him come live with me. Grudgingly, I agreed. He was in the process of moving his things into my home. Please understand, the parents and loved ones of those suffering from the disease of addiction live in a hell of their own. You never know what or when to believe the one you love, and you are forced to do the tough love thing so you don't enable them. It is a miserable existence.

He moved most of his things into my home on Sunday, September 20. The final load was to be moved in the next day. I begged him to stay home with me that Sunday night, but he was determined to stay one last night with the girlfriend. The next morning, at 4:00, I was awakened by two policemen informing me that Sean had died of a drug overdose. It was the visit that every parent of an addict half expects but dreads. I waited until about 6:30 to call my mother and tell her. She drove to my house to be with me. Two hours later she collapsed in my kitchen and died. The unthinkable had happened all in a few hours' time. I spent the next couple of weeks in shock.

However, in the first day or so after the deaths, I also made a very deliberate decision. As a dentist, I had seen patients who lost children. They either came through it with grace or dropped into the abyss. There did not seem to be a middle ground. I decided that I did not want the abyss. I made a conscious decision that I would honor my son by living my best life. One of Sean's best friends came over to the house and brought me a gift with an explanation. The gift was a rock. He lives in Northern California and, as a park ranger, had close contact with some of the Native American tribes in the area. He talked to one of the elders, who explained that they believed that when a child passes before their mother, the child resides in the heart of the mother for the rest of the mother's life. The mother then experiences life with her child and should make the most of it. The rock was taken from a large holy rock that is believed to have healing properties. I have tried to live my life from that time on as if my son is with me. I set my sights on doing something to help stop the addiction crisis—but didn't feel that I was qualified to help with active addicts.

By chance, an oral surgeon whom I am friends with called me and was upset. He said that he had just heard about Sean and my mother's deaths. He asked what he could do for me. Without thinking, I said, "Stop prescribing so many opioids." He didn't say much in return and I never gave it another thought. A few months later, I saw him at a meeting, and he said that he needed to talk to me. "Do you remember asking me to curb my opioid prescribing?" he asked. "I was afraid that I would spend most of my weekends dealing with patients in pain. Guess what?

The opposite happened. I got no calls. It has been the best thing I have ever done. You not only changed my practice—you changed my life."

He thanked me. I was in shock. This was the best news ever. People heard about this, and we were asked to speak at a dental meeting. Apparently it was well received because we have been asked to speak to several dental societies all over Ohio. I am not a natural public speaker, and I struggle with it, but it gets easier every time. I think of Sean being with me—urging me on. I may not be able to help active addicts, but I am trying to help create fewer addicts in the future. I hope that I can spare other families the pain that mine has endured.

*Sharon Parsons, DDS, is an activist and advocate for safe opioid prescribing in the dental community. She is currently Vice President of the Ohio Dental Association and will become President in October 2020.*

# 39

## ALL THE NARCAN IN THE WORLD

DAVID KESEG
(COLUMBUS)

I remember my surprise, just a few years ago, as I was reviewing our cardiac arrest patient care reports—one of my responsibilities as medical director of the Columbus Division of Fire. Usually the age of the patient who suffered the cardiac arrest was somewhere north of sixty-five, but occasionally it would be someone in their fifties and I would lament the tragedy of a relatively young person succumbing to a cardiac arrest.

But something had radically changed. The ages on our cardiac arrests were more frequently in the range of twenty to thirty. Talk about a true tragedy! These were cardiac arrests caused by opioid overdoses. We were finding that heroin was being combined with dangerous opioids many times more potent than heroin, like fentanyl and carfentanil.

When the opioid epidemic hit, EMS was on the front lines trying to make sense of it all. EMS providers have directly witnessed the increase in the rate of drug overdose deaths, which are estimated to have increased by 137 percent over the last fifteen years. Opioids caused the majority of that increase. Last year, over 50,000 Americans died from drug overdoses, the highest figure ever recorded. The number of people killed in car crashes was 37,757.

We had been administering Narcan for years but never to this extent and at this volume. Emergency departments are overwhelmed, and in many cases these transports for opioid overdoses can end up to be a revolving door for the patients.

Heroin deaths alone rose to 12,989—slightly higher than the number of gun homicides. Now fentanyl, which is forty times stronger than heroin, has become the largest drug threat to the US, causing forty-four deaths every day. Deaths from oxycodone and Vicodin tallied 17,536 last year. Robert Anderson, who oversees death statistics at the Centers for Disease Control and Prevention, said, "I don't think we've ever seen anything like this. Certainly not in modern times."

Opioid deaths have taken a toll on our EMS personnel. We have been giving Narcan at an average rate of twelve to eighteen times a day, many times to the same individuals. Compassion fatigue can set in when you end up running on the same patient and saving his life over and over again. An attitude can creep in that questions whether the patient really wants help or not. Or sometimes whether they deserve help.

Part of this comes from a lack of understanding that addiction is a chronic, relapsing brain disease. As I was studying to take my board exam in addiction medicine, it was enlightening to discover just how the brain rewires itself when addiction takes over, and just how difficult it is to break away from the pattern of abusing opioids. The whole process becomes a physiological requirement of a brain and body that demands submission.

Some politicians and municipal officials, when faced with budget crises, have called for limits on the number of times EMS should be required to give increasingly costly Narcan to the same individuals. From a purely economic perspective, this epidemic has strained the monetary resources of EMS agencies. The initial two-milligram dose of Narcan has increased threefold over the last decade from $14 to $45. Combine that increased cost with a significant need for an increased supply, and it is easy to understand why some smaller municipalities are proposing to limit the number of times Narcan can be given to the same individual.

Unfortunately, this premise is fatally flawed in that it tries to quantify how many times an individual deserves to be resuscitated. Every individual who suffers an opioid overdose deserves to be given Narcan and a chance at recovery. If it is the twentieth time, it might very well be the time that that person decides to get serious about seeking help and turns their life around.

We all need to understand how Narcan works and under what circumstances it must be given. Narcan is not without side effects. It reverses the high that an opioid user experiences, and although it can save a life, it also can throw the patient into withdrawal, which can be accompanied by hypertension, tachycardia, and serious neural responses. Sometimes patients wake up in the back of the moving ambulance and try to jump out while it's moving.

We are also seeing more medical complications from chronic opioid addiction, such as sepsis, endocarditis, trauma, and cellulitis. These conditions need to be treated with the knowledge that addiction is present.

EMS providers have to be vigilant and not become opioid overdose victims themselves. The risk of exposure to certain powerful opioids like fentanyl and carfentanil are real and becoming more prevalent. Personal protective equipment is crucial at any EMS scene, but when assessing an overdose patient, EMS providers must take into account the risk of absorbing these potent narcotics. The providers are most likely to encounter illicitly manufactured fentanyl and its analogs in powder, tablet, and liquid form. Exposure routes include inhalation, mucous membrane contact, ingestion, and a needle stick.

Data collection is extremely important to be able to tell if there are pockets of the community where Narcan is being more frequently administered. EMS electronic patient care reports have begun to standardize data collection, enabling EMS to share valuable information with their public health partners to identify high-risk populations, conduct epidemiological surveillance, and pinpoint geographic hot spots for drug overdoses and activity. It is also helpful to know demographic information like average age, gender, time of day, and day of the week.

When there are spikes of either Narcan administration or opioid overdose deaths, the EMS agency should initiate a conference call with other public health or public safety agencies within their communities to determine if further measures need to be taken. There may be a supply of fentanyl, or heroin laced with fentanyl, that is causing more deaths in a certain part of the community. This needs to be discussed and action taken.

Inconsistencies with the approach and management of patients in the emergency department can result in inadequate linkage and follow-up to provide resources for family members and loved ones of opioid overdose patients. We can give all the Narcan in the world, but unless individuals seek treatment for their addiction, they are not going to find relief from this vicious cycle.

Getting people into treatment is the key and we're doing our part. We've partnered with a mental health agency to form a Rapid Response Emergency Addiction and Crisis Team, which is composed of mental health professionals who respond to hospitals with patients suffering from opioid overdose. We have established a firefighter/police team to respond to residences where opioid overdose patients receive Narcan, but do not need hospital transport, and want treatment for their addiction.

The goals of this program are to decrease EMS workload burden, reduce compassion fatigue in EMS providers, increase the coordination of patient care, increase awareness of harm reduction services, increase access to Narcan kits, and develop best practices for community care coordination.

It is for this reason that we have worked with the community to set up the Maryhaven Addiction Stabilization Center—a five-bed emergency department and fifty-five-bed inpatient detox facility that will give EMS a place to take patients who are medically stable and seeking treatment for opioid addiction. Hopefully, this center will be the first of many others. Getting people into treatment is the key. Although it is not perfect, medication-assisted treatment given in conjunction with focused counseling and behavioral modification can have a profoundly beneficial effect on opioid abuse and addiction. Yet even with the best of these treatment modalities, the success rate is low and recidivism is high. Many times, patients have to enter into treatment multiple times before they are cured.

We need to expend the necessary resources to combat the most serious public health crisis of this generation—including economic resources and competent, knowledgeable human resources. Drug companies that manufacture these opioids need to contribute to these resources to help develop solutions. We need to be creative in enlisting our EMS personnel not only to help resuscitate individuals suffering from opioid overdoses, but also to engage and direct these people toward programs that can provide an ultimate cure for their addiction.

EMS personnel should receive training on what addiction is and how best to communicate with opioid abusers to convince them to seek treatment. This training should include recovery success stories, principles of addiction science, and better communication with opioid abusers. Recovery success stories can provide encouragement to them and show how the whole situation is not hopeless.

Then they need to be informed as to the best treatment options and be able to direct those individuals to the most immediate source of help. Sometimes the best situation to get someone into treatment is when they have been revived with Narcan and escaped certain death. That can get someone's attention, placing the EMS provider in a perfect position to start a dialogue with the patient to get them to consider treatment. Obviously, this is not within the accepted scope of practice of the EMS profession, but this interaction can save more lives than many of the interventions that EMS providers are taught how to do. To reinforce what I said above, we can give all the Narcan in the world, but unless individuals seek treatment for their addiction, they are not going to escape this vicious cycle.

Silos of influence and activity hinder efforts to solving the opioid epidemic. All players, including EMS and public safety, public health, mental health agencies; addiction professionals and their practices; judicial and legal entities; and other municipal officials should all work together to identify programs and resources within their practices and share data and information to ensure that a coordinated and focused effort is ongoing to address this epidemic. All too often, organizations compete against each other for influence and funding.

EMS can provide the data and frontline experience to other experts in this field to develop a cohesive strategy going forward within the community. EMS has a special place at the table of all interested parties who hope to come up with solutions to this opioid public health crisis. Beyond intervening to rescue those dying from an opioid overdose, EMS need to be invested in directing individuals to the resources that will provide pathways out of this pernicious affliction. When EMS is working with its partners in public safety and public health, only then will we see some light at the end of the tunnel.

*David P. Keseg, MD, is board-certified in emergency medicine and addiction medicine. He has practiced emergency medicine for almost forty years and currently serves as medical director for the Columbus Division of Fire.*

# 40

## PAUSE FOR CHANGE

NANCY POOK
(DAYTON)

In June 2017, NBC News called Dayton the "Overdose Capital of America." Prescription opioids, unfortunately, have been part of so many of these overdoses. There is a great paradox in that opioids can cause both physical and psychic pain, despite their intended use as a pain reliever. As an emergency physician, I'm supposed to relieve pain, so I take seriously the potential to do harm with opioids. This sense of duty is what gave rise to Pause—an alternative pathway to medical treatment. Pause is a reminder to think carefully about patient safety when prescribing.

In 1995, when I completed my emergency medicine residency at Wright State University, I had spent three years training in hospitals throughout the Dayton area. Back then, opioids were used only for broken bones, kidney stones, and childbirth. In 1996, Purdue Pharma marketed OxyContin to US medical practices, which were rapidly beginning to use pain scales and promise patients that "no pain" was the goal. My primary care colleagues in Miamisburg remember hearing from the pharmaceutical representatives that this was a nonaddictive drug, easily stopped without any withdrawal symptoms for the patient. It was around that time that pain clinics, known for prescribing long-acting opioids, were on the rise.

A couple of years into the rise of OxyContin use, I met Margaret and her family. Like many others, she received prescriptions for escalating doses of opioids for musculoskeletal pain. She had normal MRIs, but when she felt that her pain was more than she could handle with the prescriptions provided by the pain clinic, she presented to the emergency department for care. An emergency room visit typically meant IV doses of stronger opioid medications, sometimes with the addition of Valium or similar medicine. We would later learn this was a dangerous practice.

Most of the time, these patients came to the emergency department alone. It seemed unfathomable that any condition identified as an emergency would be something that one could handle solo. But more and more families started to tell the tale of their loved one "doctor shopping" and sneaking out to get more medication. On the day that I met Margaret and listened to her story, we discovered together that the medication had been hiding the truth. That day we found cancer that she didn't know that she had; I had to tell her that it had metastasized. Could she have had a chance at treatment if her body had a chance to tell its tale earlier? We'll never know. Pain tells us when something is wrong. It's a warning sign. It can help us identify a problem before it's too late. Strong pain medicines hide the body's natural warning system. Unfortunately, there are many other patients whose pain medication helped a larger problem hide just beneath the surface.

By that time, we were dealing with a monumental problem. More patients were demanding drugs in medical practice offices and emergency departments. Patients were often overusing their prescriptions and, fueled by withdrawal symptoms, becoming increasingly violent, making patient agitation and threats to staff a daily occurrence.

In the summer of 2006, we saw our first uptick in overdose deaths. The General Motors plant in Moraine was closing. A group of employees, many in their thirties, forties, and fifties, knew nothing but the factory and its financial security. General Motors offered many of its employees generous severance packages. During this time, I met thirty-eight-year-old Robert after he overdosed on street heroin. At that time, the street drug had a longer half-life, and we watched patients for several hours after their near-death experiences because the opioid lasted longer than the antidote. Maybe he wasn't suicidal, but with that large amount of cash on hand, he would not be able to resist the next temptation. When he was brought in by EMS in the early hours of the next calendar day, it was no longer possible for us to bring him back. He died an early and tragic death. The loss of factory jobs in Ohio left a chasm in the employment market, and drug use escalated in response to a combination of factors: cash payouts, societal stress, and chronic musculoskeletal injuries related to years of physical labor.

In 2009, I learned from a Dayton detective that a patient had stolen my DEA number. Arriving with another patient in the emergency department—a red flag—Steven had copied my DEA number from a prescription written for his girlfriend. He started going to multiple local pharmacies with a "prescription" for three months of a potent painkiller. The detective showed me the counterfeit prescription, written on fraudulent prescription paper. Steven's pharmacy visits were caught on video multiple times before his eventual arrest weeks later.

Faced with the overwhelming burden of workplace violence, my team and I were fatigued. Parents were demanding stronger prescriptions for their children with sprains and strains. Despite the culture around us, with opioid use commonly touted in TV shows and movies, we began devising an opioid-free prescribing pathway. Many of the patients who visited the emergency department repeatedly had the highest rates of controlled substance use, as documented by the Ohio Automated Prescription Reporting System. One of the many challenges at that time was the inconsistency of practice. After the introduction of OxyContin to medical practice, medical students learned, erroneously, that pain-free living was a right and that opioids provided the path to this end. Physicians were not ill-willed, just misinformed. We have since learned that opioids cause pain through a condition known as "opioid hypersensitivity syndrome," where high prescription doses result in a situation in which minor physical stress causes severe pain. The only cure is eliminating the drug. The Pause program does exactly that, while continuing to provide compassionate care.

Opioids do cause pain: opioid hypersensitivity syndrome; the physical pain of withdrawal; the psychic pain of addiction; societal pain from fractured families; manipulative behaviors; increased societal costs related to criminal justice and foster care management; and violence and trauma. Pause was designed to stop the cycle of pain that had been created.

We have seen a huge increase in overdoses over the last few years. In April 2017, on one Saturday afternoon, I saw three patients who had overdosed on fentanyl in a twelve-bed, freestanding emergency room in

Franklin, Ohio. The amount of Narcan needed to resuscitate an overdose victim began to climb.

Narcan rescues, new cases of hepatitis C, and devastating infections causing brain infection, heart infection, and paralysis became a daily part of existence in the medical environment. Adolescents were buying designer drugs from the "dark web"; adult users were buying kratom from local headshops; and pressed fentanyl pills that looked identical to Xanax and Vicodin became common. Oftentimes, patients arrived at the emergency room cold, even with hypothermia, because the concerned family used ice as a noxious stimulus to try to keep the overdose victim breathing. Prolonged attempts at home resuscitation often led to real organ damage, requiring hospitalization. We were sending twenty-somethings to hospice for end-of-life care. Patients who were revived wanted nothing more than to get out of the emergency room; after all, they were forced into acute withdrawal and felt horrible.

Something had to be done. To respond to these situations, we set up our Pause treatment protocol in the hospital's electronic records system so that secure ordering of non-opioid medications was the rule. We provided ample education and worked with the marketing department to create an easily remembered visual image. Noting that some of the opioid dosing needed to be better controlled, safeguards were built into the system so that high doses of opioids became a rare exception. We established similar safeguards, warning against the concomitant use of benzodiazepines and opioids. During the experience surrounding my stolen DEA number, I learned that the detective could reference my own prescribing pattern. I wondered why this type of transparency was not built into a platform to compare prescribing habits of providers, so we built that report. We started to review morphine equivalents prescribed per patient by a provider on a monthly basis and provided education when providers hit the higher end of the spectrum, the so-called "candy man" effect. Through all of these concentrated measures, we reduced repetitive emergency department visits by over 50 percent. Despite seeing sick medical and trauma patients in our emergency rooms, the rate of opioid prescribing is down over 20 percent since 2013, and the results are sustainable.

The burnout effect of demanding, manipulative patients and threats of violence was finally dissipating. My love of the job returned. The Pause to address patient safety through prescribing became a personal and professional safety net for me and for my team.

But the work is not done. We continue to revise our methods and educate people about pain pathways and treatment options. We believe that a revised medical school curriculum is integral to the safety of our future generations. We've shared the Pause protocol on our website (https://www.ketteringhealth.org/pause) so that more providers can access it. We recommend therapies, massage, and other proven treatment modalities along with medications. Now, with DEA waiver training under my belt, I have advanced medical and pharmaceutical knowledge regarding substance use disorder and its management. Together, in Dayton, we will replace the "Overdose Capital" with a bright and sustainable community.

*All names are fictional.

*Nancy Pook, MD, is an emergency physician, community educator, and founder of the Pause program at Kettering Health Network. As a clinical faculty member of Wright State University Boonshoft School of Medicine, she has educated hundreds on emergency response protocols and community wellness education.*

# 41

## RECONNECTING THROUGH RHYTHM

### A Symphony and Recovery

WARREN W. HYER
(DELAWARE)

The young woman hastily aimed the plastic shaker toward my out-stretched open hand. She missed my palm, and the shaker, shaped like an oversized lemon, bounced to the floor. Around the circle more shakers were being passed from person to person, the laughter and the energy in the room building as we picked up the tempo of the "take-and-pass" exercise.

"Let's reverse the direction," I said, eliciting groans and hoots this time. More shakers slipped to the floor.

"The rule is you can't pick them up," I directed. "Keep the circle going!"

After a few more passes, I called for everyone to stop. There were smiles on flushed faces around the room, including a big smile on my own. There were shakers on the floor, but a few held theirs up like a trophy. This morning's intensive outpatient program participants had just completed a break-the-ice exercise called "Shaker Pass," opening up their twice-a-month therapeutic drumming session.

So what's the executive director of the local symphony (and a classical timpanist at that) doing sitting in an intensive outpatient center while plastic lemons fly around the room? Since 2013, I have been facilitating therapeutic drumming programs in our adult and juvenile courts in Delaware County. The Central Ohio Symphony began working with our local juvenile court in a program I titled "Reconnecting." Reconnecting was designed as a therapeutic drumming program for juvenile offenders with mental illness or substance abuse/addiction issues.

The Treatment Court of the Delaware County Juvenile Court helps juveniles gain control over their illness or addiction, take responsibility for both their offense and their personal development, and reconnect as healthier individuals to their families and community.

Reconnecting helps juveniles learn to express their emotions and feelings through use of a therapeutic drumming circle. A counselor from Maryhaven, a local treatment provider, and I trained in a national program of therapeutic drumming protocols and led the sessions. The goal is not to create musicians or even teach music. The goals are to give juveniles—many of whom have broken family and community relationships—positive and new outlets for expressions, and to help them find the motivation to progress positively through the phases of the Treatment Court. At its inception, Reconnecting was the first—and is possibly still the only existing—partnership nationwide between a court and an orchestra where orchestra musicians work directly with offenders.

Every year I attend the Percussive Arts Society International Convention where percussionists from around the world present on a variety of topics ranging from academic issues to performance techniques. In 2012, my wife, who works for Delaware County Juvenile Court, came running out of a session and said, "You have to see this!" She had just observed a presentation on therapeutic drumming. Later that day she pulled me into another session on therapeutic drumming—I was hooked. I approached the court about the possibility of creating a therapeutic drumming program for juveniles. Months after I first approached the court with the idea, the symphony, Maryhaven, and the Juvenile Court launched Reconnecting.

Five years later, the symphony's therapeutic drumming program has expanded to Alzheimer circles, alternative schools, and Maryhaven's Delaware-based Intensive Outpatient program.

Like much of Ohio, Delaware County is in the midst of an opioid epidemic. Like Delaware County, our participants are almost exclusively white. The county's median household income is $94,200, but our participants tend to be working-class or indigent. Many are not working and live with family members. We don't deal with those at the upper end of the economic spectrum—I assume because they're seeking private treatment elsewhere or have insurance limitations. All the same, the benefits of therapeutic drumming are universal.

Based on what the participants choose to reveal in drumming, it is my impression that the proportion of participants who are in treatment for opioids has increased steadily. We do not ask, but the participants can bring up their substance abuse issues if they want to, and often some do. Invariably, the underlying substance is an opioid.

Why is therapeutic drumming appropriate for dealing with addiction issues? Here's why: because it works. It works not as a "cure" for addiction, but as an additional tool for the participants as they try to overcome their addiction and build new lives.

There are some key factors that make Reconnecting effective. Drumming is open to all levels of ability and to all ages. Participants do not need any musical training or prior experience to benefit from the program. During the sessions, participants frequently share aspects of their lives that even their providers do not know about. Staff at Maryhaven are then able to build on this information to increase successful outcomes.

The Remo HealthRHYTHMS protocol serves as the outline for each session. It looks something like this:

1. Introducing the Program (who the facilitators are and the benefits of drumming)
2. Wellness Exercise (stretching, deep breathing)
3. Breaking the Ice (Shaker Pass, metaphors of dealing with change)
4. The ABCs of Drumming (how to play the drums—in one minute!)
5. Rhythmic Naming (performing their names on the drum and the group responding, an empowerment technique)
6. Entrainment Building (playing what evolves from the group, facilitated group drumming)
7. Inspirational Beats (moving from challenges to resolutions or goals)
8. Guided Imagery (transferring participants to a place of comfort and calm)
9. Closing Wellness Exercise (similar to opening Wellness Exercise)
10. The Finale (each participant says one word about how they feel)

The protocol is only a starting point. Each drumming session can go in a different direction. As the participants start to talk, they can set the direction of the session. We often use small objects as metaphors to set a direction. We rotate through themes, like trust, change, and triggers. It is rewarding to try a technique and see the participants run with it. It is exciting to see them gaining insights and making personal links.

I don't know who will be there when I arrive. I have no idea who is there or why, other than knowing generally that they are there because of substance abuse. As a facilitator, I put everyone on the same level. Unlike court programs in which participants progress through phases, our program has no singular starting point. There is no beginner class.

New participants may appear at each session. First-time drummers tend not to say a lot and often have a puzzled look. When we go around the circle drumming names—a reaffirming technique—a first-time participant may just say her name quietly, hit the drum once, and be done with it. As the weeks go by and the new participants become more comfortable, they tend to open up with more playing and more talk.

Therapeutic drumming is not a treatment. It is a voice. Drumming provides participants with a way to evaluate themselves and their progress. Facilitators allow participants to respond as they want. There is no judgment. Participants are not forced to respond. They can take part in any portion of the session, including none.

Often the participants start talking about a hope, a dream, or a goal—something personal—and it turns out that whatever concern they are voicing often becomes the theme for that day. Drumming can be a positive trigger for more insight into treatment.

Sometimes, participants experience immediate change. They have already been in treatment for a few hours that day. They're tired and worn out from talking and working at their other classes. Drumming gets them smiling and laughing. Participants are relaxed when they drum. They're calm. Their facial expressions and their body language reflect their changing moods. Some may open up, and the drumming helps strengthen their bond as a group. It is a time to express, share, and learn from each other.

Everything we do is metaphor-based. Take the Shaker Pass: we change directions, we change tempos, we rely on each other and build trust that the shaker is coming and going smoothly through our hands. Change is something the participants have to learn to deal with in their lives. If change with a plastic shaker is hard, just imagine the changes participants face in treatment. When someone drops a shaker, we instruct them to let it go. It is hard for some to do that, a huge mental shift. Participants have to change their personal habits, letting go of old habits and old ways of life.

The mission statement of the Central Ohio Symphony is "Engage the Community through Music." Our goal is to reach every member of our greater community, regardless of whether they ever buy a ticket for one of our concerts. I am proud of the many ways the symphony strives to implement our mission. Our therapeutic drumming programs may be our greatest legacy.

*During **Warren Hyer**'s tenure as Executive Director, the Central Ohio Symphony of Delaware has grown to be a sixty-five-member professional ensemble with over 600 season subscribers and an annual free Fourth of July concert that attracts over 8,000 people. The symphony has gained a national reputation for its groundbreaking community engagement projects.*

# 42

# RURAL CHALLENGES, RURAL SOLUTIONS

STEVEN MARTIN, AMY FANOUS,
AND KATIE WESTGERDES
(ADA)

## CONFRONTING THE CHALLENGES
## (STEVEN MARTIN)

As a pharmacist and the academic dean at Ohio Northern University's Raabe College of Pharmacy, I've observed the tremendous challenges that exist in rural areas. There is a lack of focus on education, prevention, and increased access to treatment resources for prescription and nonprescription opioid drug use. People in Hardin County have to travel thirty miles or more to access a physician or clinic that provides treatment for addiction. Efforts are underway to provide education in the schools and establish prevention and early intervention services, but the infrastructure is sufficient only in the county seat, Kenton. There is no structure, and there are often no resources, in the many satellite communities that dot the county. A high school student who suffers from depression because of a difficult home life may turn to substance abuse to self-medicate his anxiety and depression. When that student is caught with illegal substances and the court orders substance abuse treatment instead of prison, there is often nowhere for him to receive that treatment. Even if there was a facility somewhere in the surrounding counties that could accept him, the student would have to rely on parents or family to get him to treatment, and the family was often the cause of the substance abuse problem in the first place. Upwards of 50 percent of the adult population in the county does not have a car or other means of transportation.

Opioid abuse touches all aspects of life in this community. Poverty is rampant in Hardin County, and access to adequate housing, food, and transportation is a daily concern for a large percentage of the population. A quarter of children in the county live in poverty. More than two-thirds of adults are overweight or obese. Rates of tobacco use and binge drinking exceed state averages. In our county, there are some well-paying factory jobs at an International Paper factory, but most of the other jobs are low-skilled, low-wage, and seasonal—mostly farm—jobs. It's hard to live (not to mention afford treatment) on those types of jobs, especially for families. That employment situation leads to unstable family situations and single-parent households. More than half of the births in the county are to single mothers. These factors all affect drug use.

In response to rising rates of opioid abuse, there has been a concerted statewide effort to reduce the prescribing of opioid medications. This effort has reduced the number of "pill mills" and other illicit outlets for opioid prescriptions. But it has driven many people who were addicted to prescription medications to illegal drugs like heroin. Overdose deaths have exposed high rates of fentanyl, carfentanil, and other synthetic opioids mixed in with the supply of heroin. To complicate these concerns, "cocktails" are commonly used to enhance the effect of the opioid, including the addition of benzodiazepines, gabapentin, cocaine, marijuana, and methamphetamine. Patients may present legal prescriptions to the pharmacy but then mix them with illegal substances bought on the street.

As a pharmacist and the dean of a pharmacy school, I've encountered these problems firsthand. There is a woman in the county—unemployed, single, living with her two children—who every day sends her son to school, packs her daughter in the car, and then travels to Columbus to buy heroin. She grew up in a poor, broken family and didn't complete high school. She became addicted to Vicodin after she sustained a minor injury when she was in her early twenties, and her addiction ended any interest in employment. Her drug use escalated through Percocet, Dilaudid, and then OxyContin. When her supply of prescription opioids was stopped, she turned to heroin.

We recognize that illicit drug use is a law enforcement problem, but we also know that it is a health concern. In response, we offer our students the opportunity to obtain mental health first aid certification so that they know how to recognize substance abuse and behavioral health risks.

Hardin County is a federally designated health professional shortage area, which means that very few primary care providers, psychiatrists, or psychologists practice in the area. This is an underlying cause as to why our county law enforcement is disconnected from its medical community.

In 2010, Hardin County Juvenile Court received $1.2 million to implement a "Reclaiming Futures" Juvenile Drug Court, whose mission is to "set a new direction and sense of purpose for young people and their families in juvenile court by reducing substance abuse and delinquency." This drug court is focused on moving inmates with substance use disorders into addiction treatment services, but a lack of easy access to drug-screening services, medication-assisted treatment programs, or public transportation makes transitioning to outpatient treatment difficult.

Ohio Northern University has tried to bridge the gaps. I believe that is a role that all universities should be playing in their communities. We engage students in service learning projects. The university participates in a county coalition to address substance abuse, and we have even established a task force to bring together the many campus programs, services, and people who are providing prevention, treatment, or recovery services for the community. Through grant funding, we bring together the local agencies that play a role in reducing substance abuse in the county. Our goal is to unify the efforts of our local agencies toward a common set of goals. We recognize that without coordination among all stakeholders, it's unlikely that real progress can be made.

At the College of Pharmacy, we are particularly excited about our federally funded mobile clinic and our community pharmacy. We hope that by supporting these projects, and others, we will be doing our part.

## A ROLE FOR MOBILE CLINICS
### (AMY FANOUS)

As director of the ONU HealthWise Mobile Clinic, I have observed firsthand the risk of substance abuse that patients in rural areas experience due to their socioeconomic status. Poverty, unemployment, and poor housing lead to increased anxiety and all the other behavioral health problems we see in the mobile clinic. To better serve our area, we go where we can get the best attendance—community centers and other places that provide services, such as free dinners, for the economically disadvantaged. At these clinics, we provide care for people who have had, or are currently dealing with, addiction to alcohol, methamphetamine, cocaine, heroin, and prescription drugs.

The mobile clinic operates out of a customized medical motor coach. The clinic was originally designed to provide an entry point into the health care system for Hardin County residents in need of primary care. Those who come to the mobile clinic typically don't have a consistent primary care provider. The clinic offers a nonthreatening option for health care to those who do not want to share their addiction concerns with their regular doctor, and to those who know they need help but have nowhere else to turn. We are in the process not only of expanding our services to persons with substance abuse problems but also of enlarging our geographical service area—which now includes the rural areas of adjacent Hancock and Allen counties. We will now screen for substance abuse and behavioral health problems among junior-high- and high-school-aged children. We are finding ways to evolve.

We recognize that most people don't want to be addicted or live the chaotic life that addiction brings. All too often, the only place for rural residents to go is an emergency department—which is expensive and often requires going to another county or being arrested. We are trying to break down barriers to access. In addition to screening services, we provide interventions and connect patients to treatment services in the region. We also provide case management to improve adherence to treatment and reduce relapse.

But as we expand services and screenings, I worry about the lack of follow-up services to manage those problems. When we identify a junior high school student who uses marijuana and who is at risk for progression to prescription drugs or other illicit agents, where do we refer them for care? We don't even have a full-time pediatrician in the county, let alone someone who specializes in pediatric substance abuse. When we identify a young man who is suffering from depression, who will manage his care? We also lack psychiatrists in the county, and a nonemergency psychiatric appointment can require months of waiting for availability in adjacent counties. In 2017 we began offering free hepatitis C testing because of the risk that exists among the substance abuse disorder population. We regularly see patients who use injectable drugs, but the county doesn't offer a needle exchange program.

One goal of the mobile clinic is to improve access to health education for children and adults. Substance abuse and behavioral health problems are often not spoken about in families or in schools; the topics are still taboo in rural, conservative areas like Hardin County. The education we provide to students is valuable only if parents and teachers are also involved in discussing these same problems. Depression and anxiety are not uncommon among our community's youth, yet children may lack the ability to openly discuss these concerns with adults. We will begin offering Mental Health First Aid certification this fall to give residents the skills to help others who may be developing a mental health or substance abuse problem or who may be experiencing a crisis. We hope that as more members of the community understand the risk factors and warning signs, the negative outcomes of substance abuse will decrease.

## THE ROLE OF COMMUNITY PHARMACIES
### (KATIE WESTGERDES)

Community pharmacies serve an important role in health care. People visit them primarily to fill medication prescriptions, but also to receive medical advice from pharmacists—typically provided at no cost and with no appointment. They are the most accessible place for people to see a licensed and reputable health care provider.

In the past, community pharmacists have played a role in identifying and preventing illegal prescriptions for controlled substances from being dispensed. I've had someone hand in a prescription for Vicodin that was originally written for ten tablets, but a zero had been added to make it 100. I've seen prescriptions that had unusually high quantities of Percocet or OxyContin. I called the physician's office to confirm the amount, only to find that their prescription sheets had been stolen. Oftentimes these people go to many different pharmacies using the same tactics. I've also had patients come in with legitimate prescriptions for pain medications from physicians who are well-known pain pill prescribers. Pharmacists know which physicians prescribe a lot of narcotics—patients figure that out pretty quickly too.

With the prescription-drug-monitoring programs now in place in forty-nine states, we have more tools available As a result, there has been a significant reduction in illegal prescriptions, and I've had fewer experiences like those described above. Today, however, greater societal and health-related issues confront the community pharmacist.

Access to quality care in Ohio is not sufficient to meet the needs of the opioid epidemic. There are limited providers and a wide variability in the quality of substance abuse care. Quality care requires that clinicians treat the whole patient.

I had a patient who came to the pharmacy with very high blood pressure, nearly in hypertensive crisis. Unfortunately, the addiction specialist who was providing that patient's medical care refused to manage the blood pressure. This is a common occurrence, and it affects the patient beyond their physical health. It's hard to motivate a patient to care about his or her entire health, and not just the substance abuse concerns, if the care provider does not show interest in treating *all* the medical and psychological concerns of the patient.

The current crisis in opioid abuse is perpetuated by the disconnect in our health care system. Physicians who are not certified as behavioral health providers often won't prescribe medications that treat those conditions, and in some instances they are by law unable to. In turn, addiction and behavioral health specialists usually won't manage medical conditions that go beyond their specialty. This fragmented system requires a patient to have multiple physicians to manage their health. That means multiple doctor appointments, multiple trips to medical offices, multiple days off from work, multiple copays or out-of-pocket expenses, and physicians who don't coordinate care with each other.

Substance abuse treatment is not standardized, and because of the many varied treatment paths, patient adherence to therapy, and the success of those therapies, are poor. Without structure and clear participation requirements, patients are likely to resume drug use or begin abusing the drug that is treating the addiction—replacing one addiction with another. As a community pharmacist, my hands are often tied. This is a prescriber issue, and I struggle to get the prescriber to change the patient therapy. I can refuse to fill the prescription, but that could push the patient back to street drugs. I can demand that the prescription be filled only one day before the patient runs out, but that isn't as impactful as lowering the dose. I can notify the prescriber of red flags, but again, that doesn't address the real issue. What I can offer is education. Whenever I can, I help patients understand the best path forward—if they are interested in listening.

Treatment can be tedious. I've worked with many patients who experience fatigue from working with the "health care system." Patients must wait for prior authorizations and drug test results before they can get their medication. Some patients go for days or weeks without medication or have to buy just enough to "get through." I had a patient who was given a prescription for one week's supply of medication at a time. It took so long to obtain their required insurance company's prior authorization that they had to come in each day to buy just one tablet, even though their prescription was written for the medication to be taken three times daily. Without insurance, the patient could afford to buy only one tablet at a time. By the time the prior authorization was approved, it was time to go back to the doctor's office and get a new prescription.

We have to think broadly. After all, substance use disorder doesn't just affect the patient. In our community pharmacy, we provide care for the entire family. The lack of care for children by addicted parents often leads to changes in dietary, physical, and mental health for the children—and it can result in situations of child abuse and neglect. All of the negative changes in family dynamics have a direct effect on our communities. Not only does the opioid crisis increase crime and violence, but it stresses resources.

Pharmacists must provide care coordination and social service assistance and must also serve as a backstop for inappropriate or illegal prescribing. As integral parts of our communities, we see the impact of the opioid epidemic firsthand. We have an obligation not only to help educate the public about this epidemic, but also to help our patients and their families heal. When kids come into the pharmacy, I make an effort to talk directly to them, to say hello, or to show them what's going on behind that big counter. I want children to grow up knowing that they can always come talk to a pharmacist.

*Steven Martin, PharmD, is Dean of the Raabe College of Pharmacy at Ohio Northern University. Amy Fanous, PharmD, is Director of the ONU HealthWise Mobile Clinic. Katie Westgerdes, PharmD, is Manager of the ONU HealthWise Community Pharmacy.*

# 43

## A WAY FORWARD
## FOR MOMS AND BABIES

RICHARD MASSATTI
(COLUMBUS)

"You won't believe what just happened." I had just returned to the hospital bedside, where my wife was recovering from a cesarean section. No one, neither patients nor staff, was in the area, so I could not imagine what had unfolded while I was in the nursery with the twins. "A woman came in here and was looking through all of the drawers and cupboards. . . ." I was confused, "You mean a nurse?" My wife continued, "No, a patient. She was in a gown. She had just given birth and was looking for drugs in the cabinets." A million questions flitted through my mind: "Are you okay? Where is she now?"

Thankfully, security had discovered the woman and taken her to a locked ward. My wife was safe and had never been touched or threatened by the intruder. But the event left a mark on both of our hearts—our joy discolored by someone else's suffering. And that's what this woman's behavior indicated: suffering. The intense cravings she was experiencing meant that she was compelled to seek an opioid or else she would soon be suffering the effects of withdrawal. No one would willingly abandon their newborn or root through someone else's belongings if they were in the right state of mind. But the disease of addiction does not care about a newborn child, a family, or employment; it only cares about feeding itself.

I was certainly no stranger to the epidemic, but rarely had my experience been so up close and personal. In 2010 the Ohio Department of Alcohol and Drug Addiction Services hired a small team to restart the Ohio Substance Abuse Monitoring Network. Our goal was to monitor emerging statewide drug trends by conducting interviews with persons in treatment, clinicians, and law enforcement personnel. As the program's coordinator, I managed teams who went out to do face-to-face interviews and helped regional epidemiologists prepare their narratives for our final reports.

Early on, there were stories about the hardships facing pregnant women with opioid use disorder. Many of these women were poor. Housing, transportation, childcare, and employment were all challenges. Pregnant women were concerned about the health impacts of drug use on their babies. Those who had just delivered discovered that some of their babies had neonatal abstinence syndrome (NAS), or drug withdrawal that could result in extended stays in the neonatal intensive care unit. Common symptoms include low birth weight, respiratory problems, feeding difficulties, and seizures or tremors.

We could see that the drug epidemic was getting worse, but no one really knew what the impact was specifically on moms and babies. Even our own research was limited because so few pregnant women participated in our interviews. Moreover, there had never been a statewide investigation, so no one could explain the extent of the problem. In partnership with the Ohio Department of Health, our organization collaborated to find out the scope and breadth of the problem.

It did not take us long to understand that the problem was growing worse every year. The number of pregnant women diagnosed with a substance use disorder at time of delivery grew nearly every year, from 1,554 cases in 2004 to 4,013 cases in 2015. Likewise, the number of admissions for infants diagnosed with NAS grew as well from 199 in 2004 to 2,174 in 2015. Treatment costs for these babies were staggering: over $133 million in 2015 was spent on the infants because most ended up in the neonatal intensive care unit for about fourteen days. In fact, datasets from every state agency were showing the same trends; not only was the opioid epidemic getting worse, but it was growing for all populations.

We learned the scope of the problem through our research and began speaking with state officials about solutions. But solutions were difficult to find because there were no preconceived ideas on which one could reliably and safely solve the problem. Certainly the research indicated a need for an array of services to wrap care around both mother and child, but there was no solid evidence-based program to plan and implement. It would take something new and innovative to address the issue. So a group of stakeholders from the governor's office, the Office of Health Transformation, the Department of Medicaid, and our department began planning an initiative to address the growing needs of pregnant women with opioid use disorder. The state's response to this crisis was the Maternal Opiate Medical Supports (MOMS) program, a $4.2 million program to fund innovative services. The primary goal of this two-year pilot program was to develop and implement a model for coordinated care through a maternal care home for this population. Four programs across the state were selected to provide a team-based delivery model that emphasized care coordination, provision of wrap-around services, and other appropriate medical care and case management. MOMS teams were led by care coordinators who ensured consistency in communication between clients and program partners, no matter whether that partner was an obstetrician, a behavioral health provider, an insurance case manager, a justice professional, a child welfare professional, or some other entity.

MOMS turned out to be a success on many fronts. Over 300 women were involved in services over the course of the project, and they had significantly better outcomes than similar women who did not receive support. Women involved in this program had better behavioral health treatment retention and were more likely to use medication-assisted treatment before and after delivery. They also engaged with obstetric providers earlier in their pregnancy and had more prenatal appointments than those not in the program. Family stability also appeared to be improved. Within eighteen months of delivery, women in the program experienced fewer cases of abuse and neglect and fewer cases of foster care. Outcomes for infants were mixed. While most pregnancies (95 percent) were successfully delivered, cases of NAS were slightly higher for MOMS participants than babies of similarly situated women. Low birth weight and admissions to the neonatal intensive care unit were about the same for all infants. Interestingly, MOMS participants with medication-assisted treatment in the third trimester had babies with significantly fewer days in the neonatal intensive care unit than MOMS participants who did not receive medication-assisted treatment in the third trimester.

The MOMS project had clearly improved many outcomes for women and infants. The project's success drew upon an intensive process of self-reflection and communication with other sites. Frequent technical assistance calls helped all the sites understand what was and was not working, and it helped all of the projects refine their programming in real time. Here are some of the key lessons that can serve as a template for creating similar programming:

1. Managed care Medicaid insurance plans are part of the solution: insurance plans are typically regarded by behavioral health care providers and patients alike as bureaucratic institutions characterized by red tape. But in reality, we've found that they can be very helpful. Some behavioral health organizations contact managed care plans only for billing issues, because they are unaware that they offer additional patient services. Others are unaware that they could use the state's bargaining power to help change the system. In order to capitalize on the potential of these public insurance plans, we need to educate behavioral health providers and patients about services. For example, our providers now are trained to enroll women in high-risk case management plans and to connect women with treatment incentives and transportation benefits. We also found that change was necessary because women were currently experiencing a delay in receiving medication-assisted treatment. Our statewide steering committee invited managed care plans to help navigate such barriers so that physicians were allowed to have "gold card" access to medication, saving the patient from any delays in treatment.

2. Care coordination is essential: pregnancy is a difficult time for any woman to navigate the health care system, let alone a woman with a substance use disorder. Imagine being pregnant and struggling every day with cravings for alcohol and other drugs. Then add in the complex systems in which these women are involved: the court system; the behavioral health system, which may have two or more providers; the child welfare system, if the woman is not a first-time mother; the Medicaid system; and the physical health care system. We found that it was common for the women to have six or more persons trying to coordinate their care. The MOMS program funded a position to coordinate care among these entities, and those positions proved critical to help-

ing women navigate the complex myriad of services. Care coordinators ensured that the appropriate release-of-information documents were signed so that all parties involved in patient care could easily communicate through individual and or team-based calls and meetings.

3. Co-location of health care services is important. Silos are common in health care: everyone is located under a different roof, and programs are generally not in close proximity. This situation created a lot of challenges for women enrolled in our program because many did not have transportation. Even the ones who were lucky enough to live on or near a bus line did not necessarily have a clear route to all of their needed services. Some people might challenge the advantages of co-location, saying that "the obstetrician is just located one mile away," but that type of thinking ignores the transportation coordination that needs to occur in the mother's life. What is one mile for you might as well be one hundred miles for her on a bad day.

4. Questions about basic needs should be reiterated at every visit: women with substance use disorder usually have chaotic lives. Our programs had women who slept on friend's couches, on boyfriends' couches, or in parents' homes. Some of these women simply could not find a recovery residence that would take them and their children, while others had debt problems and a history of evictions that served as a barrier to securing housing. In addition to housing, our programs found that women had other basic needs. Food insecurity was common. Safety issues with abusive partners were also present. All of these factors only served to make recovery that much harder.

5. Certain health topics need to be addressed: tobacco use was prevalent among MOMS participants, with over two-thirds smoking in the third trimester, on average eight cigarettes a day. Women reported that they frequently smoked to relieve stress. Some were hesitant to give up smoking because they had no other coping skills. Unfortunately, this issue resulted in poor infant health outcomes like low birth weight. Behavioral providers should address tobacco use as early as possible to ensure that each pregnancy is as healthy as possible.

Health providers should also help women think about planning for the next pregnancy. Some of our women became pregnant with another child during the course of our pilot program. Many pregnancies are greeted with joy, but it can be more complicated for women in the early stages of recovery. Long-acting, reversible birth control is an important option for women at risk of having an unplanned pregnancy. Birth control helps women put their recovery first, so that they can begin the next pregnancy on their own terms.

6. Child welfare agencies play an important role: it was hard to raise the topic of child welfare on our calls. Some physicians in our project were hesitant to refer to child welfare because they were concerned that women would stop all prenatal care. Counties have different child welfare policies and procedures, which makes the system confusing. The Department of Job and Family Services was quick to help our teams navigate federal and state legislation as well as develop a common way for our system to engage in discussions that were more uniform. We began to brainstorm ideas with local child welfare partners about better ways to integrate services. Some of our sites began to host quarterly meetings with local child welfare offices so that women could meet the staff and ask questions. These meetings left women feeling empowered because they allowed them to address their fears without worrying about reprisal. Child welfare staff were able to educate clients about special services available through their local departments. Staff also reassured clients that they could collaborate on the development of a "plan of safe care" between child welfare staff and expectant mothers that would foster the mother's recovery while ensuring child safety.

7. We must carefully follow the infant's health: women need to know what to expect after the delivery of their baby. Oftentimes, women believed the myth that their babies would not develop NAS if they were on medication-assisted treatment. Medical staff had to educate them that the development of this condition was complex and that their babies may still develop it shortly after birth. During our project the Ohio Perinatal Quality Collaborative developed a wonderful set of resources for women on topics ranging from swaddling to the basics of NAS. We disseminated these materials to all of our sites, and women found them very helpful. That said, one of our lessons was to underscore the importance of pediatric care, because many of the women did not

meet the American Academy of Pediatrics standards of infant care during the first six months. Drug-exposed infants may have complicated health outcomes. Therefore, it is especially important for parents to attend all of the pediatric wellness visits and let the physician know about any unusual symptoms.

The opioid epidemic will subside over time, but substance use will always be present during pregnancy at some level. By developing programs that focus on integrated care like MOMS, we can help women and babies achieve better outcomes. My desire is that the hard-fought changes we make today will be preserved for the women of tomorrow, so that those who suffer in darkness will more easily see the light of hope.

*Rick Massatti, PhD, MSW, MPH, LSW, is the State Opioid Treatment Authority at the Ohio Department of Mental Health and Addiction Services. Currently he is coordinating the efforts to bring new opioid treatment programs into the state and implement a workforce development strategy to increase interest in medication-assisted treatment.*

# 44

## FROM THE FRONT PAGES
## TO THE FRONT LINES

DARREN ADAMS
(PORTSMOUTH)

Though you don't always hear them in the media, there are many positive things to say about Portsmouth. This city has a lot of history. It was known in the past mostly for its foothold in the steel and shoe industries. And at one time it was a thriving town. We're right here on the Ohio River and are famous for the murals on our floodwalls. The cost of living is good. The people down here are totally amazing. Southern Ohio Medical Center, the hospital that I work for, is topnotch, really a gem. All of these things make being here almost perfect. Plus you get all the benefits of a small town, but you're only two hours from large metropolitan areas: two hours from Cincinnati, two hours from Columbus, two hours from Lexington. Portsmouth truly is an amazing place.

Of course, our city has gained national attention because the opioid crisis hit it so hard. I have a unique perspective to share because I'm not only an obstetrician-gynecologist but also the county coroner. I get to see what's out in the field while doing coroner work, but I also get to see what's out in the field because I deliver babies with neonatal abstinence syndrome, or NAS. So I get to see what's happening in both places.

Being in this dual role, I am in a position to try to help the situation. I was one of the first obstetrician-gynecologists working on new approaches in Southeast Ohio so that we could have healthy babies born without much withdrawal. One of the first new approaches involved weaning mothers down to the lowest tolerable dose of buprenorphine before delivery. This approach has allowed newborns to experience less withdrawal. They may still go through withdrawal, but not as bad a withdrawal as when their mothers were on heroin or other opioids. More recently, we've tried another approach to establish an opioid-free pain pathway after C-sections. There are two different ways of doing it: (1) by using a transverse abdominis plane (or TAP) block which anesthetizes the nerves around the abdomen; or (2) by infiltration of the muscle, above the fascia. This opioid-free pain pathway has the potential to decrease the risk of moms being exposed to narcotics and lowers their chance of being addicted down the road. As we have learned, with some people, all it takes is one dose of narcotics and they get hooked.

So if we can avoid that first contact, hopefully we can prevent addiction from arising down the road. And now we have most of the obstetricians in our county on board with this new approach. Our results have been very positive: after a C-section, about 65 percent of women at our facility are requiring either zero or just one dose of narcotics, so we have greatly reduced the exposure rate. We're doing everything we can to prevent future addiction as well as help people who are currently struggling with an addiction. We've got tons of resources, but even tons of resources is not enough. We don't have enough mental health practitioners to deal with the emotional side of things. We also need more doctors who can do MAT.

Even as we are addressing the present situation, we need to think about the future. For example, it's important to think about young medical professionals coming up in the state. My life has been a little different from most because I was an older student when I went to medical school. Before medical school I assisted on autopsies, so my perspective is a little skewed. But I do think that if we want physicians to be part of the solution, then medical students and other upcoming health professionals have to receive more training on alternative pathways for pain control—other than narcotics—so we can prevent them from even starting down that road of addiction.

Increasingly, I tell many of my patients, "I know you're in pain, but if I can treat your pain with non-narcotic pain relief so we don't go down this path, being in pain is better than being dead." Oftentimes, they laugh. But they also understand what I mean. Some pain is better than the alternative. To learn these dynamics in our state, more medical students need to be exposed to hot areas where addiction and overdose are happening. More students need to be in the trenches and see what's going on. It's an eye-opener if you've never seen it. If you come from an affluent place and you've never worked a real job, or if you went through undergrad right into medical school and you see this for the first time, it's an eye-opener.

We've gone through a real reckoning in this crisis. It is affecting everybody. The problem is that everybody thinks they're immune. But I can tell you from experience that it doesn't matter if you're rich or poor or where you live; it's most likely going to affect you eventually in some way. My experience in Portsmouth has been that we are about ten years ahead of everybody else in terms of the effects this crisis has had on our city. Now that the big centers in the big cities are being affected, people say things like, "Oh, man, there's a problem." No, there's *been* a problem—they just didn't see it. And it will continue to be a problem until we can educate our children that another lifestyle is possible, that there's a different way out there. Even if your mom and dad are taking opioids, you don't need to go down that path. But we've got to start early, and it's got to be comprehensive. I'm talking education, infrastructure, transportation, health care—comprehensive.

I was appointed to the Ohio Commission on Infant Mortality, and there, too, we find exactly the same problems. One additional problem, however, is that all of our agencies have not yet connected, and if they don't connect, we're never going to be able to address the social determinants of health that lead to these poor outcomes. We have a beautiful health coalition in Portsmouth. It was established because it had to be. It's big, but it's still not big enough. We need things to click not just at the local level, say, in a four-block radius in certain hot spots, but you've got to have everybody on board, from the state down to the community—everybody fighting as a unit. You've got to have the churches involved, too. We need the county level, the state level, the federal level—we need everybody to be able to talk just to make sure we know where we are. But that's not happening yet. We're getting there, but we're not there yet.

As coroner, if I send a body out for an autopsy and the autopsy shows that the death was either drug-related or a direct drug overdose, then I plot that data on a map to see where certain hot spots are. It may or may not be useful, but I feel I have to do something and that's what I can do as coroner. Similarly, if there's a hot batch of heroin that we know is laced with fentanyl or carfentanil, an alert will be sent out to warn people to be on the lookout: "Hey, there's some bad stuff out there." Occasionally, though, the warning backfires because some of the addicts want that hot stuff because it makes them feel really good.

When only the traditional opioids were being used, we had something of a handle on the problem, and things were getting better. Our rate of overdoses was beginning to take a dive before fentanyl came out. And now carfentanil has made it even worse. It's frustrating. But we keep fighting.

My primary job as coroner is to speak for the dead because they can't. It is my job to learn exactly what happened to them, and I do my best to figure out a cause and manner of death. I do that to the best of my ability. I take it seriously.

The sheer magnitude of the crisis presents challenges, however. Some people get upset if one of their loved ones passes away and it looks like it's a natural death. Since Scioto is a small county, our budget is limited. This means, realistically, that I cannot send every decedent for an autopsy. If I did, I would bankrupt the county, since autopsies now cost almost $2,000 each. So if the death appears to be natural, if it's not a suicide, a homicide, or a death resulting from a fire or a car accident, sometimes I won't have the body autopsied. Is it possible we are missing some drug overdoses? Maybe. But most of the time if the decedent had health problems that I can attribute the death to, then I won't take the death as a coroner's case. Of course, if the person was under fifty, and I don't have a very good reason why it happened, I send the body for autopsy. We've got a huge, and ever rising, number of overdoses, or at least drug-related deaths. So that puts a lot of strain on the system.

Just recently, in the last three weeks, three children under six weeks died, and I don't know the outcome of those autopsies yet. But that's the first thing that runs through your head: What happened to those babies? Were they drug-related? Were they opioid-related? As a coroner I find these questions running through my mind. It's really unusual for a county of our size to have three six-week-olds die in three weeks. So until I get the autopsies and the toxicology back, I won't know. Could they be SIDS deaths? I don't know. Could it have been something more sinister? Given what our state, and our county, have been through, that's what I wonder.

It makes sense that since we were in the forefront of the crisis, especially because of the pill mills, we should be at the forefront of treating these problems on the obstetrical side of things. The obstetricians here at Southern Ohio Medical Center decided to do universal drug screening of the pregnant women who come into our labor room so that we can take better care of their babies. Our nursery has done an amazing job weaning these babies off these substances. We have some of the best hospital stay rates for these babies; we have narrowed the rates way down. We can get the babies in and get them out pretty quickly, and doing so leads to better outcomes.

Until we get this taken care of in a larger way, these kinds of interventions are what we need. This is a multifactorial problem. The problem starts well before the drugs. We know that Scioto County is well at the bottom of the rankings of Ohio's eighty-eight counties in health outcomes. The reason is our socioeconomic conditions, the social determinants of health: transportation, education, jobs, single-parent families. The problem is that you need to address all of them, and you can't afford to address all of them. In the end, we just do what we can.

But there is also reason for optimism. Because of the challenges we've faced in Portsmouth, we are also now at the forefront of efforts to address these issues. Our hope is that other people can use what we have learned. But our success does not overshadow the fact that there is a real need for resources. We're doing amazing things down here, but there is hardly any research being done on our use of the TAP block in postpartum women. I'm one of the very few obstetrician-gynecologists in the whole country doing it. I get calls from people wanting me to help train other doctors to do this procedure because not a lot of people know how to do it yet. So we're finding ways to make it work. It's just because of our size—we're so small and flying by the seat of our pants—that I don't have time to go out on the road and teach or do research. But really, this is a shame. The nurse manager of obstetrics or maternity services here at SOMC, accompanied by others, go all over the country and tell medical professionals how we wean babies off opioids and how well they do. Then these professionals also become part of a bigger group, the Ohio Perinatal Collaborative Group; they use some of our techniques, and we use some of theirs. But they're talking and really honing our methods to reduce the length of stay for these babies. They do amazing stuff. After all, we're seeing it first because we've been the epicenter for so long. Portsmouth has a lot to share with others.

*Darren Adams, DO, is an obstetrician-gynecologist. He is currently the Scioto County Coroner.*

McCormick Farmall M—Hessville, OH 2013. Credit: Terrance Reimer.

# PART FIVE

# CHALLENGING ASSUMPTIONS

Our contributors have provided powerful examples of how ordinary people have stepped up in a time of need. They have made clear that, to meet the challenges of the opioid crisis, many Ohioans have embraced a different role from the one in which they had been trained. As a result, bills have been passed, treatment facilities and safe houses built, and communities strengthened. Nonetheless, Ohio is still in the midst of a protracted grieving period and faces significant barriers to stemming opioid abuse and the long-term consequences of addiction. And while the solutions presented in the preceding section are vital to moving forward, we also know that questions and conversations that are even more difficult remain to be raised. This section shows that the problems that opioids have brought to our communities will not be addressed merely by making financial investments or changing laws. Rather, the larger question for the long-term health of our state—if we are to come out of this historical moment stronger and more humane—will be answered only by our willingness to change how we think. Such a transformation requires wrestling with some protracted and entrenched questions.

Contributors in this section emphasize the toxicity of stigma, racism, and unacknowledged privilege in how we think about addiction. They also remind us that the rise of addiction and overdose in certain regions has been used—inadvertently or not—to stereotype rural Ohioans. The good news is that throughout this section—and really this book—we have testimony from Ohioans who have had to acknowledge how easily those narratives fall apart. Opioids have transformed Ohio. And some of the very people and institutions that will help bring us out of this epidemic are unexpected, and sometimes highly stigmatized. The question is whether we are prepared to reflect critically on how we got to this point and explore how stigma and assumptions have prevented us from exploring creative and enduring solutions to both individual and social pain. Contributors in this section ask us to reconsider how we think about ourselves, our neighbors, and our fellow Ohioans—no matter how different our backgrounds may be.

# 45

## A GOOD FAMILY

CHRISTINE HUNT
(RUSSELLS POINT)

My husband and I were high school sweethearts at Columbus North High School. We met in the back of a friend's car as we were headed to a high school football game. We married a couple of years later, forty-five years ago. I never smoked, drank very little, and never used drugs. After marriage, we both joined the US Army under the "buddy" system and served together until after our first child was born. We decided we wanted our children to grow up around grandparents and family, so we returned to our home in Columbus. Dennis went to work, and I went to Ohio State to study landscape architecture. We bought a small house in Galloway. It was a struggle financially, but we had family support and support from our church. After graduation, I found a job, and we moved to northwest Columbus. Our children attended what we thought were the best public schools in our area. When our children were little, and on through their teenage years, they did baseball, basketball, football, cheerleading, and Taekwondo. We supported any extracurricular activity that they wanted to try and accompanied them for pizza and Dairy Queen at postgame gatherings. We bought a pop-up camper and spent free weekends camping, hiking, canoeing, swimming, fishing, and visiting historical sites and museums. In other words: we really enjoyed family life. One year we had an Ohio Historical Society pass, the next year COSI, and the next year the zoo. For us, life was about either work or

family. I believed that if I gave my kids a stable environment and surrounded them with a rich family life and a church home, they would
grow to be good people.

However, when Ian went to school at Indian Run Elementary in
Dublin, he started having some problems. At the age of seven, he was
getting upset with a classmate and leaving the building. I didn't know
it then, but he was being bullied. The school recommended we get him
into counseling, which we did. The counselor felt that there had been
some inappropriate intimate contact between Ian and one of his cousins.
We . . . I . . . probably overreacted. Probably because I thought it was
my fault. We wouldn't let the boys see each other, stopped all contact,
and demanded family counseling. The situation drove a wedge between
family members that still exists today. We kept Ian in counseling until
we were told they no longer needed to see him. Ian seemed fine and I
was relieved. We could relax and enjoy. He was doing well at school aca-
demically, and he had gotten into Taekwondo in a big way. He excelled
at it and went to Master Pak in Linworth where he earned his brown
belt, competing in and winning both the Battle for Columbus and the
State of Ohio competition. I have to admit that I was amused and proud
to see a little kid out there on the floor doing his forms and breaking
his boards. Ian went on to represent Ohio in the Junior Olympics. I
felt really good about our home and our family and what I thought the
future would bring.

When Ian entered Davis Middle School, we were told he had attention deficit disorder. We didn't quite see it, but they wanted him on
Ritalin. In those days, you just called the family doctor and got a prescription. I remember noticing that the prescription did not last as long
as it should have. It never occurred to me that Ian and his friends might
be using those pills. He befriended a boy who lived a couple of streets
over. Around the age of thirteen, Ian started not coming home, sneaking
out of the house, skipping school. We had no choice but to report him
for truancy. He totally disregarded our rules and did what he pleased.
We felt that if there was no consequence for this behavior, it would only
escalate. We realized that he was going to this boy's house, but we were
being told by the parents that he was not there. We were powerless to
stop it. The police officer told us he knew Ian was there but had no
search warrant and could do nothing about it. Ian's behavior spun totally
out of control. He was always one step ahead of us. He knew what
authorities would do. He knew there were no consequences.

We went through doctors looking for a physical problem, and mental health professionals looking for a psychological cause. We tried to let him pay the consequences for his behavior. We tried to find something that he might be interested in. We sent him to special-interest camps and even tried military school. Nothing seemed to affect him or change his trajectory.

Within months of coming home from one of these programs, he was arrested for burglary. He and two friends were caught stealing from the grandfather of one of his friends. Part of what they stole was a gun collection. At the age of nineteen, Ian was sent to prison for ten years. While he was incarcerated, I saw subtle signs he was changing. "Putting on the armor" they called it, and it scared me to see him become so hard and so guarded. After five years, he was released on probation. He seemed so happy to come home, and he genuinely tried to make it work. We found a bong under the couch and that was that. We asked him to move out.

The next several years were characterized by unsteady employment and relationships. He had a child shortly after coming home, but the mother and her new boyfriend would not let him see the child even though he had had a DNA test that proved paternity. Ian and I searched for this child for years before we finally found her. Through the court, he was finally able to meet her and instantly fell in love with her. The mother wasn't able to maintain sobriety, and Ian wanted custody. He entered rehab because we told him we would do nothing for him until he had six months of sobriety under his belt. He did that and more. His daughter became his focus. I had hope for the first time in a long time that she would be the thing that would change his life. And she was.

What has always bothered me is that we didn't drink, spend time in bars, or do drugs. My husband was a supervisor, and I did design work for a state agency. Education was important to us. We worked hard, focused on our family, and put our children first. Yes, we had problems, but we faced them and did everything we could to address them. Two of our three children are doing well. They have pursued degrees and obtained good jobs, and one has started a family. We thought that if we held the line with Ian, he would return to the values we taught him. And he did.

I saw him fewer than forty-eight hours before he overdosed, in the front room of the little house we helped him buy because he wanted to get custody of his daughter. We hugged each other, and I told him I loved him. "I love you too, Momma," he said. "Stay safe," I said. "Okay, Momma," he said. Then he was gone.

I am grateful for the six months of sobriety during which we had our Ian back. The happy-go-lucky, charming, generous, and hardworking son we raised. I am grateful that he was the father of our granddaughter and that they had the opportunity to meet each other. He knew we loved him and that we believed in him. She is, of course, heartbroken that she won't get to grow up with him in her life. Every time I look at my granddaughter, I see Ian's face, his physique, his mannerisms. We tell her that her family is here. And we love her.

*Christine Hunt was born and raised in Columbus. She is author (with Dennis Hunt) of* Letting Go: Our Family's Journey through Opioid Addiction and Beyond *(2017). She now lives with her husband in Russells Point.*

# 46

## FERAL

JESSICA HARPER AND SARAH BENEDUM
(MADISON)

### INTRODUCTION
### (JESSICA)

"Feral" was the word often used to describe us Benedums—and maybe we were. Perhaps that label is inevitable when you have a group of children discarded by society and raised by an elderly grandma who lost her husband a week after we lost our mom to a drug overdose. For Grandpa it was a heart attack, no doubt brought on by the heartbreak of having his only son turn out to be a drug addict. No one walks away from addiction whole, and our family is no exception.

Shortly after Mom's death, our father, Rodger Benedum, remarried and introduced us to our new stepsister, Sonny (Sonya). Sonny's bright personality and sunny disposition helped chase away the darkness of grief for a group of kids still shell-shocked from their losses. Sonny quickly became a beloved big sister and friend. Her quick wit and lighthearted ways combined with a beautiful smile were too much for anyone to resist. Even our brother Arnie (Aaron), whom we all teased and called "Shy Skye" because he barely talked to anyone and tended to shy away from others, could not help enjoying himself in her company. Soon after our families merged in 1980, our baby sister, Sarah, was born, tying us together in what we believed would be an unbreakable bond. Life wasn't easy, but it was good for a while.

Unfortunately, a year later our dad's drug habit would again take precedence over the well-being of his own kids. Dad was incarcerated, leaving us as wards of the state. Sonny was sent to live with her biological father, and the bonds holding us together frayed but never severed. Sonny moved to Boston for many years and had two kids before her life spiraled out of control and her journey led her back to Ohio. Aaron's path led him out West, where he would join me, his big sister Jessica. He thrived in his new role as an uncle to my three boys until he moved back to Ohio after our dad died at the age of fifty-seven.

Though the passage of time had separated us once again, we were reunited in the spring and summer of 2016 through tragedy. The widespread heroin epidemic in the state of Ohio had claimed more victims: we lost our Sonny and Arnie. They died months apart from the same drug, neither knowing that the other used. Over and over our hearts have been broken, our lives forever altered because of drugs. But once, many years ago, we "feral" kids of Fern Drive had a brief moment under the stars where we dared to laugh, play, and dream of becoming Army men, doctors, firemen, even Sandy from the movie *Grease*. But none of us dreamed of becoming an addict.

*The following poem by Sarah recounts the experience of writing her sister Sonny's obituary, which follows. The final pieces are obituaries, the first written by Sarah for Sonny, the second by Jessica for Aaron.*

## TODAY I WILL WRITE MY SISTER'S OBITUARY
## (SARAH)

Everyday on the news we are exposed to stories of the ongoing
    and seemingly worsening drug epidemic in our area. And for
    the past two days I keep coming across the story of a sixteen
    year old Akron boy who was found dead.
My heart aches for his family. I know their pain.
No news coverage for my sister.

Or the young woman who died with her.

Today I will write my sister's obituary.

The night before last she lost her battle with addiction along with another young woman.

Although she was my sister we were not close. By any means. Her addiction kept us distant.

I hope her dealers slept well last night.

I know my mom didn't.

Only on occasion did I get to spend time with my sister, not the addict. She was really pretty awesome. Quite the character, could always keep you in stitches. A few times we truly had a blast together.

But the addict put miles and miles between us. Kept me skeptical. Always.

And bitter. Very bitter for the way I watched my mother suffer. Always blaming herself. Always wondering where she went wrong.

And hateful for the pain on her son and daughter's faces when she really fell hard.

I hope her dealer fed his family well on her dime last night.

I'm certain her kids were probably too sick to eat.

My sister was an amazing woman. The addict cheated the world out of that.

I'm sure my sister was an equally amazing sister. The addict always left me wondering.

My sister was an outstanding and loving mother. She loved her children more than anything in the world. Of this I have NEVER been uncertain. But the addict convinced her they were better off without her.

My sister was an amazing daughter. But the addict never failed to leave my mother shaken.

My sister WAS amazing. And selfless and caring and compassionate and I could go on and on. Was . . .

I hope her dealers are proud.

Today I will write my sister's obituary.

I pray it's my last.

## SONNY'S OBITUARY
## (SARAH)

Sonya "Sonny" L. (Fulaytar) Sheppard passed away unexpectedly on Wednesday, April 6, 2016. She was born April 20, 1969 in Cleveland. Sonny loved her kids, dogs, reading and cooking. Sonny is survived by her spouse, Don Sheppard; daughter, Nichole Atkinson; son, Corey Atkinson; step-daughter, Rachel Sheppard; mother and step-father, Nola and Dennis Lawrence; sister, Sarah Benedum, and several step-siblings. Sonny is preceded in death by her father, James Fulaytar; sister, Cherie Allie; and brother, Jimmy Fulaytar. Memorial services will be held at a later date.

## AARON'S OBITUARY
## (JESSICA)

Aaron Skye Benedum, 42, passed away August 20, 2016. Our brother died alone in a cold dark basement. His body was not found until the next day. There is no wife or children he left behind to console. No mortgages, property or finances to look over. His worldly possessions will fit into a trash bag, not even good enough for donating. Our brother was a heroin addict who, like many others before him and sadly many more after, died becoming just another statistic. His dealers will continue thriving off the lifeblood of the weak while Aaron's siblings mourn his loss and remember the person he was, the person they loved. He is survived by his siblings, Jason (Gabriejela) Benedum, Jessica (Anthony) Harper, Zachary Benedum and Sarah Benedum; nieces, Sydney Forristal, Gracie Benedum; nephews: Dale, Josh and Jeremy Harper. He was preceded in death by his parents Rodger and Janet Benedum. Memorial service will be held, Friday, August 26, 2016 from 4 to 8 p.m. at his sister's home. Arrangements by Blessing Cremation Center, (440) 352 8100.

*Jessica Harper* currently resides in a beautiful farming community in rural Pennsylvania with her husband of twenty-five years, Anthony, their three sons, two crazy Bengal cats, and one spoiled Havanese. ***Sarah Benedum*** resides in Madison, Ohio, with her family. She works with the local mental health community.

# 47

# RECOVERY SHOULD BE CELEBRATED, NOT JUDGED

## LACEY WHITLATCH
### (ATHENS)

> The very least you can do in this life is figure out what you hope for. The most you can do is live inside that hope, running down the hallways, touching the walls on both sides.
>
> —Barbara Kingsolver

## MONDAY, MARCH 2, 2018
### Meet Sarah*

Sarah is at Hopewell for her eighth injection of Vivitrol. I walk in the room and shake hands with her, taking my seat on the provider stool.

"Happy belated Easter. How was your holiday?"

"We had the most fun! I could hardly believe it but I told myself to keep on believing; the way they told us to in recovery group.

"Remember I told you how my older one, Sierra, had been scared of her shadow and not even wanting to play or leave her room? She was all over the Easter Egg hunt, whooping around, and picking up ones to share with Riley—kept saying the eggs she put in Riley's basket were for her *almost t'ird* birthday."

Sarah tears up. "Lacey, I'da been dead instead of Easter egg hunting with my girls if you hadn't given me Vivitrol. I thought of heroin, nonstop, from the time I woke up, to the time I went to bed, and now I'm not even thinking about using. That is one miracle drug!"

Sarah and I clasp hands for a time and then laugh and high-five. I remember the day I first met Sarah, and I can tell she still remembers it as well.

## MONDAY, AUGUST 2, 2017
### Sarah meeting with Lacey for the first time

The nurse informs me that my 8:00 is here inquiring about Vivitrol. When I enter the exam room, I see a young woman in acute withdrawal. Her hands are trembling and she is terrified. As I look at this young woman, I see behind her pale gray eyes someone who has come to the end of her capacity to hide her addiction. I see a young woman who needs to not be judged. A young woman who needs someone to pick her up from the bottom and hold space for her to believe in her worth, to listen to her, to hold on to hope for her until she can grasp it herself.

### Meet Lacey

I am from Nelsonville, once a thriving community, now covered
   in bones—the bones of the lost skeletons, the skeletons in the
   closet, generations of closets.
I am from the space between. I am from addiction. I am from
   despair.
I want you to know that I care.
I wear your crown covered in shame.
Trust me when I say that it is not you I blame.

I am from a place of trauma. I am from a place of peace.
I am grace.
I am light.
I am healer.

I am holder of hope.

In the decade since I've been a registered nurse, I've participated in numerous aspects of caregiving, all of which have brought me to an understanding that my greatest calling is in the field of public health. This focus led me to complete a Doctor of Nursing Practice (DNP) degree with the intention of improving chronic disease in my place of origin, the Appalachian Mountains.

I was drawn to Hopewell Health Center's mission of providing "access to affordable, high quality, integrated health care for all." Hopewell meets and treats patients with compassion, empathy, and kindness, the same values that drew me to a career in nursing in the first place.

Sarah is now living with hope because of her consistent contact with healers who believe in recovery. Her treatment consists of integrated care, a blend of behavioral and primary health care. Licensed social workers, therapists, psychiatrists, and peer support specialists work in tandem with primary care providers, offering a tapestry of services, interwoven with strands of compassion. Hopewell provided Sarah transportation, psychiatric services, case management, group counseling, wellness services, and a registered dietician. It also connects Sarah to cutting-edge community resources, such as Natural Freedom Equine Therapy and the Athens Photographic Project.

As Sarah's story makes clear, medication-assisted treatment is a critical part of her treatment. The form of medication I prescribe is Vivitrol, a once-monthly injection used to decrease opioid cravings and prevent use. Vivitrol is a non-opioid medication that blocks the opioid receptor sites in the brain so that when heroin is used, the user does not feel reward or pleasure. Although there are other forms of medication-assisted treatment, such as Suboxone, my experience has been solely with Vivitrol.

Despite controversy over medically assisted recovery, we are seeing great results. The controversy rests largely on the argument that the treatment is teaching addicts to simply substitute one drug for another. Another argument that I've heard against Vivitrol is that it will cause them to substitute their initial drug of choice with another, such as crystal meth. I favor Vivitrol because it is non-opioid with minimal abuse potential.

Sadly, even as medication assisted-treatment aids people in recovery, Sarah and others still have to combat the stigma of being "drug users." My colleagues and I combat this stigma by educating others about how the medicines save and stabilize lives while patients work on the underlying issues that trigger the addictive process. As a provider, I believe there is no such thing as false hope. Storytelling helps patients reweave their lives into a whole. Their recovery requires that we listen to them.

Addiction is treatable, people recover, and recovery should be celebrated. I am dedicated to working alongside patients and changing the story of "hopeless addiction" to one of "hopeful recovery."

*Sarah is not an actual patient, but a composite of many patients I have seen through my practice.

*Lacey Whitlatch, DNP,* is a family nurse practitioner at Hopewell Health Center.

# 48

## SERVE AND PROTECT

DENNIS WHALEY
(TOLEDO)

My first posts with the Lucas County Sheriff's Office were in corrections and the courts, where my job was to keep inmates and the courthouse safe and secure. In 2015, the sheriff's office asked me to join the Drug Abuse Response Team as an officer. Because of what I had seen in the jails and courts, I couldn't say yes fast enough.

Many of the court cases I had observed had some intersection with addiction, from burglaries to robbery to things as small as petty theft. When I first joined the unit, I didn't realize how bad this epidemic was going to be or how this unit was going to change the way people look at addiction. In the early days we would come in each morning and our sergeant would go through the previous day's reports. If there was an overdose, we would try to locate that person to see if they wanted help with their addiction. Finding someone in this manner was not easy to do, so the sheriff and other officers discussed ways to streamline the process. We worked with fire and police forces and encouraged them to let us know when there was an overdose. When EMS transported an individual to the hospital, we were notified and would meet with the person to see if we could connect them to resources.

This experience made it clear to me that the biggest hurdle was distrust. Most addicts just thought we wanted to arrest them or ask them about dealers and where they got their drugs. This was not our goal at all. Nonetheless, people were initially very hesitant to talk with us, which made it hard to get people the help they needed. But slowly the stigma started going away, and talking with them became easier. When they found out we were there to help them, and weren't taking them to jail, all of a sudden so many began looking for help. We had only sixteen detox beds available in Lucas County at this time and approximately 10,000 people addicted to opioids. We were overwhelmed.

In our office we started to compile a list of overdose survivors. When we learned of a bed coming open, we would start calling the people on the list. It was a first-come, first-serve basis. When new centers opened, it made our jobs easier, but recovery housing beds remained at a premium. Stable recovery housing is critical because if individuals go back to the same situation after they detox, the addiction will just start over again. Recovering addicts need to be around other people who know what they are going through. People who have never experienced addiction simply don't understand it. Being in a recovery house around people who understand can really help.

Those who think addiction is a choice need to be educated about the physical effects of this disease. Even if they can't believe it's a disease, they should know that addicts don't want to be this way. Some people think that these people are just junkies and ask why tax dollars should go to help them. I hope these people never have to deal with the pain and anguish of knowing someone addicted to opioids.

I often think of the mother whose son became addicted after an injury and was given opioids for pain. It became so bad for him that he left a note saying the demons were just too much to fight. And after being in at least four treatment facilities, he put a gun in his mouth and took his own life. Or there is the gentleman who, after taking opioids for an injury, turned to heroin when his dealer couldn't get him his pills. He went to treatment twenty-eight times, but still he overdosed and ended up on a ventilator for a few days after using five dollars' worth of heroin.

He is now two and a half years clean and sober. We know that interventions can work.

These are just a few of the many people we have encountered through this work. For me to tell a parent, wife, husband, son, daughter, or grandparent that their loved one is not worth saving is something I can—and will—never do. When I first joined the unit, I took a woman to detox seven times. The first six she would leave and go back out and then call saying she wanted help again. But the seventh was the one: she has been clean almost three years since she checked herself in that day.


*Dennis Whaley* *has served in law enforcement for twenty-seven years. Currently a deputy sheriff, he has worked in the Drug Abuse Response Team of the Lucas County Sheriff's Office since 2015.*

# 49

## WHAT DO LIBRARIES DO?

NICK TEPE
(ATHENS)

When I moved to Chillicothe in 2012 to take the job of Director of the Chillicothe and Ross County Public Library, everyone knew that there was a drug problem in Southeast Ohio. The drug of choice varied over time, and at that point heroin appeared to be on the rise. There were concerns about drug houses and the role that landlords played in perpetuating the problem. Law enforcement did what they could with the resources they had, usually just arresting and putting away anyone they could catch. The response that I heard from many people was "What do you expect? It's Chillicothe." However, I also encountered many people who were dedicated to taking on the challenges facing the community—people who not only expected but also demanded better, people who had hope for the future of the town. But no one I encountered thought that the problem was anything more than a side effect of generational poverty in Appalachia and the decline of the rust belt.

In early 2015, I was ordering books for the library, and a new book—*Dreamland* by Sam Quinones—came across my desk. The book's blurb made reference to the "pill mills" in Portsmouth in the late 1990s. I remembered hearing about those busts while living in Columbus. Curious to learn more, I flagged the book to read later. When I finally got around to doing so a few months later, I was blown away. The book makes it clear that this crisis was the result of forces outside any individual's control and that any solution was going to require collaboration among a wide swath of community groups. Not only was I convinced that everyone in Chillicothe needed to read this book, but I was equally sure that libraries had a central role to play in overcoming the crisis.

Around the same time, Chillicothe made national news due to reports of missing women, with national media attempting to turn the story into the hunt for a serial killer. Most of us who lived in Chillicothe were very frustrated by such reporting, for we all knew that the only serial killer was the drug trade. But the national attention did help get the real story of the opioid crisis out there. Combined with the release of *Dreamland,* more and more people within and without Chillicothe began to realize that this problem went beyond stereotypes of junkies, pimps, and dealers. This was societal.

As I continued to evangelize for *Dreamland* among the residents of Chillicothe, others began to make efforts to understand and overcome the epidemic. Local officials convened the Heroin Partnership Task Force and hired a well-respected former corrections administrator to coordinate efforts between different agencies. Out of that group grew a post-overdose response team made up of law enforcement and social services aimed at getting help to families and addicts in the wake of an overdose.

A wealthy graduate of Chillicothe High School pledged to buy a car for a graduating senior who committed to going drug free. The local Rotary funded an effort to introduce a drug-free program to all the county schools. The editor of the local paper committed to reporting that would get the real story out there. I saw my community pulling together around this issue. By early 2016, I was able to bring together multiple local organizations to fund a community-wide reading of *Dreamland,* culminating in a visit by Mr. Quinones. With the assistance of our Friends of the Library organization, we sold over 300 copies of the book at cost. Multiple events were held around the city, highlighting the epidemic, educating the public, and raising awareness of how it touched every person. I saw participants' attitudes shift from blaming addicts to seeking a community solution. Mr. Quinones was so impressed by our efforts that he brought his family along to see a community that was getting it right.

As more and more stories about the involvement of libraries in the crisis come out, people often seem surprised that libraries have been so greatly affected. But as my experience in Chillicothe underscores, libraries are at the center of our communities. Our leaders and staff members are active in their communities: we have the resources and information to be able to assist the community in responding to a crisis, and we are one of the few remaining public agencies that are open and staffed throughout the day for everyone, regardless of their situation. Libraries don't have a choice: we are on the front lines of the crisis. And because of what we do and how we are trained, our first instinct is to find resources that answer the questions and address the problems our patrons bring to our doors.

The most basic response we have to provide to the crisis is the training of and care for our staff. Since the library is a public space that is open to all, any problem in the wider community will inevitably find its way through our doors. Our staff has to be prepared to address those challenges. Almost every library in Ohio has trained its staff on the issue at some level, but the training program undertaken by Toledo Lucas County Public Library (TLCPL) is a good example of a comprehensive approach.

TLCPL has worked to increase their staff's general awareness of mental health through a series of video trainings that help staff understand the issues facing their patrons, establish positive relations with disruptive patrons, answer concerns about individuals affected by mental health issues, and take care of themselves in addressing these challenging issues. The library has also offered trainings on issues faced by ex-offenders reintegrating into society and is helping staff understand the challenges faced and how the library can help.

In addition to general training on issues that have arisen from the opioid epidemic, TLCPL, along with many other libraries around the state, has conducted trainings to educate its staff specifically about opioids and drug abuse. This training includes information on how to identify drugs and drug paraphernalia and how to handle and dispose of suspected drug paraphernalia. The sessions also teach staff how to use information from law enforcement and health workers about the extent of the epidemic and how their agencies are responding, and they provide training for staff on how to identify someone who has overdosed and what steps to take at that point. As libraries are quiet public spaces where someone can linger for an extended period without being bothered, trainings also explain that by providing excellent customer service—greeting every patron, roving around to maintain awareness of who is in your building and who needs help, checking restrooms frequently—staff can make the library a less appealing place for drug users.

Libraries have also responded to the crisis by offering programming in-house for those directly affected and for those seeking additional information about the crisis. As information professionals, it is our job to answer questions brought to us by our communities with the best information and resources we can find. But libraries are also neutral and nonthreatening. An individual with a drug problem, or someone concerned about a loved one with a drug problem, is not likely to go to an informational session held at the courthouse or government offices. Libraries lack such barriers to participation and do not carry as much stigma.

In Athens County, where I am now director, we have tried to make use of this unique place in our community by partnering with other agencies to provide information and support to those who are affected by the crisis. One of the most successful programs has been a series of family support sessions offered by the Athens County prosecutor's office at one of our branches. Every other week, family members of those fighting addiction can meet with experts on the front lines of the crisis to get answers and find solutions for the problems they and their loved ones are facing. Among the participants is a mother who had been bankrupted by her son's heroin addiction. He wiped out her entire life savings through theft and fraud. We also helped a grandparent whose grandson had been born with opioid dependence find information on drug addiction in babies. For every one of the stories that we get to hear, there are many others who quietly come to the library to take advantage of the information and services we can provide.

We also offer a recurring program with a pharmacy professor from The Ohio State University to answer questions about prescription drugs from anyone who drops in. Again, offering the information in a nonthreatening way in a neutral space lowers the barriers for participation and encourages community members to find the information they need. Similar programs and partnerships can be found at libraries throughout the state.

Libraries have also made use of their position within the community by offering informational flyers from a wide variety of community resources for recovery and support. In some cases, they even stock physical items like prescription drug disposal bags that allow individuals to safely dispose of excess prescription drugs without having to drop them off at a law enforcement agency. Library meeting rooms are also frequently used by recovery counselors who need to meet their clients in a neutral and nonthreatening space for regular check-ins.

One of the most significant barriers to addicts and their families seeking help is the stigma that accompanies drug addiction in our society. As the crisis was coming to the surface in Chillicothe, someone pointed out to me that you could spot the obituaries of individuals who had overdosed by looking for people in their twenties through forties who "died unexpectedly." This reluctance to talk about the issue very likely delayed effective responses to the crisis, as well as clouded the issue with stories like those about the "missing women" in Chillicothe. Libraries have an important role to play in lowering the stigma surrounding addiction that prevents individuals and families from getting the help that they need. The more that people have correct information about drug addiction and how it affects their community, the better positioned we will be to respond well to the crisis.

The most common way libraries address this sort of effort is by starting community conversations, a role we are uniquely positioned to play. A good example of how libraries have created this sort of program is the Troy-Miami County Public Library's "Opioid Awareness Week" event. In September 2017 the Miami County Recovery Council, Miami County Public Health, and Tri-County Board of Recovery and Mental Health Services partnered with the library to present programs over the course of three days in order to demonstrate the different ways opioid addiction affects different parts of the community. By convening experts in an accessible space where people from different parts of the community can come together without feeling out of place or threatened, this library facilitated open discussion about the problems facing the community and brought the issue out of the shadows.

Libraries across the state are convening similar groups, holding similar trainings, and working with their communities to find information and make connections that will help them overcome the challenges they are facing. Ultimately, the opioid crisis is about the lack of information about two things: how individuals can overcome pain and isolation in ways that are not dependent on drugs, and how communities can overcome the isolation endemic to our society. We are perfectly positioned to address both of these problems. We can bring people information about how they might overcome the problems in their lives, health-related or otherwise. We can break down the barriers between different segments of society and help people talk to each other about how the epidemic has affected them. We can connect those directly affected by the crisis find the resources they need to heal and keep healing. And we can help our communities overcome the stigma associated with addiction.

In his book *Chasing the Scream,* journalist Johann Hari says, "The opposite of addiction isn't sobriety. It's connection." Connection is what libraries do. We connect people to information. We connect people to community resources. Maybe most important, we connect people to each other.

*Nick Tepe is Athens County Public Libraries Director and 2018 Chair of the Board of Directors of the Ohio Library Council.*

# 50

## CONFRONTING STIGMA
## IN PORTSMOUTH

TRACI MOLLOY
(PORTSMOUTH)

I first worked with students in Portsmouth from 2013 to 2014, creating several collaborative projects and a public art installation. During my initial visits, which were made possible by outreach funding from the University of Rio Grande, I encountered teenagers enduring the effects of poverty, unemployment, parental addiction, and loss. The community was still dealing with the OxyContin epidemic, though many of the pill mills had shut down years prior. Heroin was just beginning to take hold. I was struck by the incredible resiliency of the youth I worked with. In spite of their difficult life circumstances, they possessed a genuine curiosity for learning, joy for living, gritty determination to achieve their life goals, and a sense of hope that things will get better.

It came to my attention in 2016 that the Portsmouth High School art teacher, April Deacon, was working with visiting artists on a large-scale public sculpture project she called the Human Rights Sculpture Garden. Deacon is an extraordinarily talented arts educator, someone whose work I deeply respect. I wanted to return to the city to partner with her and her students again. I knew this project would be dynamic and important. I proposed facilitating an extension to the garden, thereby creating new collaborations with more students, which would add to the Human Rights discourse. Together we received additional grant funding from the University of Rio Grande, the Ohio

Arts Council, and the Puffin Foundation. I returned to Portsmouth in 2017 to 2018 to once again work with area adolescents on a series of collaborations.

The new collaborations were designed to explore themes of identity, poverty, and regionalism. Addiction was an unavoidable topic. I posed a series of questions to the classes I partnered with, which became the starting point for our collaborations: What does it mean to be growing up in Portsmouth today? What is it like to be from this community, this region, this state, this part of America? I was struck by some of the responses I heard, so I started asking follow-up questions. How many of you are missing your father, mother, or both parents? The results varied slightly in the different classes, but on average three-quarters of the students were missing their father, a third were missing their mother, and a quarter were missing both parents. How many of you have a family member who is an addict? Every single student in the first class raised their hand. I asked this again in the other classes. The results were the same. No matter how resilient, determined, creative, or intelligent these children are, they're going to be impacted by the ripple effects of trauma, disenfranchisement, loss, and neglect. It is inevitable.

The imagery included in this book reflects two of the five collaborations I facilitated in Portsmouth. The images will become permanent four-feet-by-seven-feet stone monoliths in the Human Rights Sculpture Garden. The sculptures were designed to be diptychs, with a composite photo accompanying a poem. The two poems were written collectively and collaboratively. Initially, every participant wrote their own sixteen-line poem. The poems were read aloud anonymously to the class. Passages of interest were selected by their peers. I then took the highlighted passages and pieced together a rough combined poem using the selected stanzas. Later, I presented this rough version to the group, and collectively we adjusted the lines until a final version was actualized. Every student has at least one line of their original poem in the final version. These poems reflect a collaboratively constructed but still first-person account of what it's like to grow up in Portsmouth.

The poems, as readers will see, are honest, gritty, and real. The first poem was written by Tayler Zempter's twelfth-grade Women's Studies Class, composed of sixteen young women. The second poem was written by ten young men from Noah Fannin's twelfth-grade Honors English Class. We framed the poems similarly: what does it mean to be a boy or girl growing up in Portsmouth?

The photos that accompany the text are composite portraits of each respective group of students. I photographed every student in the same location and pose and then layered the photos on top of each other to create a singular prototype—the outcome is a representation of what a boy or girl from Portsmouth looks like. The students determined the pose and location for the composite. The boys wanted their pose to reflect determination and strength. They have one foot slightly in front of the other to show they are taking a step forward toward their future. The girls also wanted their pose to reflect strength, as well as intelligence. They have one hand clenched in a fist by their waist, while the second is pointing to their mind. Both groups chose to include the bridge that spans the Ohio River, connecting Portsmouth to Kentucky, in their photo. This bridge, one of the signature landmarks in town, is also the main artery for the drug trade. The boys' image, taken from Kentucky, features Portsmouth in the background. The girls' image, taken in Portsmouth, shows the Kentucky mountains in the background. The students' names follow the poems.

## What It Means to Be a Woman

What it means to be a woman is important to the balance of the
    world

Being a woman in Portsmouth is like a merry-go-round
Or should I say see-saw because it's full of ups and downs

This town full of addiction, bad intention, and temptation
Sadly, paving the way for the rest of the nation

A river community once full of industrialization
Now rusty and dusty, people with no occupations

A place that everybody hates, but nobody seems to be able to
    escape
Sometimes it feels like a black hole that you've been sucked into
Small town, big dreams. Will I succeed?

Despair beyond repair, with only your mother there.
A daughter without a father: he never truly cared.
In his eyes, I was unwanted

Now, I look in the mirror and see nothing but imperfection
Ashamed of myself as I gaze at my reflection.

Not too rich, but way too poor
We are oppressed, suppressed, and depressed, but at least we are,
    well, dressed

There are drugs, prostitution, and young pregnancies.
Girls disappearing. Mothers, sisters, daughters overdosing daily.

To men, we are inferior objects to please, something to catcall,
    play around with, and tease.
No matter where you go, you never feel safe—you're watched and
    harassed
"Just wait until you're eighteen"—they don't even ask

Being a woman means you are compliant. To men, we are a client
We are silenced, and God forbid, we are defiant

A woman who is resilient is a woman who is brilliant
We are beautiful and powerful, intelligent and strong
and don't you dare tell me that I'm wrong.

Though the work is never done, together we are one
We are warriors because of the battles we take on

Why do they set our throne too low—discriminate and walk all
    over us?
Little do they know—we are more.
We are the creators.

*Authors: Hannah Adkins, Janayah Dickey, Alleria Dorsey, Allison Douthat, Grace Emnett, Alyson Ferrara, Aiden Fields, Brooklyn Greene, Sharia Kearns, Skyilynn Kidder, Rylee Moorhead, Jenny Perryman, Lynsey Shipley, Emleigh Smith, Lyda Spencer, and Andrea Thomas. Facilitators: Traci Molloy and Tayler Zempter.*

Student Composite Photo, Girls. Credit: Traci Molloy.

## What It Means to Be a Man

What it means to be a man is important to the balance of the
    world.

Growing up male in Portsmouth is hard.
A man has to climb steep obstacles and overcome challenges.

Who needs skyscrapers when you have mountains
Though kids can't play in polluted fountains.

Walking down the streets you see plenty of poverty.
Boarded-up windows and doors on every other property.

Roaches, drugs, lice, and famine envelop the homes.
Hidden everywhere, between each tooth of the comb.

Full of fear, scared to go out at night.
Vulnerability will attack like a wild animal.

It clings to you without your knowing.

I'm not so worried about dying young
I'm more afraid of not getting out and becoming someone.

You have to live day by day.
But don't live in the past—live each day like it's your last.

Who will teach me what it means to be a man?
Who will help me interpret life's ever-changing plan?

Here, life can get rough.
Here, you have to be tough.

Cracks and calluses on hard working hands.
The hills whisper his name.
A name given by his father, the same.

A man needs to stand steady and strong, present and proud.
He needs to protect his family from harm and the growing
    crowd.

But where I come from, you rarely see this type of man
Instead, you see men abusing and mistreating, addicted and gone.

These are not men—they are cowards.

I will not be this kind of man.

I'm just a hard-working kid looking for his glory.
Single mom, same old story.

I go for a drive to clear my mind. Everything is drenched in
    bleach.
Crying about the past. Tears latch on like a leech.

You laugh and tell me to get over it.

But that's okay.
Because I've come a long way from where I was to where I am
    today.

*Authors: Broc Bumgardner, Adam Earley, Anthony Ferrara, Jadan Josey, Isaac Kelly, Zack Kinney, Wesley Mullet, DJ Pearsall, Kendal Reynolds, and Adrian Soard. Facilitators: Traci Molloy and Noah Fannin.*

*Traci Molloy is an artist and education activist based in Brooklyn, New York. For more than twenty years she has worked throughout the country on large-scale public art pieces in collaboration with adolescents and young adults who have experienced trauma. For more information, visit www.tracimolloy.com.*

Student Composite Photo, Boys. Credit: Traci Molloy.

# 51

## EVERYBODY PLAYED ALONG

ANONYMOUS
(COLUMBUS)

Given the scope of the opioid epidemic, it seems almost banal to place my story alongside the others. Yet the obvious needs to be called out: the fact that this epidemic has directly reached my demographic—the white, suburban, middle class—has allowed it to attract a sympathetic spotlight compared to other recent drug crises. Testament to this is that my life in Columbus contained a great number of supposed firewalls to addiction: private schooling, insular suburban living, no financial worries. But if these barriers were not sufficient, then what was the root cause? Is it the monotony of my upbringing, or perhaps something about Ohio specifically? And how should I process all the sympathy my situation has garnered in light of those who instead of being cared for were stigmatized and even incarcerated for similar choices?

Allow me to trace the path.

My first opioid, at age seventeen, was an innocuous five-milligram Vicodin after dental surgery. Forget ice cream after a tonsillectomy—this was the real stuff. Here I was, a loner who took solace in books and the internet, and I had found in post-surgery painkillers the one friend who didn't let me down. Friday nights in high school, without plans or phone calls, began to seem less sad. Then, when I realized that the medicine cabinets of parents, friends, and family were stocked full of the stuff I wanted, a deeper connection was made. My teenage experimentation, the usual drinking and pot smoking with friends, was wholly unsatisfying in comparison to the relief I had found in prescription painkillers.

The fact that I didn't take opioids regularly during high school made it easier to dismiss the idea that I was developing a habit. Years of erratic relationships and irresponsibility at work and in school were restructured by what appeared to me, at the time, to be the incredible rationality of drug use. The highs, however, were fleeting. My social isolation only grew, and I felt increasingly alienated from the world. This makes sense, I suppose. After all, they call them "painkillers" for a reason, even if my pain was mostly emotional. In college, as I began to explore my passions and made friends, this pain persisted. I continued to use drugs.

A small dose of fentanyl during my sophomore year marked a dangerous transition. Here was a drug that removed pain while being easily hidden. It obliterated my inhibitions, especially while working a tedious job. It made class fun, debates lively, and the experience of writing feel like I was churning out award-winning prose (I wasn't). My previously intermittent use became a daily habit. But the initial bliss was gone, as higher highs meant lower lows. My mother used to jokingly describe an ordinary morning as "shit, shower, shave." By the summer of 2012, my schedule had an added necessity on top of that—as drug seeking became as routine as getting out of bed. My commute to class included an additional pit stop. Breaks at work meant a quick rendezvous with my dealer. All of these signs pointed to the mounting tension between my life and my addiction.

My ability to maintain this breakneck pace was short-lived, as was my ability to confide in others. I recall sharing a line of broken-up heroin known as "brown sugar" with a friend toward the last year of my use. What I found so riveting and so essential did nothing for him. I was rattled by the notion that what I considered to be so sensational could be boring to someone else.

Even some years later, I've yet to understand how the innocuous use of my late teens could escalate to snorting lines off a soap dispenser in a workplace bathroom. Only looking back did I realize how grievously hooked I was. I'm still struck by how easy it was—certainly not dealing with unpunctual dealers and finding the cash flow and the other difficulties of maintaining a costly drug habit—but what child's play it seemed to be to hide the whole ordeal. When I think of hardened drug users, I catch myself slipping into the habit of conjuring those dramatic "before and after" pictures that are circulated in the media and that are supposed to mark a clear transition. I don't believe the contrast would have captured my trajectory. For me, body maintenance was part of the game and a key reason why nobody around me seemed to notice what was happening. I refused to be a sunken-eyed, pockmarked junkie. Instead, I was pumped full of heroin with clean teeth, nice skin, and a sincere smile. I looked the part of a middle-class white kid, and everybody played along.

Why, then, has it taken the growing, drug-addled struggles of a person like me to attract a sympathetic public? I, like many other Ohioans from the white middle class, have "benefited" from biased thinking about the problem. In my story lies an example of deeply ingrained prejudice in a society that claims to be color-blind. Ignoring questions of social inequality and racial oppression continue to reinforce the epidemic status of drug abuse in this state.

When I think about my experience with opioids, and Ohio's experience more generally, I think about those "Ohio Against the World" T-shirts I see around the state. While they have been appropriated as symbolic for the trials and tribulations of Cleveland sports teams, I see something deeper at work. To me, they represent an attempt—conscious or not—to veil the harsh reality of drug use in Ohio. Is it really true that we Ohioans are taking on everyone else? And what does the world know of or care about Ohio anyway? When we blur the link between a troubled society, on the one hand, and drug addiction, on the other, we fail to uncover and understand that society's inner logic. Creating a fictional battlefront—"us vs. them"—blurs the fact that I and so many others are in fact against the world—of disappointment, tedium, and hopelessness—that Ohio offers us. Such conditions are ripe for harvesting addiction. Sports fanaticism provides solace. Being white lets you hide. But ultimately neither one counteracts the intense sadness on which addiction feeds. I wonder what it will be like when it's "Ohio Against Opioids" and we start battling addiction for all people, and not just those who look like me.

*The author is a central Ohioan in his mid-twenties.*

# 52

# THE MAKING OF A PUBLIC HEALTH EMERGENCY

YVONKA MARIE HALL
(CLEVELAND)

Opioid addiction has recently become a hot-button issue across America. While communities have been devastated by this epidemic for years, it seems as if policymakers and the media are finally waking up to the realities of the crisis. Much of the recent attention is focused on white communities, especially in rural and suburban areas where addiction to legal painkillers has soared. Yet African American communities have long suffered from the diseases of addiction with little to no help. I wonder why.

In January 1995, intravenous drug use in African American and low-income communities was at an all-time high. Then mayor of Cleveland, Michael White, declared that drastic action was necessary to curb the spread of HIV. An emergency order was issued approving tightly restricted needle-exchange programs. Although controversial, needle exchanges are effective in reducing the spread of HIV among intravenous drug users. The number of people with HIV/AIDS had increased so dramatically that the city knew it had to respond in a way to help get to the heart of the problem.

Though intravenous drug use in African American and low-income communities was at an all-time high, the only people speaking up were those in urban areas. It wasn't deemed an "emergency" until the inner-ring suburbs began to be impacted.

In 1996, after much turmoil, I was appointed the first African American to serve as director of a harm reduction program in the state. We worked to ensure that the program sites were in the best possible locations. I met with police chiefs to ensure the safety of their deputies and the safety of the community that sought our services. We wanted to make sure that people didn't feel intimidated by and fearful of seeking help. It was a tough road to climb. We had to deal with police patrols doing ride-throughs and church groups protesting our immoral actions, when our entire goal was simply to provide an opportunity for people to come and exchange needles without fear of repercussions.

Adding to this frustration was the length of time it took to really find support for this work. As long as African Americans were the ones dying, it seemed as if there was no one to help them—they were put off as casualties of their own reckless behavior. Then white suburban housewives started using. And then we just had to do something.

The thinking seemed to be that if white communities were using drugs, there had to be a clinical problem. In hospitals and doctor's offices, African Americans who presented with pain were simply addicts not worthy of receiving pain meds. On the other hand, white communities became the drug companies' best consumers because of the large quantity of prescription drugs that were written for them—whether they needed them or not. When black people were addicted to drugs or painkillers, they were swiftly and forcefully given a new address and an orange jumpsuit.

The "Godfather of Soul" James Brown released his cautionary anthem "King Heroin" in 1972, citing its devastating effect on black communities. Forty-five years later, the harsh truths he spoke of remain true. Instead of treatment for this disease, black communities have seen increased incarceration rates—resulting in broken families, fewer opportunities, and an endless cycle of addition. Black families weren't given appropriate support or provided with treatment options. Our untreated drug addiction, fueled by unacknowledged cultural trauma and racism, made us an easy target. Black community members were given sentences—not sympathy.

The rap song "The Message" by Grandmaster Flash and the Furious Five highlights the media narratives and racial disparities that impact the communities embroiled in a national war on black and brown communities. African American health problems didn't begin with doctor-prescribed painkillers; instead they are rooted in the racism touched on in that song. But there is little to no sympathy or empathy for black families who face these issues. Among whites, addiction is blamed on the greed of pharmaceutical companies that used white communities as a cash cow, but addiction in black communities isn't afforded the same leniency.

Beyond the framing of addicts in black and white communities, additional differences persist. Black overdose victims tend to be older, with the largest share occurring among users between forty and fifty-nine. Yet the public health implications of opioid addiction go even deeper. Since 2004, Ohio has seen a 750 percent increase in the number of babies born to mothers with opioid dependency and then diagnosed with neonatal abstinence syndrome—the aftermath of an addiction developed in the womb. This issue disproportionately affects African American communities where infant mortality rates outnumber those of whites three to one. Unintended use and illegal resale exacerbate the cycle of addiction and relapse that prevents communities from recovering and rebuilding.

As Director of the Northeast Ohio Black Health Coalition, I work to educate, advocate for, and empower the community on health disparities. Our communities have been disproportionately impacted because of the criminalization of addiction. Make no mistake, white communities did not face the same rate, or kind, of criminalization.

African American families have been torn apart, with many children placed into public systems when we should have been working to get parents with addictions the help that they needed. We have penalized children for their entire life by placing them in foster care and then releasing them to the world on their eighteenth birthday, just so they could be abused and traumatized even more. Many of these children were born addicted themselves. And yet we offered no treatment options as they came of age and began to experiment with alcohol and other drugs. In my work I saw many young people who had aged out of foster care systems who were now in the streets and addicted to the very drugs that they were born addicted to. The great news is that we have finally realized the mistakes that were made in sentencing people instead of ordering treatment for them. An example of this reckoning is Ohio Senate Bill 66, passed in 2018, which makes rehabilitation one of three factors weighed during sentencing, in addition to punishment and protecting public safety. It also:

- Eliminates automatic prison terms for technical parole violations such as being late to a meeting.
- Allows someone with an unlimited number of fourth- and fifth-degree felony convictions to apply to have his or her record sealed.
- Expands eligibility for drug and alcohol treatment in lieu of conviction to third-degree felons.

Addiction with no sympathy or treatment is a lonely road that many African Americans have been forced to walk down. For white folks, there was a way out that was never offered to the black community. This bill changes the lives of many African American offenders.

If we are to truly combat this problem, especially in communities of color, state officials must improve coordination in their public health and law enforcement branches. Currently, those two groups are as different as two trains passing in the night. They are literally on different tracks. Along with this necessary interdepartmental coordination, the implicit racial bias within our systems must be addressed on all levels if we are to make any inroads in the opioid crisis.

As the US Congress works to create legislation to address the nation's opioid crisis, I can't help thinking of the many lives that have been torn apart during the years of inaction, and sometimes downright complicity, on the federal level. This inaction has certainly caused a lifetime of trauma and behavioral issues in the African American community—all of which has culminated in a never-ending cycle of addiction that has become a generational crisis impacting grandmothers, grandfathers, mothers, fathers, and children. Is this action by politicians too little, too late, or will the approved legislation be a solution to a problem that has needed attention for decades?

It's a peculiar feeling—an issue you've been aware of for so long finally being recognized. I remember walking through my neighborhood of well-manicured lawns and well-kept houses in the early 1980s where the street club hosted meetings at neighboring homes and the neighbors blocked off the streets for block parties. Then, in the late 1980s, while driving through the neighborhood, I looked at those same homes. This time there were no flowers, no people, no life; the drug epidemic had taken away street club meetings because of the fear of having your home broken into by neighborhood addicts. Many families lost their sons to either the jail or the cemetery. Those who could afford it spent lots of money and even put their homes up as collateral hoping to keep their children from going to jail.

Early one morning while driving to work, I looked at the cars to the left, right, front, and back, and I noticed that there were no men, just all women, heading to work. Drugs had taken a toll on my community. Who would be there to help the parents as they were aging, who would be there to raise the children, who would help protect the vulnerable? James Brown urged us to "get [our] mind[s] together and get away from drugs." We want to end the opioid crisis, not replace it with a more pervasive one. Our communities demand greater action on this issue. As I look at the legislation coming down the pipeline, I sometimes close my eyes and remember my neighborhood before the unanswered crisis came knocking. I remember the people sitting on their porches; I remember the gardens. I remember the lives that were lost and the impact of drug use. I open my eyes and those homes are gone, torn down. Those families are gone, and to where I don't know. A homeless man once lived at the house across the street, but drugs sent him to jail. Then his arrival back home was met with deceased parents and with siblings who had long been separated and placed into systems.

I am glad that we have finally figured out that we needed to do something to address the opioid crisis. It is just too bad that we couldn't figure out what needed to be done when black families were on the other end of the needle.

*Yvonka Marie Hall, MPA, is Executive Director of the Northeast Ohio Black Health Coalition, the first organization in Ohio dedicated to addressing health disparities in the African American community.*

# 53

# THE ADDICT, A HUMAN BEING

STEPHANIE KENDRICK
(ALBANY)

When I think about the women
who make it to us
who make it
through detox, still willing
I am scared.

Not of them, they will resist
losing control (who wouldn't?)
They will not trust others
(they have been hurt too much)
They will take note of what we say
then cry when waking
from dreams so vivid they swear
they smell the heroin burning
through their pillow. Some will run

and some too fast and when I think
about those women
I am terrified
and sad.

And tonight after working with these women
I might pour a 2nd (maybe 3rd) glass
and remember that I've been hurt (too much)
and I am not so different from them.


*Stephanie Kendrick lives in Albany, Ohio, with her son and husband, and works for the Athens County Board of Developmental Disabilities. She empowers herself through art and jiu-jitsu, while giving a voice to others through her work and her poetry.*

# ACKNOWLEDGMENTS

This project, with its more than fifty contributors from around the state, required the support of a large and generous group of individuals. We are grateful to our colleague Dr. Jane Balbo, Assistant Professor of Family Medicine at the Heritage College of Osteopathic Medicine, for her help in conceptualizing the project. Jane helped edit and provided feedback on some of the early submissions and was instrumental in connecting us with various social and patient services groups around the state.

Kacy Gaddis, M.Ed, Curriculum Coordinator at the Heritage College of Osteopathic Medicine's Dublin campus served as Managing Editor for this project. Kacy played a key role in early and ongoing conversations about the book's conceptualization as well as the logistics of compiling, organizing, and completing it. Jory Gomes, Health Policy Research Assistant at the Heritage College of Osteopathic Medicine helped with initial edits of submissions and helped pull the final manuscript together. Dr. Matt Taylor, then a fourth-year medical student at Ohio University, provided helpful feedback on the glossary of pharmacological terms.

Dr. Ann Dietrich, Associate Clinical Professor at the Heritage College, connected us with first responders and clinicians in the Columbus area. The Ohio Poetry Association helped by connecting us to some of the talented poets featured in the collection, as did the poet Brian

Spears. Becca Lachman, Communications Officer at the Athens Public Library, and Nick Tepe, Director of Athens County Public Libraries, helped us recruit contributors and develop relationships with libraries across the state.

Generous contributions from several sources at Ohio University enabled us to reduce the cost of the book, include color plates, and expand the book's reach to readers throughout the state. The co-chairs of Ohio University's Opioid Task Force, Dr. Ken Johnson, Executive Dean of the Heritage College of Osteopathic Medicine, and Dr. Randy Leite, Dean of the College of Health Sciences and Professions, both graciously provided support for the book. Dr. Nagesh Rao, Interim Chair of the Department of Social Medicine, supported this project by making departmental funds available, as did the Heritage College's Office of Research and Grants, directed by Dr. Darlene Berryman, Associate Dean for Research and Innovation. Finally, we are grateful for funds provided by Ohio University's Vice President for Research and Creative Activity. This project also would not have been possible without various kinds and levels of support from our Heritage College colleagues, including (in Dublin) Dr. Bill Burke, Pam Dixson, Maureen McCann, and Brian Thompson; and (in Athens) Angela Mowrer and Cassie Tritipo.

We thank The Ohio State University Press, especially Director Tony Sanfilippo, for supporting this project from its inception and helping us see it through to publication. Finally, we thank The Ohio Humanities Council for funding the opioid-related community conversations that we will be facilitating in Ohio in 2019. The council's support will make it possible to use this book as a foundation for community discussions across the state. We hope that the stories included in this book are just the beginning.

# GLOSSARY OF DRUGS
# MENTIONED IN BOOK

benzodiazepines: a class of prescription medications used to treat anxiety, muscle spasms, and seizures. About a quarter of Americans who experienced opioid overdose in 2015 were concurrently using a benzodiazepine.

Buprenex (buprenorphine): a prescription opioid medication used to treat pain or opioid withdrawal symptoms and opioid dependence.

carfentanil: a synthetic opioid medication that is intended to treat pain in large animals. It is, on average, 10,000 times stronger than morphine and 100 times stronger than fentanyl.

cocaine: an addictive stimulant drug created from the Coca plant. Cocaine is classified under the federal Controlled Substances Act as a Schedule II drug, meaning that it is a street drug but can also be administered for limited medical purposes.

crack: cocaine that has been mixed with baking soda or ammonia, producing a highly addictive substance that can be smoked.

Demerol (meperidine): an injectable prescription opioid medication used to treat pain.

fentanyl: a synthetic opioid medication used as a surgical anesthetic or to treat uncontrolled severe pain.

heroin: a highly addictive opioid drug derived from the poppy plant that can be smoked, snorted, or injected. Heroin is classified under the federal

Controlled Substances Act as a Schedule I drug, meaning that it has no legitimate medical use.

hydrocodone: a prescription opioid medication used to treat severe pain.

K2/Spice: herbs or leaves that have been coated with synthetic tetrahydrocannabinol (THC), the active ingredient in marijuana. It can be smoked or infused into a tea.

marijuana: a psychoactive drug harvested from the flowers of the cannabis plant. It can be smoked, cooked, vaporized, or infused into tea. Although Ohio legalized medical marijuana as of 2018, marijuana is classified under the federal Controlled Substances Act as a Schedule I drug, meaning that it has no legitimate medical use.

methadone: a prescription opioid medication used to treat severe pain or to prevent withdrawal symptoms in patients receiving medication-assisted treatment for opioid dependence.

methamphetamine: an addictive, stimulant drug that can be snorted, smoked, eaten, or injected. It is classified under the federal Controlled Substances Act as a Schedule II drug, meaning that it has limited legitimate medical use.

morphine: a prescription opioid pain reliever that is naturally derived from the opium poppy plant.

Narcan (naloxone): a prescription medication that reverses the effects of opioid drugs, including overdose. Can be administered through injection or nasal spray. Naloxone can also be combined with medications used in medication-assisted treatment to block the pleasurable effects of opioids and discourage misuse.

Neurontin (gabapentin): a prescription anticonvulsant medication used to treat seizures or neuropathic pain, such as fibromyalgia or pain from Shingles (a skin rash caused by the herpes zoster virus).

opiates: a type of opioid derived naturally from the opium poppy plant. Examples include heroin and morphine.

opioids: a class of drugs that includes naturally derived opiates, synthetic opioids (such as fentanyl), and manufactured prescription medications. Opioids are primarily prescribed for pain relief, including anesthesia. When opioids attach to receptors in the brain, they reduce the perception of pain. Opioids stimulate the reward centers of the brain, producing feelings of pleasure that can cause cravings for more opioids. Chronic opioid use can result in addiction.

OxyContin (oxycodone): a prescription opioid medication used to treat severe pain.

Paregoric: a prescription medication derived from opium that is used to treat diarrhea.

Paxil: a prescription antidepressant medication used to treat mood disorders, including depression, and anxiety disorders.

Percocet ("Percs"): a prescription opioid pain reliever composed of oxycodone and Tylenol (acetaminophen).

Percodan: a prescription opioid pain reliever composed of oxycodone and aspirin.

speedball: an injectable combination of cocaine and either heroin or morphine.

Suboxone: a prescription medication comprised of buprenorphine and naloxone to treat opioid dependence. Often used as a primary medication in medication-assisted treatment.

Talwin: a prescription pain reliever combining pentazocine (an opioid) and naloxone.

Topamax (topiramate): a prescription anticonvulsant medication used to treat seizures or migraines.

tramadol: a prescription opioid pain reliever used to treat moderate pain.

Valium (diazepam): a prescription benzodiazepine medication primarily used to treat anxiety, muscle spasms, and seizures.

Vicodin (hydrocodone acetaminophen): a prescription opioid pain reliever combining hydrocodone and acetaminophen (Tylenol).

Vivitrol (naltrexone): a prescription medication often used to treat opioid dependence in medication-assisted treatment. Blocks the effects of opioids on the brain to discourage relapse.

Xanax (alprazolam): a prescription benzodiazepine medication primarily used to treat anxiety and muscle spasms.